The New History of Scotland

General Editor
Jenny Wormald

Advisory Editors
G.W.S. Barrow and Christopher Smout

7

The New History of Scotland

Industry and Ethos

Scotland 1832–1914

Sydney and Olive Checkland

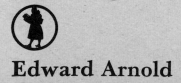

Edward Arnold

© Sydney and Olive Checkland 1984

First published in Great Britain 1984 by
Edward Arnold (Publishers) Ltd, 41 Bedford Square, London WC1B
3DQ

Edward Arnold (Australia) Pty Ltd, 80 Waverley Road, Caulfield East,
    Victoria 3145, Australia

Edward Arnold, 300 North Charles Street, Baltimore, Maryland 21201,
    U.S.A.

British Library Cataloguing in Publication Data

Checkland, S.G.
    Industry and ethos: Scotland, 1832–1914.—
    (The new history of Scotland; 7)
    1. Scotland—History—19th century
    2. Scotland—History—20th century
    I. Title   II. Checkland, Olive   III. Series
    941.1081   DA815

ISBN 0–7131–6317–8

Text set in 10/11 pt Baskerville
by Colset Private Limited, Singapore
Printed and bound by Richard Clay (The Chaucer Press) Ltd,
Bungay, Suffolk

Contents

For
S F C

Preface

The historical literature of Scotland has been marvellously enriched over the past quarter-century, especially as it is concerned with the years covered by this book. It has, moreover, been infused with insights from the social sciences which have burgeoned again in Scotland, the country which can lay claim to having been their seedbed in the eighteenth century. To this scholarship the authors are deeply indebted. It has made available a range of studies new in quantity and in kind. But it has also created the very difficult problem of doing justice to so many excellent monographs, within the rounded statements to which such a study as this must confine itself. We apologize for the superficialities of contraction. As the writing proceeded we have become increasingly conscious of the question: how do you encompass and integrate the entire experience of a nation over a significant period of time?

Among those who have written on Scotland in the Victorian and Edwardian periods, and to whom we owe most in scholarship and in friendship are Bernard Aspinwall, Callum Brown, John Butt, Roy Campbell, Robert Cage, Michael Flinn, William Forsyth, Hamish Fraser, Malcolm Gray, Tom Hart, John Hume, Gordon Jackson, Masami Kita, Margaret Lamb, John Lenihan, John McCaffrey, Ian MacDougall, Joseph Melling, Michael Moss, Ian Muirhead, Charles Munn, Forbes Munro, Peter Payne, Eric Richards, Alec Robertson, Anthony Slaven, Norio Tamaki, James Treble, Christopher Smout and Gavin White.

Other debts are owed to Gordon Cameron and to Jean Robertson and Anne Good of Glasgow University Library and to Mary Manchester of Baillie's Library, Glasgow. Essential help, as on previous occasions, has come from Isabel Burnside both as secretary and as general family support aided by her husband Bill.

Our editors Christopher Smout and Jenny Wormald have provided guidance that is much appreciated. Aileen Forbes Ballantyne
has provided the index.

SGC
EOAC
Cellardyke,
Fife
Scotland

Introduction

The Scottish Identity

Two themes interacted in the formation of Victorian and Edwardian Scotland, namely the material one of industry and empire and the impalpable one of ethos. The immense industrial development of the country both corroded and renovated the older pattern of life and assimilated the economy of Scotland to the ascendant one of England and her Empire. In consequence Scottish identity was threatened not only by the new age of industry and urbanization but also by the dominant culture and polity of England. In this way industry and ethos are the two great aspects of Scottish evolution between 1832 and 1914. To them all else can be related. In the earlier Victorian years the urge for a distinctive identity faded in the face of shared industrial and commercial success, but as Victoria aged the desire of a good many Scots to be once more distinct revived. By then industry and trade had so worked upon Scotland as to make it not easy to know wherein Scottishness lay.

As with all small nations, the question of identity is a crucial one for the Scots. It is what distinguishes them in their own eyes and in those of other nations. By its nature it derives from an interpretation of the communal past. In the Scottish case that past included sharing in the world's first industrialization and participating in one of its greatest empires. Scotland passed, yoked with England, through the great arc of world ascendancy in trade and power to the challenges at the turn of the century of industrial maturity and of trade and imperial rivalry. It is for these reasons that the history of Scotland in the long reign of Victoria, and its coda, the relatively brief reign of Edward VII, hold a special interest for the Scots and those who are intrigued by them.

It was in the three-quarters of a century following the Queen's accession in 1837 that the Scottish character assumed the form that still makes it distinctive in the time-lagged perceptions of the world: the Scot as seen from abroad is still largely Victorian. Within Scotland through the inter-war years the Victorian inheritance was still fundamental. For though challenged, it continued to dominate Scotland's value system and much of her industrial structure. In the second post-war age since 1945 the late Victorian and Edwardian inheritance have constituted the basic point of departure for Scotland's response to runaway, science-based technology and to the accompanying shifts in social values and discipline.

The question of the identity of the Scot can be approached from two perspectives. The one is extrinsic, in terms of the image held of him abroad. The Scot from Victorian times and earlier had been known in the world to a degree far greater than the size of his country might warrant. This was because, for reasons which were part of his history, the Scotsman had gone to so many parts of the world, had been so effective in action, and had generated so strong an external projection of himself. The second way of viewing the Scot is intrinsic, that which he might hold of himself.

Broadly speaking the view of Scottish identity from outside, as with that of any other nation, loses sight of detail, generating a kind of ideal type, almost a cliché. But this is not without its meaning: it represents a kind of quintessence; it is an attempt by those who cannot know the inner workings of Scottish society to assess its product, to summarize and synthesize the Scot in terms of his strongest characteristics. The Scot, in this conception, so largely drawn from the Victorian age, had a considerable nobility. This was based upon steadiness, reliability, judgement and a formidable range of skills: the Scot has been seen to excel in medicine, science, banking, engineering, soldiering, teaching, preaching and philosophizing. In this perspective he has a Presbyterian reserve, but with a powerful confidence: certainly there is no sense of having to live with defeat and insult, no need for aggressive assertion or for diffidence and deference. All of these imputed characteristics of strength are taken to be part of the Knoxian inheritance, the outcome of an austere view of man's functions, responsibilities and dignity. They are seen as being accompanied by their obverse qualities, namely an intransigence, a humourlessness linked with assertiveness, a tightfistedness, a tendency to the sanctimonious and a liking for whisky. The external image of the Scot is signalled especially by speech: it is the first word exchange that evokes this dual picture of the Scot in the minds of others.

The great names that reverberated far beyond Regency and Victorian Scotland reinforced this austere pattern for observers. Sir Walter Scott, though indeed a romantic, worked with great self-discipline at his writing, and saw it in terms of social responsibility: indeed he killed himself labouring at the pen to pay off debts that were not his fault. Dr Thomas Chalmers who had so earnestly sought a basis on which church and state could be reconciled, split the national church, the only organized expression of the nation, doing so on the ground of conscience. James Mill, (1773–1836) born near Montrose, his youthful sermons abandoned in a saddle bag in an attic, joined Bentham in trying to reduce society to rule. Thomas Carlyle was a morose indicter of human and societal follies, a Victorian sage, casting a wide shadow of moral earnestness over the English-speaking world. Samuel Smiles of Haddington was the quintessential voice for the Victorians of the doctrine of self-reliance and self-help, the distillation of the protestant ethic as it should function in secular life. David Livingstone destroyed his wife and himself in an effort to Christianize and commercialize East Africa, seeing these two aims as mutually supportive. Robert Louis Stevenson set Mr Jekyll loose as a warning that the evil side of man was real and could too easily be released upon society. Behind them all stood the stern and admonitory figure of John Knox, bearer of Genevan Calvinism to Scotland, and father of her reformation. He was as powerful in his influence in Victoria's reign as in the sixteenth century, and was carried abroad by Scots to the empire and elsewhere as the father figure of their society, a sort of theocratic Jefferson.

But if the eye is turned to the internal working of Scottish society under Victoria and Edward, the impression is very different. Here is revealed a people divided by their past, to which their corrosive industrializing experience was added. The differences ranged widely over many issues, and were often bitter.

First came religion. The Scottish Kirk split in 1843 in such a way as to fracture Scottish life for the rest of the century, weakening the culture and releasing unforeseen forces. The influx of Irish, especially from the famine of the 1840s onward, produced additional religious and cultural conflict. The continuing Catholics from pre-Reformation times had not been numerous enough to threaten Presbyterianism, but Irish Catholicism in Scotland was a different matter, especially in the west. Whereas the Catholic incomers were firmly within their church and in the care of their priests, much of the Scottish working class lost its contact with the Kirk: Chalmers spoke of 'excavating the heathen' as being the great challenge to churchmen.

The modernizers, who were also the Anglicizers, especially in education, became locked in a struggle with the protagonists of the traditional Scottish view. Those who took advantage of the opportunities offered by the union with England and the Empire seemed to many of those who did not to be betraying Scotland. There were those who accepted rule from Westminster and White-hall, and there were those who resented such remoteness, often ill-informed and obtuse, and so often an affront to those sensitive to Scottish self-esteem.

Highland and Lowland Scotland became very different societies as the Highlanders faced defeat by the forces of the modern world, to which the Lowlands were so notably contributing. Within the Highlands there was much resentment as lords and lairds sterilized vast areas for sheep raising and deer hunting. Emotionally too, there was a difference between Highlander and Lowlander: this was reflected in a contemporary view of the character of Mr Gladstone, a pure-blooded Scotsman with a highland mother and a lowland father. His extraordinary responses to the challenges that confronted him, with their mixture of passion and caution, were described as those of 'a Highlander in the care of a Lowlander': thus the intuitive, impulsive actor, relying on responses from his Celtic blood, was controlled by his lowland component, that of the measured calculator, pausing, referring action to both general principles and to particular circumstances. Those who sought to restore the greatly diminished Gaelic tongue found little sympathy among those who were more interested in the fact that English was the language of the Empire and North America, and who too often regarded the Gaelic as a barbarous archaism.

The monarchy too had a divisive aspect. There were perhaps a few Scots who were republicans, rejectors of the mystique of heredi-tary continuity. More generally, there was a mild degree of equi-vocal feeling about the descendants of the Hanoverian kings who, having displaced the Scottish line of the Stuarts, had put down the risings of the '15 and the '45, and then mounted an attack on High-land life and culture. George IV's visit to Scotland in 1822, so splendidly stage-managed by Sir Walter Scott, had caused much disrespectful hilarity as the majestic bulk strained against the High-land dress, with the pneumatic royal legs protruding from the kilt.

Finally there was the rising confrontation between labour and capital in the central industrial belt, as real in Scotland as anywhere in the industrializing world. Scotland generated its own distinctive form of the conflict between capital and labour: some of this was projected onto the broader British stage by such men as Keir Hardie.

All in all, it might seem that by the time Victoria was celebrating her diamond jubilee in 1897 Scotland was a confused and deeply divided society. But was this really the case? There were two sets of counter-circumstances.

Firstly there was the sense of identity that geography, history and shared myth had generated in the Scots over the centuries. Victorian Scots felt, with some justice, that Tweed and Solway defined a distinct people. There was the folk memory of the Bruce and the Wallace, of Mary Queen of Scots and of the '45. The latter was echoed in the wistful Jacobite songs of Victoria's time that fitted so well the nation's sense of loss. There was a Scottish literature, unique but with a universal appeal, its tone set by Burns and Scott. There were distinctively Scottish thinkers, especially David Hume and Adam Smith, the latter presenting a view of man and society that Scots could recognize as arising from the experience of their own country. There were the great inventive engineers – especially James Watt (who in the myth of his persistence in watching his mother's kettle was in the same tradition as Bruce and his spider). There were differences in the pronunciation of English, of idiom and cadence that distinguished Scot from Sassenach (and indeed the Scots of one region from those of another). There was a belief among the Scots that they were less deferential and more democratic than the English, that the master and servant relationship that was so pervasive in English life had never invaded that of Scotland. Neither the 'lad o' pairts' nor the 'independent working man' (both of whom were strongly held Scottish notions) did English-style obeisance to the boss. Finally the extrinsic ideal image of the Scot held abroad may have had a feed-back effect on the Scots at home, for, with such a diaspora, the Scots could hardly fail to be aware that abroad at least they were a distinct race, as sharply drawn as the Jews, but largely free of the hostility that could assail that other, less fortunate, peculiar people. The Scots, so long believing *in Calvino veritas*, in the sovereignty of God, and in their responsibility to God, could acquire a sense of absolute rightness, the accompaniment of their steadfastness.

Secondly, there is often a sense in which differences are permissible because they rest upon a substratum of agreement. The debate on education was recognized by many to be not a question lying between England and Scotland, but between two views of how Scotland should respond in educational terms to a rapidly changing world. There was a common acceptance of Presbyterianism in its fundamental aspects of the rejection of bishops and the assertion of a particular view of church government which stressed the rightness and benefits of control at a local level by parishes and presbyteries. The Calvinistic inheritance was common to most of the nation. The Scots as a people had either to reaffirm Calvinism, to adapt it or to consider the route of escape and how far to travel along it. In this sense most Scots were involved in the question of the validity of the Westminster Confession of Faith of 1643. They were buffetted by the new Biblical scholarship coming from Germany, with its critique of the old fundamentalism that had been at once comforting and terrifying, and by Darwinian biology with its challenge to the first chapter of the book of Genesis. The union of sects of 1847, forming the United Presbyterian Church, and that of 1900, merging it with the Free Church showed that, with the passage of time, unity could reassert itself. The Presbyterian churches, in surrendering their various systems of schools to the School Boards after 1872, were tacitly recognizing an increasing sense of common ground. Moreover for the Scots, schooling was by the 1870s too important a matter to be impaired, as it was in England, by religious differences between sects. The loss of religion by a considerable proportion of the working classes inspired the church extension movements of the 1830s and the 1880s, together with a range of religion-related activities in which Scotland was a prominent innovator: both the YMCA and the Boys' Brigade were Scottish inventions.

Scottish politicians who, like Lord Rosebery, took an active part in British and indeed English affairs (he helped to remake the government of London as well as being briefly prime minister), could also demand greater autonomy for Scotland. The sense among Scots that they were ruled from London could, partly at least, be offset by the feeling that London was ruled from Scotland, not only because Scots politicians were prominent there, but also because Scotland, with its liberal radical tradition after 1832, provided a power base, first for the Liberal Party and then much later for Labour. Lowlanders gradually became aware that the

Highlands had produced a distinctive life and culture that had been under official and philanthropic attack, but which represented the background not merely of those living in the Highlands, but of the large numbers whose forebears had come from north of the Highland line. The hostility between labour and capital could exist without impairing Scottish national sentiment.

As to the monarchy, despite criticism its magic and mystique found much support in Scotland. The Scots had always lived under monarchy, and had a profound sense, fed by the Old Testament, of anointed kingship. For in spite of the democratic part of their outlook and inheritance, many Scots had a pragmatic sense that monarchy was a way of keeping questions of the legitimacy of state power safely in the realm of abstract debate: they were aware that the constitution of England was consistent with Scottish historical experience. Though Victoria had retired from public life in 1861 after the death of Albert, she spent a considerable part of her time in Scotland, at Balmoral, among Albert's tartan wallpapers. When William McGonagall, poet and tragedian, made his pilgrimage to the gates of Balmoral to pay homage to the Queen (he got no further), he was saluting her as his sovereign, as many another Scottish working man was prepared to do.

In the matter of experience shared with England, there was the question of the empire. Here a comparison between Scotland, at the northern extremity of Europe, and Italy at the southern, is perhaps not out of place. In nineteenth-century Italy ineluctable poverty at home was not relieved by the opportunities of empire abroad. Thus there could continue the immemorial paradigm of Italian behaviour that arose from this, namely a deep pessimism, forged almost into an instinct by the endless struggle for survival, characterized by oscillation between imposed order, resistance, the seeking of alternatives, chaos and the re-imposition of order by force. The British empire (including England itself) to which the Scots gained access after 1707, opened to them, already an outward-moving people (who had taken over much of Northern Ireland from the seventeenth century), a much wider horizon of opportunity: they moved into it to explore, to garrison, to trade, to rule and to colonize. In so doing these migrant Scots not only carried Scotland abroad, they also had profound effects on society at home, both stimulating economic development there and limiting by emigration the increase in population among whom the national product was to be divided. Scots could thus enjoy a frontier of opportunity on a world-wide scale, while at the same time making Scotland itself an economic frontier, with the opportunities and agonies this presented.

Finally, though much of the Victorian working class was by the mid century deficient in its attendance at the Kirk, leaving it largely to the middle classes, God was securely in his heaven, perceived in a distinctively Scottish way. Scottish heroes were to be found as soldiers, missionaries, authors, men of science, philosophers and divines: the Scots had no difficulty in following the injunction of the Book of Ecclesiastes to praise famous men, their own prominent among them.

It is thus possible to draw up a kind of balance sheet of Scottish ethos and identity, with elements of division and conflict on the one hand and elements of shared feeling and experience on the other. But these must be fused rather than juxtaposed. This task lies squarely in the field of the historian.

The principal themes can be listed. As the prime mover there was the industrializing process, impelled by the inventors and innovators, operating on the long continuities of the Scottish past. With it came the new urban and rural experiences, each with its own internal diversity within a tiny country. It brought division and stress in terms of class, power and politics. The labour force with its organization, earnings and welfare, together with its changing aspirations, contained the matters which most concerned the mass of the population. Ideology, both religious and secular, was of intense importance to the thinking Scot, high and low. Crucial to the nation was the working of the intellect in the arts and sciences, a phenomenon that related to the national life as both cause and effect. On the wider scene Scotland as a participant in the newly integrating world must be set within the larger frameworks to which it related, namely the British, the Imperial, the European and the global. Finally there was the partial loss of Scottish identity, and its rediscovery, a strand that is woven through the book. This sequence of themes is principally pursued over the 64 years of Victoria's reign.

The 13 years between the new century and world war, most of which was the Edwardian age, provides an opportunity to bring these aspects of Scottish life together in terms both of the mature economy and the industrialized society, and to envisage the nation on the eve of a vast discontinuity.

Part I

The Victorian Generations

1

Entrepreneurs and Industries

1 The Conditions and Scale of Industrialization

The Scottish national ethos, like all others, must rest ultimately, though subject to complex timelags and tangled interplay, on the bedrock of the economy. Adam Smith had given a good deal of thought to the relationship between the two as he contemplated the condition of his native land while writing *The Wealth of Nations* of 1776. He was struck with the general poverty of his countrymen in the past and even in his own day, and compared the listlessness of many Scots with the vigour of their more bustling English neighbours. In the manner of his time he seems to have thought that vitality was a constant among men, but that it could be released in varying degrees, and so lift a society from the poverty trap, depending on changes in the appropriateness of the business environment. Smith believed that the best result would be obtained if men were allowed by their government to operate freely and securely in a widening market. The necessary resource base had of course to be available: in this Scotland was not deficient. For Smith, lowland Scotland, though behind England in economic progress, was a civil society fully capable of participating in the European intellectual tradition. But it was hardly likely to play a part in world industrial leadership.

The economic success of Scotland in Victorian times would have astonished Smith. But it was consistent with his general ideas. It was the result, in considerable measure, of releasing Scottish energies by the easing of traditional poverty through a widening of market opportunity. The extension of markets due to the opening to the Scots in 1707 of England and her empire had rapidly accelerated in its effects by 1832. This was combined with the increasing harnessing of the value system of the early reformers to the new industrial and commercial achievement. Scottish Calvinism had always laid emphasis on popular education, on individual responsibility, and on answerability to God for his gifts (which condemned waste and so favoured thrift). These virtues, so appropriate to survival under traditional Scottish poverty, could now work powerfully in the nation's escape from it. They provided a labour force with a significantly higher level of literacy than in England, together with a system of values appropriate to economic success.

To the wedding of market opportunity with a favourable ethos were added the favours of nature. She had supplied Scotland with the resources most called for by the new industrial technology of the day, chiefly coal and iron in quantity, appropriate in quality, and readily accessible. There were the two great estuaries, those of the Forth and the Clyde, the one giving access to the traditional markets of northern Europe, and the other to the vastly expanding Atlantic economy. There were separated by only some 40 miles, and could relatively easily be joined by canals and railways, so that the waist of Scotland could become a unified band of commercial and industrial achievement, containing compactly within itself the fuel and mineral resources on which all else rested.

One further condition was necessary to generate the Scottish Victorian economic miracle. It was that a race of industrialists, traders and bankers should arise from the traditional agriculture, small-scale production and modest trading of earlier times, capable of forming and conducting enterprises of the scale and sophistication required by the new technology. This indeed happened.

The simplest indicator of the effects of the new entrepreneurial energies on Scotland is population change. The forces of rapid population growth had been released from the later eighteenth century: they continued to operate. Scotland's greatest percentage increase had come in the decade before 1832 at the rate of 15.1 per cent. The population, without the entrepreneurs and the growth forces they released, would, as so often in the past, have been cut back to the levels supportable by agriculture. Instead, between the censuses of 1831 and 1901 the increase in numbers continued, carrying the population from 2,373,561 to 4,472,103, not far short of doubling. But the rate of growth was erratic: it fell sharply in the 1850s, (6.0 per cent) recovered in the 60s (9.7 per cent) and 70s (11.2 per cent), fell in the 1880s (7.8 per cent) and recovered in the 90s (11.1 per cent). This performance was related to net losses by emigration: in spite of industrial and trading achievement Scotland could not hold her natural increase in population at its prevailing rate of growth. The peak emigration decade of the century was the 80s, with Scotland losing 41 per cent of natural increase or 218,274 persons. In all between 1861 and 1901 just under half a million Scots went abroad (including to England).

Moreover the population redistributed itself. It steadily concentrated in the central belt. Both the western and the eastern lowlands dramatically increased their numbers between 1831 and 1901. The eastern region, centred on Edinburgh, grew from 785,814 to 1,400,675. This represented, however, a decreasing share of Scotland's population, falling from 33.2 per cent to 31.3 per cent. The west, with Glasgow as its metropolis, grew even faster, expanding from 628,528 to 1,976,640, increasing its national share from 26.6 per cent to 44.2 per cent, thus becoming the dominant region. The losers were the Highlands, peaking in 1841 and then declining, the far North doing so in 1861, the Borders in 1881 and the North East in 1911. Thus was the demography of Scotland remade.

The level of productivity more than kept up with the increase in numbers. Scotland, though still poorer per capita than England by 1850, was closing the gap. Thereafter, though Scotland north of the Tay lagged, the central belt, from being a region in which wages were below the national British average, achieved parity by the 1880s, and was by the new century one of the four highest out of 13 wage regions in Britain, bringing, in spite of slums and slagheaps, higher incomes to the working classes. An inquiry during Lord Salisbury's second ministry (1886–92) showed that Scotland was fully self-supporting in terms of yielding a tax revenue to meet government expenditure, with a slight surplus.

By 1901 Scotland was predominately urban with all city dwellers sharing the same experience. In another sense, however, there was variety. Scotland produced four major cities, strongly distinct from one another. They, with their city-regions and satellites, gave a new kind of diversity to Scottish life.

There are no figures for the growth of Scottish national income from 1832 to 1914. The money and credit system may serve as a kind of proxy. Whereas the Scottish banks had total liabilities of some £24,500,000 in 1825 (or £11.07 per head of population), by 1914 they stood at £167,840,000 (or £28 per head), with slightly falling prices. Scottish overseas investment had probably reached about £60,000,000 in 1870; thereafter it rose rapidly to some £500,000,000 by 1914. Money, like men, was going abroad on an increasing scale in the later nineteenth and early twentieth centuries, though out of a larger quantum.

2 The Men of Business

The new breed of men of business gradually took the fate of Scotland into their hands, wresting it from the landowners. Many of them, including the most creative, were impelled by the excitement of discovery and development, with profits as a necessary but secondary incentive. Certainly it was essential for them to read the markets in which they bought and sold, making the best bargains in each, for this was how the business system was made to cohere and extend. But there was much more to their role. By trial and error in the midst of unknowns, by contributing to or drawing upon the available pool of inventions and by the ploughing back of profits they created a new economy and society. At the same time they disciplined and trained their workers to the new forms of production, keeping the labour force within wage levels that left a substantial surplus for investment, as well as for their own rising middle-class expenditure. All this assertiveness was subject to its own disciplines, namely the ruthless amputation of bankruptcy, together with resistance from the labour force.

These men, engrossed in their atomistic tasks, guessing about the actions of other business men, and in a continuous contest with their workers, were scarcely aware of what they were doing to the nation. They had no conspectus of the new industrial and urbanized society they were bringing into being, decade by decade, by their competitive efforts. Much less did they understand the effects of their actions on the nation's beliefs and ethos. Beyond the affairs of the firm they were, in large measure, blind actors.

Such men ranged from the titans of heavy industry to the masters of small works and the petty shopkeepers. Great names appeared among the engineers and shipbuilders, including Napier, Elder, Stephen, Thomson, Denny, Pearce, Dubs, Howden and Beardmore. There were the magnates of coal and iron and later steel: Neilson, Dixon, Merry and Cunninghame, Houldsworth, Dunlop, the Bairds of Gartsherrie and David Colville. In chemicals there was the Tennant family. In cotton there were the Monteith, Dunlop and Coats families. In linen and jute there were the Baxters and the Coxes of Dundee. Wholesale trade produced James Arthur and the Campbell brothers. Though most of these men, especially in the earlier phase, had come from families that had been tenant farmers or perhaps coal masters on a small scale, or who had had a modest urban background as artisans or merchants, by the 1870s they and their families had become an industrial élite. By contrast the Scottish banks retained a kind of democratic character in terms of recruitment: they took in young men of good modest middle-class families to man their many branches; the lad o' pairts could work his way up from one stool to the next, with that of the general manager the ultimate prize.

There can be no doubt of the dedication, courage and hard work of many of the industrialists of the formative phase. Samuel Smiles was not altogether wrong in seeing something heroic in such men. Down to the 1860s, and indeed later, some of the engineers and ironmasters of Scotland, rather than the maximization of profits being their governing motivation, often had to be called back from romantic and indeed sometimes obsessive technical ingenuity and perfection to profit considerations. They felt the exhilaration of creation: with this in many cases went the excitement of contact with men of science, as with Lord Kelvin. This was the atmosphere that generated Elder's compound engine of 1853, A.C. Kirk's triple expansion engine of 1874, the construction of Denny's ship testing tank in 1888, the replacement of wood by iron, followed by steel, all done while reconciling the demands of safety, speed, carrying capacity, crewing requirements and fuel consumption.[1]

It was sometimes, especially from the mid-century onward, the

[1]See section 4 below.

threatening liquidators and their agents the accountants who enforced economic realism upon the founders of firms. Thus the accountant, having been called in, would impose at least rudimentary costing procedures and might insist that production be aimed at a specified market. The inventive employer (who was also responsible for the labour force he had attracted) would be brought under discipline by the grey men far removed from development and production, namely the accountants and the lawyers. As the employer disciplined his workforce, so he in his turn was disciplined by these representatives of economic reality. In this way a rationalism based upon calculation could be imposed; the founder of the firm could be subjected to the limitations of costs and markets. This necessity did not end with the advent of very large scale: William Beardmore, later Lord Invernairn (1856–1936), made of himself a titan of such size as to defy even the disciplinary power of shareholders: Beardmore, indeed, was never really subdued to commercial discipline, but continued to be expansive to the last.

There were too, the obverse phenomena, whereby the head of the firm suffered from deficient rather than excessive assertiveness, or lost sight of the demands of changing markets: These deficiencies could come with hereditary management. These might bring oblivion to the firm, or the replacement of top management: the latter became easier in the later nineteenth century as companies went public, using limited liability.

Down to the mid-nineteenth century the firms that composed a relatively simple Scottish economy, for the most part based on small-scale production, did not need elaborate structures or record keeping, either for their own purposes or those of the tax collector. For most businesses the solicitors or 'writers' could provide such professional services as were required. The single trader or the simple partnership constituted such business structure as was necessary. But limited liability from 1856 brought change. Firms became larger, with shareholders to satisfy, needing better business methods. The accountant expanded and generalized his role over much of business. So too did other providers of business services, including surveyors, stockbrokers and insurance men. Business thus developed round itself a set of service professions, of which the law continued to be an essential but no longer dominant component. These men became an important part of middle class society. Around them, in turn, but at a lower level, there was the growing army of male clerks, sharing the general outlook on society of their employers.

A harbinger of the new economic age for Scotland had been the company promotion mania of 1825, the effects of which were still felt in 1832. Edinburgh was its centre. The old capital, so conservative in so many ways, had demonstrated a new potential for irrationality. It was the point at which much of Scotland's money was concentrated, where the three chartered banks attracted the lion's share of deposits, and where landed wealth held its liquid balances. For the first time Scotland learned what could happen when there was a heavy concentration of liquid funds seeking an outlet, and finding one in a wide range of new and tempting promotions. In these the docks, canals and railways were prominent, but also included were steamship companies, banking and insurance and gas and water companies, together with industrial projects in iron, glass, textiles, distilling and brewing. A poor harvest put an end to the speculation, causing falling values and indeed collapses. Thus did nature remind the precocious money market of Scotland of the continuing dependence of the economy upon the yield, in real terms, from the soil.

Glasgow, in spite of great efforts, was never able to wrest the leadership in banking from Edinburgh. But it was the Glasgow scene that largely determined the behaviour of the Scottish money market. Glasgow contained both the produce markets (especially cotton and iron) with their inherent instability, together with heavy industry, so liable to the fluctuations of the trade cycle. Money shortage and rising rates of interest, heralding crisis, appeared first in Glasgow. Scottish bankers knew that Glasgow was highly speculative: they were usually relieved to be transferred to the more tranquil atmosphere of Edinburgh.

The business men by the 1890s provided the targets for socialist and trade union attack. Certainly their behaviour was such as to make it essential that their workers provided themselves with unions. Indeed Scottish employers were in general opponents of unionism, especially down to the 1870s, some of them, like the Bairds and the Neilsons, bitterly so. Many of them used the incoming Irish and Highlanders against the unions. But this was often accompanied by a form of paternalism. Not a few of such men became assertive and inflexible, self-regarding magnates with a hauteur that could rival that of the landed noblemen, crassly sure of their judgement and brooking no interference or advice.

  Success often, perhaps typically, meant losing sight of the conditions being created for the workers. By the 1870s and indeed in important cases earlier, much Scottish management, especially in the larger enterprises, had become insensitive to the lives and needs of those over whose livelihood they presided. This was especially so in the basic elements of the Scottish economy, namely coal, iron, chemicals, shipbuilding and shipowning. Like all men who had arrived at positions of power, whether by economic or political means, the masters of these industries often tended to distance themselves from the fate of those who were casualties of the system they were operating. Moreover they believed, with some justification, that the primary need for all concerned, including the workers, was that the firm should prosper. In spite of the marvels of new technology, most tasks were still labour intensive: it followed that any excessive solicitude about wages would raise costs sharply, to the peril of the firm and its capacity to employ, especially when competing in world markets. The great entrepreneurs were admired as they created jobs; they were less admired when they resisted wage claims, or when they failed. There was in any case no alternative to them: who else could bring investment and employment?

  Yet human sympathy was not wholly lacking. Indeed Dr Thomas Chalmers had attracted to himself a notable group of young men, his 'boy elders', who carried on his evangelical work in Glasgow from the early 1820s. These included William Collins publisher, George Burns (shipowner partner of Samuel Cunard), David Stowe and others. Later in the century the evangelical tradition among business men continued with Hugh Matheson and William Mackinnon. There was considerable philanthropic endeavour among the business classes; Scotland achieved as much in this respect as anywhere, especially perhaps with the YMCA (1841) and the Boys' Brigade (1883). Moreover, it was the business men who ran local government until late in the century, often inspired with a sense of civic pride as well as self-assertion. When these men sat in their presbyterian pews on Sunday listening to the minister expounding (perhaps guardedly) Christ's injunction that they should care for their neighbours and brothers, and discreetly warning of the perils of default that threatened men of wealth, unease could be pushed aside by the reflection that they provided employment and a modicum of charity for the deserving poor.

  In spite of the immense changes for which they were responsible, the view of life of most men of business was essentially passive and determinist: most of them, though often amazed at the changes that had taken place in their lifetime, and taking credit for some part of these, accepted the Scotland they and their kind had created, phase by phase. They saw its evolution as being in the inevitable course of things, for which they had no responsibility beyond the functioning of their own enterprises and a degree of ritual giving to charity.

3 Industry by 1832

In addition to the study of the business man there are two other ways of viewing industrialization. There is the sectoral perspective, looking at the evolution of the industries brought into being by business initiative, together with the interlocking pattern they formed. Secondly there is the pattern of city-regions which was the spatial expression of industrial development.

In 1832 the potential of the new industrial forces had only begun to manifest itself. The steam engine that had been so vastly improved in 1769 by James Watt (as instrument maker to the University of Glasgow), had yet to make its full impact on industry, mining and transport. The steamboat was still a small-scale novelty on the Clyde and Forth. There were no real railways in Scotland except for the 8¼ miles of the Glasgow and Garnkirk, opened in 1831, though the steamboat network was pretty well established up the west coast. The coal industry was largely a local affair, though the coming of the canals in the central belt had begun to change this. The most·important element of the iron manufacturing industry was the Carron Company; shipbuilding was a minor activity on the Clyde, based on wood and sail.

The attempt at a regional development policy for the Highlands had been abandoned. The winding up of the Board of Trustees in the 1820s had meant that the Highlands had no governmental support. In spite of the extent of urbanization by 1832, most Scots still thought of themselves as a people of the countryside; indeed most city dwellers had country origins and country connections. Sir Walter Scott sustained them and those who followed them in the cities in their self-identification with the uplands, the mountains and the glens, the rivers, the coasts and inlets and islands.

And yet by 1832 the power and intoxication of new industrial possibilities were indeed powerfully felt. Steam-powered cotton spinning mills had sprung up from the early 1800s, especially in

Glasgow and the West of Scotland, demonstrating the marvels and the horrors of the factory system: cotton, indeed, was well on its way to becoming the principal industry of the region. Linen, its predecessor and to some degree parent, had faded. Cottage industry in the form of spinning flax and wool, so long a major support of Scottish rural life, was virtually dead. The handloom weaver, once so prosperous in his combined home and workplace, was by the 1840s seriously threatened in cotton, linen and wool, in that order, though there were still tens of thousands of them in all branches of textiles. The Scottish handloom weavers probably peaked in 1840 at 84,560; by 1850 there were only 25,000 of them, declining to 8,000 in 1880. In their place, men, women and children were gathering to the factories, many of them from the Highlands and from Ireland. The textile-related chemicals industry was thriving: the St Rollox chemical works in Glasgow was the largest in the world, a massive and essential source of alkali, but by its dissemination of sulphurous waste a terrible pollutor of land, air and water. Iron foundries and machine shops were multiplying in the city, in Kilmarnock, and in other neighbouring towns, providing engines and gear for the cotton factories and for sugar processing. In Ayrshire, too, ironfounding and engineering had received a stimulus from the textile industry, though a good deal of cotton-making machinery came from Lancashire. Whereas the Edinburgh foundries specialized in architectural castings (rainwater goods and the like) for the New Town, those of Glasgow were strongly oriented toward the engineering trades. The Scottish share of United Kingdom pig iron production had been 5 per cent in 1805: by 1835 it was nearly 30 per cent.

It was the manufacturing activity centred upon cotton that had given the necessary primary impulse to West of Scotland engineering, ironfounding and blacksmithing. For the factories required machines, engines, shafting and cast and wrought iron components. The West Indies, that connection from the eighteenth century, as well as providing raw cotton, required sugar processing machinery: here the West of Scotland soon had the lead. From engineering and its auxiliaries the linkages quickly spread. By 1832 the demand for fuel, both industrial and domestic, had stimulated coal mining, causing it too to demand engineering products including engines for pumping and for winding gear.

4 Industry and Infrastructure: Shipbuilding and Engineering

From 1832 the forces of industrial change extended and accelerated in dramatic fashion. Among them was the impetus to improve communications. Transport facilities progressed step by step with industrial and commercial achievement; each in turn outran the other, each stimulated the other to further and improved provision. There were to be no more canals built in the industrial belt of Scotland after the 1820s; the second phase of the Scottish transport revolution was to be dominated by the deepening of the Clyde and the creation of the railway system. In 1825 the Clyde could carry ships of only 300 tons to the docks in the centre of Glasgow; by 1857 it could bear ships of 3,600 tons. The primary object in 'making' the Clyde in this way by public expense was to bring seagoing ships to the heart of the city, but in so doing the Improvement Commissioners made possible the building of ships of all sizes along its course, and so linked shipbuilding with the growing engineering and iron working complex of the city. The Leith docks, serving Edinburgh, were greatly improved as the trade of the Forth abandoned the little outports of Fife and East Lothian and concentrated there. The improvement in coastal shipping made possible by the steamship lowered the cost of water carriage from Scotland to the seaport cities of England so that by the mid 1830s Scottish farmers could ship produce to London as cheaply as an English farmer producing within 20 miles of the city: Scottish agriculture responded to this opportunity, as well as that provided by its own urban centres.

Traditional wooden boats were being increasingly powered by steam and paddles, an activity which the Clyde had pioneered. To the expanding engineering industry thus stimulated was added from the 1850s the building of railway locomotives. From the 1860s came iron ships, though most owners still preferred to power their ships by sail. The pioneers of iron shipbuilding were a new breed, with little or no experience of building in wood. The widening and deepening of the Clyde progressed further, in step with the growth of Glasgow, not only providing new sites for the shipbuilders but allowing them to create ever larger craft. The adoption of the screw propeller from the mid-1840s made possible much sturdier and more efficient ships. It was those builders who specialized in steamships who seized the lead when the shipowners were finally converted to steam power. In 1860 the sail tonnage launched on the

Clyde was still twice that of steam, though the iron ships were almost all steam powered. The steamship was not secure in its victory over sail until the later 1870s. In the meantime the sailcloth makers of Dundee and Arbroath could flourish. The Clyde made its contribution to the final efflorescence of sail with the *Cutty Sark* built at Dumbarton in 1870 and sailing until 1895. The new phase of Clydeside shipbuilding ascendancy was heralded in 1879 when William Denny, also of Dumbarton, launched the world's first ocean-going vessel with a steel hull. In 1831 the Clyde yards had employed 3 per cent of the British shipbuilding labour force; by 1871 the Clyde share was 21 per cent (that of Scotland 26 per cent). The Clyde in that year launched 48 per cent of the industry's output (which had itself increased by more than four-fold since 1831). Clydeside's shipbuilding achievement was by 1900 moving to its final phase, providing much of the world's merchant tonnage, together with the building of naval vessels to outdo the vast effort being made by Germany to match Britain on the high seas. To add to the many challenges confronting the shipbuilders, their industry was a classic example of a capital goods industry subject to vicious swings in demand. Between 1822 and 1879 the industry went through seven major cycles averaging 7 to 9 years.

At the heart of the West of Scotland engineering complex from 1818 to 1853 stood the yard of the cousins David (1790–1869) and Robert Napier (1791–1876). It was a place of high inventiveness and efficiency: David was the great inventor and adaptor, the father of marine engineering as a distinctive profession. Robert excelled as the man of efficient construction and effective business: he achieved the extraordinary status of being wholly trusted by the Admiralty, as well as by Cunard and other shipping companies. Out of the Napier yard came an extraordinary stream of new developments in the powering of ships, together with a flow of men who, trained and confident, spread over the industrial complex, founding or managing other firms. Napier's yard was thus a kind of college for discovery and dissemination. In the highly competitive context thus created, the Govan yard engined the entire Cunard fleet from 1840 to 1865, as well as building for many other companies. It was to Napier's yard that the young samurai, Yozo Yamao, came in 1866 to learn at first hand how the new Japan should build ships. But by the 1860s Napier's yard was losing the initiative, for a phase had been reached in shipbuilding in which technical achievement was becoming relatively less important than marketing decisions and a location favourable to the demands of increasing scale.

The leadership in inventive terms passed to another genius of the industry, John Elder (1824–69). He was a brilliant man, who combined delicate health with immense energy. His father David in 1817 had been drawn from Kinross to Glasgow there to set up as a mechanic and millwright. Five years later David had become manager of Napier's engine works. He realized that the need for economy in fuel use was enormously greater at sea than on land, for the ship had to carry its own energy, displacing paying cargo. His son John grew up in the atmosphere of a search for fuel economy. In 1852 John left Napiers to join what became Randolph, Elder and Co. He and Charles Randolph in 1853 patented the marine compound expansion engine: when combined after 1862 with the 'Scotch' boiler of James Howden, another Glasgow engineer, it revolutionized the powering of ships, driving about three-quarters of the British merchant marine by 1876. Elder had the courage in 1868 to begin again, moving down-river from the now congested and limiting stretch to a greenfield site at Fairfield. J. and G. Thomson decided in 1870 to challenge for the North Atlantic market; they too moved downstream in 1871 to Clydebank. Sir William Pearce, successor to John Elder at Fairfield, brought the adventurous touch. Before 1879 the Atlantic crossing took generally a fortnight. Pearce, with his *Arizona*, reduced the journey to seven days. A long run of Fairfield ships was to hold the record.

The peak of Edinburgh engineering achievement was the provision, by the Stevenson family, of a set of lighthouses constituting the 'northern lights' of Scotland; they also built a complete ring of lighthouses around Japan. These structures and their brilliant illuminations were marvels of civil, mechanical and lighting engineering. Robert Louis Stevenson (1850–1894), possibly to propitiate his father's annoyance at his rejection of the family profession, celebrated the achievements of his grandfather and father in verse:

> Eternal granite hewn from the living isle,
> And dowelled with brute iron, rears a tower
> That from its wet foundations to its crown
> Of glittering glass, stands, in a sweep of winds,
> Immoveable, immortal, imminent.

Meanwhile civil engineering had begun to replace stone with

iron as the basic material for bridges and other constructions, especially for the railways. As the cities grew, together with the connecting links between them, the civil engineers and contractors strove to provide infrastructure and public utilities. They were the builders of the waterworks, aqueducts and pipelines that brought water to the cities, and of the sewers that carried it away laden with human waste. They constructed docks, railways, tramways, roads and bridges. They struggled with the earth and its wilful drainage, tunnelling, shoring, fighting against flooding, and stabilizing the subsidence caused by the coal mines and by the activities of other civil engineers. They battled too with their labour forces, and with the insolvencies of sponsoring companies. They swept through communities large and small with their armies of navvies, temporarily boosting local incomes and disturbing the social peace, leaving behind facilities that permanently changed the tenor of life and work. All these things the civil engineers did piecemeal, at the call of private companies and local authorities. Among their great names was that of William Arrol (1839–1913), builder of the second Tay Bridge, the Forth Bridge, the Tower Bridge and capital works in various parts of the world. Arrol, the son of a cotton spinner, was a classic example of the lad o' pairts making his way to the fore from being apprenticed to a blacksmith in Paisley, a man whose inventiveness could suggest pre-assembling the elements of bridges and drilling and rivetting by hydraulic power.

5 Coal, Iron and Steel

In a sense the fundamental basis was coal and iron. Coal had been dug from Scotland since the Middle Ages. Its production had accelerated before 1832; thereafter it increased at a striking rate, being necessary for growing domestic consumption and for the whole range of industries, especially those working in iron, together with the new converter of heat into energy, the steam engine. Scottish output rose from 7.4 million tons in 1854 to 38.8 in 1914, or from 11.5 per cent of United Kingdom output to 14.5 per cent. Employment rose from 39,200 to 146,200. Coal exports grew in importance. The coalfield of West Fife had enjoyed a traditional predominance, but Lanarkshire and Ayrshire now took the initiative: nearly 70 per cent of Scottish coal by 1870 came from these western fields. To them a large Irish labour force was attracted. The expansion of output and the difficulties of union organization worsened conditions in an industry in which they had always been bad. The 1842 Mines Report revealed a terrible debasement and deformity of life in Scotland as in England. Though women and children were at once brought above ground, life for the man was not to be greatly changed before 1914. Safety regulations did not come until 1861; even then they were feeble.

The Scottish coal-field villages were dismal places, standing among the detritus of the pits. But out of isolation and shared danger there developed a real communal life, together with a strong trade unionism. It was out of these that the leadership of Scottish and indeed British labour came: Alexander MacDonald and Keir Hardie from the 1860s and 1890s were figures of a new stature. The colliery owners, often remote from their workers and concerned over costs in highly competitive markets, fell into a fatally confrontational relationship with their miners on a good many occasions, using Irish against Scots.

The iron industry of Scotland, a major user of coal, was even more dramatic in its growth. Though the Carron Company continued to thrive, it was to be eclipsed by the extraordinary development of the blackband ironstone of Lanarkshire, using unprocessed coal instead of coke in the new hot blast technique developed in 1828 by J. Beaumont Neilson (1792–1865). Iron production in Scotland was now possible at extraordinarily low cost. The record was remarkable. In terms of iron ore raised the output was no less than 2,500,000 tons in 1857 (6.5 per cent by value of UK output); thereafter with the exhaustion of the ore bodies it declined, reaching 538,000 tons in 1914. Pig iron was better sustained, using imported ores: output rose from 797,000 tons in 1854 to peak at 1,206,000 in 1869; after severe contraction in the 1880s it was at about the same level in 1914. A high proportion of the new Scottish cheap iron necessarily went abroad or south to England. With this hectic growth came the explosion of frontier towns east of Glasgow like Airdrie, Coatbridge and Motherwell; in such places, murk, brutalization and social incoherence produced fearful drunkenness and violence, against which struggled Chief Constables and their police forces.

The very high proportion of iron output that left Scotland meant that the masters were not greatly interested in processing what they produced. The foundries of Glasgow and its region absorbed a great deal of iron in castings, but there was relatively little interest in producing malleable iron, largely because of earlier failures with it. Three malleable (puddled) iron companies failed in the 1840s; the Scottish iron masters thereafter tended to concentrate on the lucrative primary production of smelting pig iron. But the demand for forgings by the mechanical engineers, shipbuilders and civil engineers meant that they themselves developed great forges, notably the Parkhead Forge founded in 1837 by Robert Napier and the Lancefield Forge. Output ranged from the heavy to the intricate.

The age of cheap steel dawned in the 1870s; in the course of the 1880s steel superseded wrought iron in the shipyards, in the railways, and in civil engineering. The Steel Company of Scotland, founded in 1872, brought the new beginning. It was formed by Sir Charles Tennant and others of the chemicals industry who had set up the Tharsis Company to work pyritic ores in Spain for copper. They sought to exploit the tantalizing iron residues from their ores, the 'blue billie'. But even with the help of William Siemens, the metallurgy did not work. The Steel Company turned to the more usual sources of iron; in spite of early losses and many subsequent difficulties the company flourished. Beardmore's of Parkhead went into steel in 1879, as did David Colville in 1880. These leading steel producers bought their pig in the British and indeed the European market where they could find it most cheaply. By 1881 Scotland had surpassed South Wales in the open hearth production of steel. Scottish steel output reached half a million tons by 1895. The ironmasters, instead of integrating forward into steel, did so backward into coal; so powerful did ironmaster families like the Bairds become in the coalfields that by the early 1890s some two-thirds of Scottish miners worked for them.

The dominant ethos of the west derived from heavy industry. It was held in its various forms by owners, managers and men. This industrial complex was Scotland's chief generator of wealth, and of its social problems.

6   The Railways

The railways too made an immense contribution to the economy. The 1830s and early 40s had been a time of tentative beginnings, consisting of short lines, largely providing links between the coal fields and the cities. Even the Edinburgh and Glasgow railway opened in 1842 was conceived mainly in these terms. Joining up with the English lines as they moved northward began with the

North British Railway, formed in 1844 to link Edinburgh and eastern Scotland with Newcastle; in 1845 the Caledonian Railway began the connection from Glasgow and the west over Beattock to Carlisle. The completion of the dense lowland network, and of the English connections, took some 30 years to the 1870s. But amalgamations and consolidation had been carried a long way in the 1860s, with five companies operating 98 per cent of the Scottish system. Of these the North British and the Caledonian held the palm of pride and performance. In the famous railway races beginning in 1895 the west and east coast trains competed from Euston and King's Cross respectively to Aberdeen; the race culminated between Perth and Kinnaber, the first train to get to Kinnaber proceeding in triumph along the single route to Aberdeen.

The estuaries of the east, those of the Forth and the Tay, were great natural obstacles to contact with Dundee and Aberdeen. Their bridging brought Scotland to the notice of the world, the Tay by the tragic collapse of 1879 and the replacement of 1887, and the Forth by the superb achievement of the great cantilevered structure of 1890. The West Highland Railway, the last important development, was opened for traffic in 1889, 5,000 men having blasted their way for five years through the glens.

The capital invested in Scottish railways was in 1850 £26.6 mn and in 1900 £166.1 mn. Its flotation was a major factor in the formation of the Scottish stock exchanges and in accustoming the Scots to a market in shares. The Scots financed the early mineral railways largely themselves, but English capital became significant in the Glasgow–Edinburgh link, and even more so with the trunk lines joining Scotland and England. As with the canals of an earlier generation, the capital cost of railway building was almost invariably calculated too low, though in most cases this was compensated by an underestimation of revenue arising from the great stimulus to trade, and particularly of passenger revenues.

7 The Pattern of Interaction

The industries that used the new transport facilities increasingly formed by the 1860s a complex in close interaction. All required the products of the coal mining, iron and steel, and engineering industries for their energy and machine inputs. The mills provided female employment to counterbalance the masculinity of iron and engineering. Shipbuilding was both a massive user of metal and a continuous challenge to the metallurgists and marine engineers, as well as requiring highly developed finishing trades, especially carpentry for passenger liners. The breweries and distilleries provided for the labour force, as did the rapidly growing food industries. As the cities grew the warehousemen and wholesalers thrived, creating vast repositories and distribution points within the cities.

8   Scottish Textiles

Cotton underwent a cycle of rise and decline, mainly in West Central Scotland, but also in Aberdeen. By 1840 steam-powered mills provided the principal industry of Glasgow. The earlier mills had been for spinning; by the 1850s power dominated weaving also. In so doing it intensified working class radicalism, especially among its leaders, the handloom weavers, present as early as the 1790s. By the 1880s Scottish textile manufacturers, with cotton dominant, employed 100,000 workers, of whom two-thirds were women, whose dexterity was rewarded with low wages. But cotton could not hold its place in the industrial pattern of the west of Scotland. The American civil war of the 1860s weakened it. There was an inability to continue to compete, perhaps due to a failure of management to adapt. The coarser counts were abandoned first, with a retreat to the finer cloths and more specialized markets.

Scottish woollens had become highly specialized in the upper range of the market much earlier. From the 1820s the tweeds of Galashiels and the borders were made popular by Sir Walter Scott, setting a new vogue in the informal wear of well-to-do men; the romantic of Abbotsford was an inadvertent promoter of many things, including the woollens of neighbouring entrepreneurs. There was also frame-knitted hosiery and underwear: indeed the high-grade knitwear of Hawick became widely celebrated. It could hold its markets over the generations, though the tweed of the Borders became subject to the competition of cheaper Yorkshire cloths. The Paisley shawl, based on Indian design idioms, achieved an enormous popularity by the 1830s, but faded rapidly in the early 1840s. In 1837 there were 6,000 looms making shawls; by 1843 there were 3,000. Hebridean Harris tweed was a new beginning in crafted quality cloth from the 1880s, to be worn by persons of social quality who were happily ignorant of the production procedures of the cottage weavers and finishers. Linen lived on in Dunfermline at the upper end of the market, providing napery for the table and sheets for the bed. Finally there was the lace making of Ayrshire, perhaps the last refuge of cottage industry, mechanized from 1875. Scottish fabrics of cotton, wool and linen were all thus forced into the quality range where changing tastes and rival producers made necessary a continuous sensitivity to consumers' preferences.

But there were three branches of textiles in which Scotland seized the mass production initiative and held it, namely cotton thread, jute and linoleum. In the making of sewing thread Coats of Paisley assumed a world lead, becoming the largest firm in British manufacturing industry, employing 6,000 people by 1890. It invaded the United States to circumvent the American tariff and dominated the American market from the 1870s and 1880s and especially after the extension by amalgamation with Patons of 1896. So much so that the firm came to the attention of America's trust-busters. It was marketing skill that made this dominance possible, permitting Coats to reap extraordinary economies of scale in production. The amalgamation with Patons gave the firm 80 per cent of the industry's world capacity. Archibald Coats (1840–1912) was known as the Napoleon of the thread trade; immense profits were generated, making no less than 11 members of the family millionaires. A more basic product thus replaced the Paisley shawl, for thread grew rapidly in importance with the mechanization of sewing. The Singer sewing machine company invaded Scotland from America in 1867, setting up in Clydebank, the first Singer factory outside the United States. The great Kilbowie factory was opened in 1884, eventually producing 12,000 machines per week. Its Scottish works became one of the great small machine factories of the world. It is one of the curiosities of Victorian business history that Coats of Britain and Singers of America whose products were so complementary, should reciprocally enter and dominate each other's national markets, doing so from bases within 5 miles of one another in the west of Scotland.

The Scottish exploitation of jute was even more dramatic than that of cotton thread. In 1832 one Watt of Dundee, having been intrigued by the possibility of jute, discovered that it could be made sufficiently pliable to be worked by machine if it was treated with whale oil, of which the city had a glut. Soon the producers of both benefited. Jute by the 1850s was the great sacking material, for grain, coffee beans, indeed anything that could be carried in the new large and cheap bags. During the American civil war fortunes were made supplying nose-bags for horses and sacking to the armies of both North and South. The boom conditions thus created were confirmed by the new power-driven machines. Dundee jute, like Paisley thread, enjoyed a near world monopoly of its product. Jute from Bengal came to the east of Scotland in vast quantities, to be worked in the factories by a largely female, low-paid labour force. The jute masters became a local aristocracy. Linen and canvas continued to be important: down to the end of the age of sail Dundee and Arbroath provided the greater part of the canvas that powered the Royal and merchant navies.

By 1866 the Camperdown jute works, the largest outside India, employed some 14,000 people, mostly women, being virtually the sole employer of the Lochee district: its ascendancy was marked by the erection in that year of Cox's Stack, 280 feet high, making the Cairngorms 100 miles away visible from its top. It was a master-piece of bricklaying, an Italian campanile dominating jutedom, discharging industrial smoke into the then pure upper air. There were in the 1870s some 72 mills and factories in Dundee employing 42,000 people.

In a textile-related field, that of linoleum (a floor covering built up on jute canvas from linseed oil), the Scots also achieved great success, with Kirkcaldy in Fife the great centre. So it was that three Scottish towns became in large measure textile based, and in a specialized manner, using the most advanced mass production methods, namely Paisley, Dundee and Kirkcaldy. Each of these places in later Victorian times was unthinkable except in terms of its basic industry and the kind of society it generated.

9 Chemicals, Oil and Spirits

Just as the demands of the textile mills had given an early impetus to engineering, so too with the chemicals industry. Out of the need for cheaper and more quick-acting bleach had come the St Rollox chemicals works, less than half a mile north of Glasgow Cathedral. It was the creation of Charles Tennant (1768–1838) a former weaver of radical inclination, and was to be the basis of an industrial family whose fine flower was to be Sir Charles Tennant (1823–1906) industrialist and financier, and his daughter Margot (1864–1945), wife of the last prime minister to govern through the Liberal party. St Rollox in its heyday was an extraordinary place, producing alkali very cheaply by the Leblanc process, but pushing much of the cost onto society by fearful sulphurous pollution of air, land and water courses. It was also, like Napier's yard, a training place for its industry.

Tennant's Tharsis Company revived Spanish mine workings that had been abandoned since the Romans: from them came copper, sulphur, iron and modest quantities of the precious metals. The Tharsis example was followed in 1873 by the Rio Tinto Company, founded by another Scot, Hugh Matheson (1821–1898), chairman of Messrs Matheson of Lombard Street, London, intimately associated with the greatest of East India houses, Jardine Matheson and Company. The copper from Spain was highly profitable; its sulphur was basic for the Leblanc process. Pyritic gold led to the discovery in 1887 by MacArthur and Forrest in the Tharsis laboratories in Crown Street, Glasgow, of the cyanide process for gold extraction. It raised the yield from 55 to 95 per cent, thus making possible an immense addition to the world's gold supply, especially from South Africa, thus relieving the global deflationary pressure exerted by gold shortage in the later nineteenth century.

Scotland also had a notable stake in oil production. In 1851 at Bathgate James Young (1811–83, known as 'Paraffin Young'), pioneered the exploitation of the shale deposits of West Lothian, the only workable shalefields in Europe outside Russia. Young patented a number of inventions associated with oil and spent a good deal of his life in litigation with the Americans. By the 1900s nearly two million tons of shale were being dug annually, employing 4,000 men, housing them in company cottages, and leaving as Young's memorial the vast flat-topped tips of waste that dominate the countryside.

In the production of spirits, especially whisky, Scotland asserted an unchallengeable dominance. In 1850 output was 10,847,000 gallons and in 1914 it was 28,024,000; at both times it was roughly twice that of England and Wales. Scots were of course enthusiastic consumers of their own product, but it also generated important export earnings.

10 The Pattern of Concentration

By 1900 Scottish industry, so largely centred in the west, had focused itself around engineering, both mechanical and civil, specializing in engines and machines, heavy castings, plate, ships to carry goods and passengers and to protect the Empire and enforce the *Pax Britannica*, together with locomotives for British, imperial and foreign railways. It was prosperity or depression in these industries that set the pulse for Scotland. All this rested on a base of iron, steel and coal. A marvellous set of external economies had asserted itself, whereby the entire pattern, sustained by world demand, was in mutual reinforcement, not only as to products, but as to management and the labour force. The elements that had provided diversity and balance in the 1850s, chiefly cotton and chemicals, though they had receded in importance, were still present. A variety of other industries flourished including brewing and distilling, paper making and printing, furniture making and the building trades, together with a remarkable growth in the wholesale and retail trades.

The overall Scottish shape of employment had radically changed between 1851 and 1901. The labour force in defined occupations had grown from 1269.9 thousand to 1879.2 thousand. Within these figures agriculture, forestry and fishing had fallen from 347.6 to 237.3 thousand; textile, leather and clothing contracted from 366.4 to 327.8 thousand. By contrast the metal trades grew from 60.8 to 205.8 and miscellaneous manufacture from 66.2 to 130.4; mining and quarrying expanded from 48.1 to 132.2. Most dramatic of all was the growth in the service trades including building from 380.8 to 845.7, approaching half of the total labour force.

11 The Pattern of Response

Within this general picture between 1870 and 1900, however, the responses of business men within the various sectors of industry were very different. Some of the coal masters, especially the owners of the multitude of small collieries, tended to be a conservative lot making little use of the coal cutters, available from the mid 80s, or of electricity or haulage machinery. Other colliery owners were progressive, especially in opening new seams in Fife. Though the coal masters had some success in export markets, they were not sympathetic to technical education and theory, believing in the work force learning on the job. In iron also there was much technical backwardness, with furnaces that were too small and poor handling gear. There was little integration of pig iron and steel. Even the steel entrepreneurs, in spite of raising Scottish output substantially, were less progressive than they might have been.

In striking contrast were shipbuilding and marine engineering. Here the men of business did extraordinary well. With them a cumulative atmosphere of adaptation and success prevailed, no doubt generated by the ever-changing technical demands that confronted them. There was a brisk adoption of steel, accompanied by advances in engineering practice, the application of longitudinal construction of ships hulls, embodying the cellular principle yielding lighter, larger and stronger vessels. Scientific designs and construction methods were introduced. Piece-work payments were extended from riveters and smiths to all manner of trades. Machines came in with punches, presses and riveting methods using power. Labour relations, so bad in the coalfields and iron and steel, could on occasion be turbulent in engineering and shipbuilding, but were not seriously damaging. The ca' canny attitude (do not be over zealous at work) was increasingly taking hold on the Clyde as workers took to restrictive practices in self-defence. The shipbuilders and engineers were beginning to turn toward new principles of education, realizing that the old apprenticeship system was not enough. But this response fell short of what was needed. Not for the first or last time a new and thrusting range of industries, its management exhilarated by their own atmospherics, could exist alongside elements of stagnation and failure to respond, rooted in the past.

2

The Urbanization of Scotland

1 The Urban Inheritance

The new generation of traders and industrialists gaining momentum after 1832, together with the professional men who serviced them, brought about a great enlargement of the cities and determined their new shape. They did these things almost inadvertently. They did not see the cities that were the scene of their activities as their responsibility. Each city-region was allowed to grow and assume its industrial form not as a planned procedure, but as the outcome of competition for sites for industry and commerce. Working-class housing was a kind of residual, its location determined largely by proximity to the workplace and the availability of 'made down' housing in the old urban cores. Thus did the choices of the business class as to where to produce and where to live dominate an evolving urban morphology, but without conscious control.

Radical variations arose between the four major cities from differences in the nature of their terrain and in their industrial and social mixes. The New Town of Edinburgh, indeed, provided an exception to the general lack of planning, reflecting the unique condition of part of that city in the later eighteenth century, though the Old Town continued to be a dramatic exemplification of spontaneous growth and shape. Private enterprise planning could produce middle-class enclaves within the cities and at their perimeters, but these too were partly at least the result of commercial calculation. There was too the influence of the Dean of Guild Court in each city which, though it did not initiate it, could exercise certain amenity controls over development.

Though a range of generalized phenomena occurred as Scotland urbanized, as of course took place in all societies undergoing this change, including that of the formation of social class, there is a rival perspective that sees important aspects of societal change as rooted in specific urban morphologies and regional patterns of industry. The distribution on the ground within a given city of occupations and of the homes of middle and working classes had much to do with determining the patterns of regional social, political and cultural behaviour, and of attitudes of class to class. With the extensions in the franchise vote-seeking politicians were not slow to discover this.

The four principal cities of Scotland had been formed long before the industrial revolution; indeed Edinburgh, Glasgow, Aberdeen and Dundee were all ancient places, where much had been enacted. Their size, shape and nature had been determined by the exploitation of their natural settings within the technology and market opportunities of pre-industrial times. The matrix thus set in each case was to have a significant continuity in the industrial age, for the compelling circumstances of the past are not easily expunged.

2 Edinburgh the Semi-Capital

The location of Edinburgh had been determined over the centuries in which the rulers of Scotland had been seeking by trial and error for that place at which the nation could be focused for coherence, rule and defence: they had hit upon a place of confluence of the principal land routes, as determined by the gaps between Scotland's hills, lying further south than Perth or Stirling and thus closer to England, combining this with access to northern Europe by the Firth of Forth. Within the site thus chosen the historical shape of Edinburgh had been determined by the ridge along which it was built. It was contained to the North in its formative phase by the Nor' Loch, and to the south by the steep hollow of the Cowgate and to the east by Holyrood Loch. These natural obstacles were to have a profound effect on the shape of the city long after they had been drained or bridged.

Edinburgh had produced on the ground a segregation of class and function dating from earlier times, which was to be ever more strongly confirmed, though changing in form through the first half of Victoria's reign. The city's topography and economy consolidated this dramatic division. It was in the Old Town that the history of the city and indeed much of that of Scotland lay. It had been the stage trodden by John Knox, Mary Queen of Scots, the

Covenanters, Deacon Brodie (the inspiration of Mr Hyde) and many others of Scotland's sombrely dramatic past. It was also in the mid-century still the place of business of merchants, bankers, lawyers and craftsmen. When everyone lived in the Old Town they traditionally mingled in the streets. But at home they had been distinct horizontally, the better off living on the middle floors of the tenements while the poor lived above them.

Though the functional base of Edinburgh did not greatly change in Victoria's reign, continuing to be professional and service-based rather than industrial, the morphology of the city did. The aristocracy and gentry, together with the leaders of the professions and of business, by a remarkable effort of planning and investment, had created the New Town to the north of the Old, beginning in the 1780s. They removed themselves thence, away from the mounting squalor of the Old Town. By 1830 the New Town had 5,000 houses and 40,000 people, approaching one quarter of the total population of Edinburgh including Leith. As the decades passed Edinburgh became more and more divided; there were two Edinburghs, not one.

By 1832 the face of much of the city was being remade. There was an efflorescence of classical buildings and monuments, with the Calton Hill as a Necropolis, in a general setting of Augustan housing, squares and streets, a celebration of Scotland's leading part in the European Enlightenment of the eighteenth and early nineteenth centuries. But as early as 1832 much of the intellectual and cultural impetus had been lost. Moreover the greatest days of patronage of the New Town by people of rank was over; there was now for the greater landed magnates the increasing attraction of a town house in London.

The accumulated confusion and incompetence of the oligarchic rule of the city was finally revealed when, in the year following the Burgh Reform Act of 1833, Edinburgh was declared bankrupt. The rate of population growth diminished thereafter: whereas it had doubled between 1801 and 1831 to 166,000, the next 50 years brought a growth of 82 per cent to 295,000; in 1901 Edinburgh had 413,008 inhabitants.

Meanwhile the condition of the Old Town, already bad by 1832, had by the mid century degenerated yet further, to become a fearful concentration of misery and vice. Bad harvests and trade depression brought uprooted people to add to the festering mass. There was a certain amount of middle-class fear that the barbarians of the Old Town might erupt from their lairs to threaten the life of the city. No new houses were built in the Old Town – the subdivision and crowding became relentlessly worse. The canyons of tall, crow-stepped houses vacated by the middle classes had become places of gross human degradation, with narrow closes, passages, holes in the wall, cheap partitioning and hidden rooms. All of this was projected in dramatic detail by the Report of 1865 of Dr Littlejohn, the first Medical Officer of Health. He described how in the Old Town the working classes and the paupers, with their human wastes, shared the confined space with the smoke, smells and effluvia, of tanneries, breweries, foundries and cow byres.

The Princes Street Gardens set in the bed of the old Nor' Loch shielded the middle classes of the New Town from the sight of the Old. Nor was the Old Town opened up by the coming of the railway to the heart of the city as in the Glasgow case: by 1846 the railway had reached Waverley Station, doing so not by replacing slums, but by sharing the bed of the Nor' Loch with Princes Street Gardens.

The Edinburgh New Town had been changing. Shopping and banking had invaded Princes Street, George Street and St Andrew's Square. Most of Princes Street was commercialized by 1875, though the exclusive clubs there held their own. A new central business district had been created in the New Town, just as in Glasgow. Similarly middle-class housing extended: the New Town had grown northward from the 1830s, with crescents fitting neatly around the hill contours; from the 1870s southern suburbs grew up. In the last decade of Victoria's reign to 1901 the outward creep of villas doubled the built-up area.

The contrast between the economic base of Edinburgh and that of Glasgow was striking. In 1861 Edinburgh and Leith, though they had a population about one-half of that of Glasgow, had less than one-third as many workers in manufacturing industry. There were almost no textiles, and hence few industrial jobs for women, though there was plenty of employment for them in domestic service. Instead it was the trades that provided services of one kind or another, or homes and furnishings and vehicles for the better off, that constituted the principal basis of business and male employment. There were cabinet makers, upholsterers, polishers, coachmakers, blacksmiths, workers in leather, glass, brass and rubber, as well as tailors, boot and shoemakers. The notable concentration of publishers encouraged papermaking, printing and the production of paper-making machinery. Brewing and distilling also thrived. This range of small-scale industries provided a more stable economic base than that of Glasgow. It catered for a prosperous upper and middle-class and the landed men and the lawyers (of whom there were five times as many in proportion to population as in Glasgow by the 1860s). The judges were a powerful clique especially at the peak of their profession as Senators of the College of Justice, often combining the wielding of the sanctions of society with an advanced eccentricity. Then there were the three chartered banks, all centred in Edinburgh. For though the Glaswegians were active in the 1830s and 40s in floating their own joint-stock banks, they could not in the long run overcome the dominance of the Edinburgh banks, with their landed deposits and their country-wide branch systems. Edinburgh confirmed its position as Scotland's financial centre with its great growth of insurance and investment companies. But the elements of industrialization that helped to make Glasgow and Aberdeen subject to speculative outbursts were absent in Edinburgh: the experience of 1825 was not repeated; Edinburgh seems to have been able to place the funds that converged upon it without exposing them to high risk.

Edinburgh, though without a secular parliament, was the place of meeting of the General Assembly of the Church of Scotland and of the other presbyterian churches. It had St Giles Cathedral, together with Scotland's order of chivalry, the Knights of the Thistle. It was the home of the sovereign's bodyguard in Scotland, the Royal Company of Archers. Edinburgh had taken the lead in Scotland in adopting the English public school system, combining the confirmation of the existing class predominance with a certain obeisance to the older Scottish tradition of seeking out and bringing on the best of the young talent.

So it was that landed wealth, together with the middle-class professionals, living in a city that had embellished itself with impressive memorials and buildings, generated an Edinburgh outlook that was self-confident and indifferent to what went on elsewhere, to a degree that could be offensive to Glasgow. Edinburgh too had its slums, but they were not by the later nineteenth century on the Glasgow scale, and were less visible to the wider world.

3   Glasgow the Industrial Powerhouse

Glasgow's rise from a modest cathedral and college town to trading and industrial eminence was the product of circumstances different from those of Edinburgh, and relied on a great estuary to the west and deposits of coal and iron to the east. Glasgow, like Venice, had her empire *ad mare* and *ad terram*, each part of the other. Her shape and density, and hence the life of her labouring inhabitants, was not, like that of Edinburgh, seriously affected by being confined by nature to a narrow strip of land, though eventually in the later nineteenth century the confines of the Clyde Valley were to assert themselves. The conditions that governed Edinburgh's location and nature help to explain why that city fell so far behind Glasgow in growth of population and output in the nineteenth century, but they were to prove more favourable in the longer run of the later twentieth century.

Glasgow was by far the faster grower: already by 1831 it had a population of 274,000 against Edinburgh's 166,000. In its internal morphology it was in a sense the simpler case. The High Street of Glasgow, the ancient spine of the city, was not constricted and defined by natural features as was Edinburgh. There the Castle on its rock was a dramatic terminal to the city in the West, and in the East there was the palace of Holyrood House set against Arthur's Seat and the Salisbury Crags. Glasgow could expand westward over the first and second of its gridirons laid out by the surveyors in the 1780s and 1820s without having to jump a natural obstacle, as did Edinburgh's New Town in overleaping the Nor' Loch. This meant that the wealthier class of Glasgow could build their squares and houses over relatively easy terrain as they abandoned the ancient core to the artisans, who in turn left much of it to the growing concentration of what contemporaries called the residuum.

By 1832 the latter existed in the dense and debased slums that landlords had created out of the high pre-industrial tenements by subdivision, cheap partitions and in-building. In 1851 nearly 13 per cent of Glasgow's inhabitants were paupers. The dwellers in the deep slums were of three main kinds: the drop-outs who had reached a depth from which there could be no recovery, the criminals (whose principal prey was property), and the miscellaneous providers for both groups, the shebeen keepers, the street traders and the low prostitutes. In Glasgow the cotton industry, the basic employment of the city down to the mid-century, concentrated first its spinning and later its weaving mills around the Green and to the east and south-east where they were interspersed with workers' housing: it was here that the factory hand and artisan lived. By 1832 this townshape had been established.

Its governing processes continued to operate thereafter. The slums of the old heart of Glasgow, between its west and east ends, sank further and further into debasement. The middle classes moved progressively westward; indeed a good many of the more substantial merchants had by the 1850s not only acquired town houses up west, but country homes down the Clyde as well, travelling in to business on Mondays by train and steamer.

Between the Old town and the New there developed a shopping centre with Buchanan Street (begun as a residential street in 1780) becoming a kind of Glaswegian Regent Street. The first gridiron steadily lost its housing function in the new century, being encroached upon for business offices. Onto this intermediate zone of shopping and business facilities middle classes and working classes converged and mingled – it was here that the owners of carriages and the beggars met on the causeway. Theatres, churches and public buildings were in shared territory. When Kossuth the Hungarian patriot addressed the liberal middle classes of Glasgow on 'The Organic Structure of Modern Europe' in 1858 he did so in the City Hall from which his hearers debouched into streets filled with pedlars crying their fish, apples and other wares, groups of drunkards, diseased prostitutes, pickpockets and street arabs (homeless children). This, then, was the shape of Glasgow reached by the mid 1860s. Half way through Victoria's reign the city though highly prosperous had produced social dereliction on an altogether new scale. Densities rose from 65 persons to the acre in 1851 to 93 in 1891; in the wynds there were 583 to the acre in 1858.

The Royal Exchange and the Glasgow clubs had been for more than a generation the meeting places of a self-assured higher bourgeoisie. The latter were indeed in a masterful position, enjoying a low tax on incomes after 1842 and none on profits, few really serious restraints on pollution and an almost uninhibited choice of industrial location. Their philosophy was that business and the state were separate spheres, and that the market system would act as the great arbiter and regulator.

Glasgow and indeed Scottish prosperity reached its peak in two international exhibitions, held in 1888 and 1901 in Kelvingrove Park, then the focus of her west end, with the new buildings of the ancient University, erected in 1870, looking down from Gilmorehill. In 1901 there were no less than a million and a half attendances, viewing exhibits celebratory of art, industry and science. The city was proud of itself, abounding in confidence and assertion.

Industrial and urban growth in the west of Scotland taken together meant that Scotland had developed by the last decades of the nineteenth century a ponderous regional imbalance. Glasgow had held 5 per cent of Scotland's population in 1801; by 1891 this had risen to almost 20 per cent. Productive capacity, employment and population focused on the Clyde Valley became an ever larger proportion of the whole. By 1901 the West Central Scotland region contained nearly two millions of Scotland's total of four and one half millions. Here was a society in which industrial urbanization had gone as far as anywhere in the world: it was classical of its kind, attracting observers from many countries, especially the United States. It contained the full range of social classes as determined by the technology of the maturity phase of the first industrial revolution: there were magnates, middle and lesser capitalists, managers, foremen, and a workforce ranging from the highest level of skill to the lifting, carrying and cleaning labourer and including clerks and shopworkers.

The growth of Glasgow reflected the fact that the British industrial revolution was not complete by the 1830s, and indeed in a sense it was not even very far advanced, but was patchy and slow, not able to generate its full cumulative force until after 1850. Thus whereas the population of the city was 274,000 in 1831: by 1881 it was 511,000 and by 1901 the figure stood at 761,000. With the acceleration from the 1850s came greater concentration on shipbuilding and engineering in its many branches; thus the diversity of the city's industrial base diminished with the decline of the cotton industry and associated chemicals. Though the mills still belched their smoke from around Glasgow Green, cotton was no longer king and the days of the Dunlops and Houldsworths as the city's industrial magnates were numbered, to be replaced by men like William Dixon, whose ironworks, 'Dixon's Blazes', lit up the night sky. The city was already by 1832 the centre of a canal system for carrying coal, iron, chemicals, timber and stone. It rapidly became a leading railway centre, beginning with the 'mineral railways' to the east. But trade and commerce were also important. Glasgow developed vast wholesale concerns, 'warehouses', which served the retail trade of much of Scotland. The city had long dealt in primary produce, especially sugar and cotton, making links with the West Indies and the United States. By the 1880s the Glasgow iron price dominated the British market, reflected in speculation in Glasgow iron warrants. Primary and heavy goods such as these helped to encourage the reckless spirit of Glasgow, so different from the caution of Edinburgh.

Banking in the Glasgow atmosphere was a much more challenging affair than in Edinburgh, both because of the elements of instability in the regional economy and because of the growing need of heavy industry repeatedly to renew what were ostensibly short-term loans. Glasgow dominated the business failure picture: between 1850 and 1879 the city's share of Scottish liquidations was never less than 23 per cent (1869) and was as high as 42 per cent (1855); Edinburgh's low was 6 per cent (1866) and her high 17 per cent (1853): though Glasgow had a larger share of Scottish business, its share of failures is greater than can be explained thereby. The risks of Glasgow business were dramatized by the collapse of the Western Bank in 1857 and of the City of Glasgow Bank in 1878. The latter was one of the most extraordinary in British banking history. In spite of these calamities Glasgow felt that though Edinburgh might *be* the capital, Glasgow *had* the capital. This was true not only in the investment sense, but in terms of the personal and family fortunes being generated. Great satisfaction was taken in the fact that by the 1890s Glasgow could claim to be the second city, not only of Britain, but of the Empire. Not only so, it was a city celebrated for its civic government, gracefully receiving guests from foreign cities to demonstrate to them how transport and other municipal affairs should be managed. Civic pride was strong in Glasgow, and was not hidden under a bushel.

At the same time Glasgow was a place where industrial tensions could be inflamed in times of bad trade. Moreover the concentration of the working-class population in the east end of the city represented a housing and welfare failure of a kind that was notorious. In the later 1880s the worst districts of Glasgow lay around St Andrews Square (with the splendid eighteenth-century church a reminder of lost days of grandeur), Calton proper, Broomfield, Bridgegate Wynds, Cowcaddens and the Gorbals. It was in this part of the city that ethnic bigotry, sustained by the Orange Order, could thrive. Yet even here the peace was kept by a magistracy and police force that did not hesitate to wield the law. The opening of the great prison at Barlinnie in 1882 was a symbol both of urban growth and of the irresolvable problem of what to do with those guilty of crimes against the person or against property.

4 Aberdeen the Versatile

Aberdeen and its region did not produce human debasement on the scale of Glasgow and Edinburgh. Because of the difficulties of its northern location it did not grow at a comparable rate. It had 57,000 inhabitants in 1831 and 154,000 by 1901. Within its growth limitations the adaptability of its business leaders saved it both from decline and from excessive specialization and narrow market dependence. Even in the phase in which cotton was at its height in Aberdeen there was no large industrial proletariat. Serious social problems there certainly were, as tackled by Sheriff Watson and others in the 1840s, but they were not comparable to those of the Old Towns of the two dominant cities. It is true that by the building of Union Street Aberdeen too acquired its New Town to which the successful business and professional men removed. But the old core continued to be the focus of their occupational lives, bringing all Aberdonians together.

From the 1860s Aberdeen manifested certain striking character- istics. Firstly, there was its economic resilience, based on business initiative, through which it could find new means of investment and employment when old ones faded. The railways, when once well joined with the improved port, stimulated and focused trade. There were diverse linkages creating secondary employments, as for example when the greatly expanded fishery enlarged the timber trade with Scandinavia for boxes and barrels. The agriculture of the region continued to be efficient and prosperous, with Aberdeen its outlet. Secondly, however, and partially inconsistent with the notion of continuous adjustment, the rate of population growth was not constant: it was much reduced in the 1840s, and especially in the 1850s, recovered strongly from 1871 to 1901, and collapsed thereafter to an absolute *decrease* in the decade after 1911. Thus even the impressive responses of the business community to the chal- lenges of change did not meet the requirements of linear growth in population.

The recruitment of the city of Aberdeen was highly regional: whereas Glasgow attracted the Irish and the Highlanders on a large scale, Aberdonians were to a very great degree northeastern stock. The result of all these circumstances taken together was that Aberdeen, though it certainly generated social problems, did so to a much lesser degree than the other three major cities. It, like others, had its areas of high congestion, making an attack on the slums necessary, as in the Shorelands in the 1870s. But Aberdeen was spared the grossest human debasement.

Because Aberdeen neither committed itself more and more strongly to heavy industrial development as did Glasgow, nor did it rest upon the professions, landed wealth and small-scale enterprises and crafts as did Edinburgh, its occupational mix differed from both. Before 1832 Aberdeen had traded to the Baltic, it had had a modest fishery, and had been the marketing and cultural centre of the agrarian north-east. As the improving farmers raised the productivity of much of the Aberdeenshire hinterland from a poverty-ridden near subsistence level to an astonishing new prosperity, aided by the development of the carriage of farm produce coastwise to southern cities by sea, Aberdeen's marketing and shipping functions grew. Then in 1832 came a new process for polishing granite, thus adding to the city's exports; in 1839 the city made a new beginning with the launching by Alexander Hall and Co., of the first Aberdeen clipper ship, bringing an air of high-seas glamour to the city's name. But it was textiles that continued to supply most employment. The city had long been the regional centre for the putting-out system of linen and woollen spinning and weaving, sustaining employment and incomes in the crofts and village cottages. With the coming of the factory system to Aberdeen small-scale subsistence farming in the region was threatened, finding it more difficult to continue without its auxiliary income. As early as 1800 crofters had moved to the city in considerable numbers; by 1832 the textile factories along the Don were the principal employers; by 1843 some 25 per cent of Aberdeen's inhabitants worked in them. Lacking coal and iron, no engineering developments of any scale ensued.

In the 1850s Aberdeen, unlike Glasgow and Dundee with their heavy specialisms of cotton and jute respectively, had a diversified textile sector, shared by wool, linen and cotton. But the distance of Aberdeen's mills from coal and from southern markets were severe handicaps. Power-loom weaving made a heavy demand on local capital, at a time when it was being attracted abroad. In the aftermath of the collapse of the railway boom in 1847 local manufacturers found themselves in severe difficulties: only two textile factories survived the 50s. In 1845 81,000 bales of textiles had left the harbour; 10 years later, with sea carriage still far more important than rail, only 9,000 bales were shipped. This collapse meant mass unemployment from 1848 to 1856, bringing a lowering of population growth and an increase in prostitution. But the business men of the city showed a remarkable resilience. Its manufacturers realized that they could not compete in the standard lines, and so sought specialisms: Aberdeen 'winceys' (a material used for skirts or overcoats, made of wool sometimes combined with cotton) made possible a modest revival of the city's textiles. Aberdeen took to the deep-sea fisheries and rapidly developed the building of steam trawlers. The opening of a new fishmarket in 1889 marked a rising trend of prosperity. The 1890s were a further testing time for Aberdeen's industries, made so by American protectionism and local labour disputes. As a response new continental markets were acquired, processes improved and purchasing and marketing made more efficient.

In the meantime, however, the city had developed a considerable investment sector: money from the North East was pumped out from the 1840s into land companies and ranches in the American west (a good deal of the wild west was Aberdeen financial territory) and into Canada and Australia. This represented the accumulation of capital in the city-region and its search for higher returns outside it. But such activities were characteristically risky: there were large losses as well as gains beginning with the near collapse of the North of Scotland Bank in 1847 after bad investments in lands through the Illinois Investment Company.

5 Dundee, the One-Industry City

Dundee in 1832 had its mixture of smaller industries, including weaving. There was also the fishery, more venturesome than that of Aberdeen, including the hunting of whales, though this element was threatened because the whale population was beginning to decline. The production of hodden grey woollen cloth and broad bonnets had given place to flax products, namely linen, sailcloth and sackings. With the new textile age came large four-storey mills. The flax was now no longer home grown, but was imported from Prussia and Russia, extending the town's overseas trade. From the later 1830s jute challenged flax as the basic material of Dundee's mills.[1] The mills, together with working-class tenements, defined the town. Flax and jute came to dominate everything. Under its influence Dundee became a polarized city, with a relatively small middle range of society between the jute masters and their factory workers. Not surprisingly the city produced a radical response. But the very success in profit making of the jute masters induced their own ultimate destruction. In 1853 certain Dundee jute men, their

[1]See chapter 1, section 8 above.

minds moving to the economies that could be gained in factories in Bengal where labour was even cheaper, began the industrialization of Calcutta by setting up factories there.

In Dundee a strong class pattern had developed by the 1860s, based on linen and jute. The tall chimneys of the mills dominated the landscape from every quarter, their smoke darkening the heavens every day except the Sabbath. The millowners of course sought clear air, finding it at the little fishing village of Broughty Ferry some three miles to the east. The building of Reform Street in the 1830s, together with some Georgian terraces, had represented the first phase of factory-master living. This was the focus of Dundee's New Town, wherein were built the Kinnaird Hall, the Albert Institute, the Royal Exchange, the High Street and the Post Office. But desperate water and sewage problems in the city, together with the smoke, impelled the exodus of the millowners, made easier by a railway link after 1839. In the 1860s the mansions of the jute magnates at Broughty Ferry assumed a new scale.

Meanwhile the mill workers remained crowded round the mills; the worst mixture of closely packed factories and unwholesome dwellings stood on ground known from earlier times are 'The Pleasance'. The labouring part of the populace disported themselves on Saturday nights near the docks round the Greenmarket where the street preacher urged salvation, his voice competing with those of the pedlar and the ballad singer. There were loud offers of sale from quack doctors with nostrums and galvanic batteries, and from vendors of beef and sweeties and from the promoters of exhibitions of freaks of nature, living and dead. In 1844 Lord Cockburn described Dundee as 'the palace of Scottish blackguardism'; the rest of the century did little to redeem this epithet, though from 1895 there was indeed an effective attack on serious crime.

Dundee, having outdistanced Paisley in the 1830s, with a population of 63,000 in 1841, ran neck and neck with Aberdeen in the later nineteenth century in claiming to be Scotland's third largest city, having 161,000 inhabitants by 1901. But it was strikingly different. Though Dundee had industries other than jute, it was the single element of jute that dominated the life of the city from the 1840s to 1914 and beyond. This brought a heavy imbalance, the fate of the city hanging on a fairly narrow set of markets, with Calcutta asserting itself as a cheaper rival. To this precariousness was added the social imbalance that stemmed from the jute labour force, in which women predominated in excess of two to one. This meant a low-wage industry, with the consequence of ever increasing congestion of labour round the mills in industrial slums. It also meant that because in so many of the working families the women were the wage earners, there was often a reversal of sex roles: masterful women dominated husbands who 'boiled the kettle'. Among the women there was fierce class distinction between the aristocratic weavers and the lowly spinners.

Between the labour force and the jute kings there was an almost absolute polarity; the world of mill girl culture and of the 'platties' (workers' tenements near the mills), and that of Broughty Ferry were antithetical. The workers were enveloped in smoke, grime and the smell of whale oil; their employers gazed across graceful gardens to the waters of the Tay. Certainly, the juteocracy created some fine public buildings in the centre of Dundee. These provided the city with an impressive core where an urban culture could express itself, but it was exclusively middle class. There was, however, an element of the middle class in Dundee who were concerned with improvement in the city based upon the search for a social philosophy. Prominent among them were young men who came to teach in the new University College, founded in 1881, virtually the sole creation of the Baxter family. In the 1880s the Dundee Social Union was a serious ameliorative movement concerned with housing, health, diet and disease.

Dundee, though so different from Aberdeen, shared with it the limitations of growth. Juteopolis, like its rival the diversified Aberdeen, was contained within the limits of a moderately sized city.

6 The Inter-City Comparison by 1900

Scotland by 1900 thus had four principal sub-economies or city-regions, and four distinctive modes of urban life. Much earlier indeed than 1832 Edinburgh and Glasgow were firmly the focal points of Scotland. Patrick Geddes, the Scottish father of the modern study of cities, used the concept of 'life forces' as applied to cities: these, he said had produced by the end of the century two Scottish regional capitals, which, though separated by only some 40 miles, and sharing a common national heritage, were distinct geographically, meteorologically, racially and spiritually. Aberdeen and Dundee were outlying urban cores. But though each of the four was distinct, and consciously so, in another sense all four city-regions comprised a single phenomenon – they were the Scottish expression of the new urban age.

Glasgow, the giant among Scottish cities, had worked itself by its self-confirming pattern of heavy industry into world stature, but also into a dangerous dependence upon the world economy. Edinburgh enjoyed the advantages of metropolitanism and the service industries, though its growth had been limited thereby to half of that of Glasgow. Aberdeen had shown a protean capacity to adjust to its circumstances and to changing markets. Dundee, by contrast, had become a city dominated by a single product and by the low-wage female labour that it had generated.

Glasgow had early seized the industrial lead, though her economic base passed from a dependence on textiles in 1851 to a commitment to engineering and shipbuilding by 1900. Her morphology did not, however, radically change, but was, indeed, confirmed. The east and west ends continued to be distinct. A large pool of labour was centrally located in the oldest parts of the city, so that as a class the poor constituted a paradox, living on the most expensive land. For this reason they had to be piled up and crowded together in tenements, accepting, because they had to, the social costs of noise, filth, crime, neglect and subdivision. To this most of the old style radicals had no solution to offer, their thoughts being a mixture of social amelioration (of which education was a chief component), free trade to sustain the local economy and attacks on the wealth of the landed interest. Proposals to solve the problem of the slums by pulling them down and rebuilding at much lower densities encountered the limitation of land shortage at the centre accompanied by impossible travel costs if the poorer classes were uplifted to parts of the perimeter. The wealthier could buy amenity and status by further migration, accepting the costs of commuting. By so doing they pre-empted perimeter land. The skilled artisans could rent a modest level of amenity in their own districts of Partick, Govan, Dennistoun and Crosshill. The middle territory of the city in its functional heart continued to be shared between classes, at least on the streets. The buildings had become more and more impressive, making the city centre of Glasgow one of Britain's Victorian architectural achievements, but by the same token reducing working-class participation in downtown street life. The City Chambers, completed in 1889, were a stupendous headquarters for a civic government that was overwhelmingly middle class.

But in spite of its business face and its class tensions, Glasgow had developed a kind of austere beauty. At its old core stood its ancient cathedral with the battle flags of its regiments, and on the bluff beyond there stood the fantasy of its necropolis, developed since 1833, on the model of Père Lachaise in Paris, wherein lay so many of the men of business destiny, their success celebrated by competitive tomb-building, a spine-chilling sight against a sunset. Further west stood the reincarnation of the fifteenth-century university, standing in gothic splendour on its commanding hillside, its tower marking the intellectual centre of Scotland's most populous city-region. The people had their park of Glasgow Green; the middle classes had created the West End Park, a place of spacious walkways ornamented by a splendid museum and art gallery. The shops of Buchanan Street and Sauchiehall Street were prosperous tributes to the city's spending power. The police were acknowledged by all classes as a source of order, but they were expected to be tough.

The Glasgow–Edinburgh differences did not diminish: indeed by 1900 they had been confirmed. Whereas Glasgow epitomized the way of life and the problems of the industrial age in something approaching a classic form, Edinburgh, like London, was *sui generis*. Edinburgh had the air of a capital and some of its institutions, being the centre of the Scottish churches, the law, education and banking and finance. Indeed it may be that the lack of political power in Edinburgh, with no parliament and no royal court, increased the self-conscious feelings of her lieges that their city was a capital, making them yet more aloof toward industrial Glasgow. Edinburgh had nothing approaching Glasgow's industrial proletariat. Physically the difference between the Old and New Towns of Edinburgh made a more distinctive break in urban morphology. But by 1900 Edinburgh had become one of the most successful townscapes of Europe in terms of architecture and layout, the epitome of how a capital city should look: an Athens had indeed been created in the North. Whereas Old and New Towns, with their radically contrasting idioms, might have created a clash of styles, the opposite had occurred, producing at once a splendid unity and contrast. From the high ground of Arthur's Seat, an eminence that Glasgow lacks, Edinburgh could be seen in its splendour with its domes and spires, its streets and their defining buildings, in a setting of land and sea.

In a sense, however, Aberdeen had a claim to being Scotland's ideal city. In the 1890s it had the lowest Scottish urban death-rate, the lowest housing density, the lowest percentage of families in one-room houses and the highest percentage of those with three rooms, the lowest level of crime and probably the highest level of literacy. Though Aberdeen, like other cities, contained pockets of serious degradation, they were on a considerably lesser scale. All this related, of course, to the economic success and adaptability of the city and its region, together with the blessing that there had been no distorting boom in particular sectors leading to a commitment that attracted a labour force that both in number and in kind could not be found jobs in the next phase. The achievement of Aberdeen was the more notable in that it did not enjoy the advantages of a metropolis as did Edinburgh, with its discharge of national functions. But Aberdeen, in terms of its role in its region did enjoy a sub-metropolitan status.

Dundee was the obverse of Aberdeen. Its economic and social pattern continued on its curious course, dependent upon flax and jute, with all that this implied. It was a grim place even by the standards of an industrial town. It had not suffered the stresses of places like Motherwell where industrial imbalance was aggravated by a mainly male labour force, but things were bad enough. The jute workers could make no effective stand against their masters: their attempts at union organization only began in the 1870s. Though there were improvements in civic government, especially policing, the standard of amenity for the workers remained dismal: as late as 1912 the 300 courts, footways and passages in the centre of Dundee were entirely unpaved.

7 The Satellite and Country Towns

Urbanization outside the major cities took two principal forms. There were the industrial towns that were in a sense satellites to the greater centres. These were chiefly in the west, with Glasgow as their focus; Paisley, Kilmarnock, Motherwell, Airdrie, Coatbridge. Paisley, indeed, in the early part of the century challenged Dundee for fourth place among Scottish cities. In these western satellites the same formative processes that operated in the larger cities were present, though because of the lesser scale of development they were so to a lesser degree. Thus something like an Old and a New Town can be traced in most cases, with class segregation and an area of concentrated debasement, together with public buildings on which the influence of the classical revival was strong, sponsored by the business class who needed them for both business and as symbols of local urban pride.

The experience of Glasgow's set of satellite towns continued to have much in common with their industrial metropolis. Heavy industry, iron and steel, textiles and mining set the tenor of life. The tenement set the framework of home and family. Each of these towns structured itself into a community and a polity, with its town council and provost. In general their working-class politics resembled those of Glasgow, especially after the widening of the male franchise in 1884, and when the Independent Labour Party after 1893 could add its growing strength to the other elements of working-class politics.

Secondly, there were the towns that remained largely agrarian, continuing to service farming regions and providing marketing points: among them were Perth, Inverness and Dumfries. Here the rate of change, though often significant, was not on the same scale. Though such places had their industries, these were usually closely related to agriculture; a town like Ayr was both rural and industrial. In places where the impact of industry showed mainly in the form of increased demand for farm products there could be modest growth, and the Old Town could be spared the ravages of large-scale middle-class abandonment and working-class overcrowding, though most towns developed a quasi-surburban element, as well as containing poor quarters.

8 The Pattern Set

The pattern of Scotland's urbanization had been largely set by the end of the 1860s, half-way through Victoria's reign. The cities were of course to grow larger in later decades, but their principal configurations and their characteristic patterns of density were not to alter to any great degree. Nor was class segregation on the ground to change significantly, except perhaps to become more obvious. Though suburbs could develop, they did little to alter the spatial concentration and debasement of the working classes. Though there were efforts at urban renewal, they could not significantly change this basic pattern of the cities.[1] But civic pride was a reality among the middle classes.

[1]See chapter 6, section 5 below.

Two leading sets of factors, common to the four cities, were to confirm this pattern down to the end of the century. The first was the grossly unequal distribution of Scottish income and wealth. This was inevitably reflected in the morphology of Scotland's cities. Low incomes among much of the working class, a budgetary preference among them in favour of food and drink rather than housing, together with the need to be near the place of work, all militated against the provision of adequate housing. Secondly there was the prevailing mode of transport: it exercised a powerful concentrating effect upon production and the location of the labour force because of a combination of cheapening long hauls for freight between cities by railway and steamship, and a rise in the cost of short hauls, largely by horse-powered carts moving along increasingly crowded streets.

9 The Escape from the Urban Cores

Where did the working-class escapees from the Old Towns go in search of a better life? To some extent in Edinburgh, as in Glasgow, middle and working-class housing were in symbiosis – the dwellings abandoned by the wealthier being occupied by those who were pursuing them in social ascent. Also, as from the 1840s house building began to reach out along the principal roads, and then to fill the gaps, sometimes merging middle and upper working-class housing.

But there was also some development of more distinctly working-class areas. In Edinburgh one such was that between the railway line to Glasgow and the canal. Central Leith also developed as an industrial quarter with working-class housing. Thus could the more skilled of the working classes, with their better incomes, exert bidding pressure on the housing supply. The relief afforded by these various means was, however, limited. There was always the possibility that such areas could degenerate into slums as the artisans vacated them and left them to the unskilled. Edinburgh, Glasgow and Dundee in 1900 were still burdened by much squalor and overcrowding. Though such matters must be viewed in the light of the standards and expectations of the times, it is clear that because of limitations of working-class incomes and of site availability, together with a consequent lack of incentive to the building trades to cater for the working classes, the Scottish cities were in serious housing default.

10 Municipal Enterprise

In Scotland, as in England, the municipalities became sources of power within the unitary state, and were seen as vehicles for social improvement.[1] The city of Glasgow was a pioneer in this on the British and indeed the international scale, acting through its Improvement Trust and its municipal enterprises; other Scottish cities produced similar responses. Always there was the conflict between the ratepayers and those who wished to carry out social amelioration and civic improvement. In sharp contrast to England, municipal enterprise in Scotland was not expected to make a profit to be used to reduce the rates; instead where profits appeared the benefit was to be passed to the consumer through price reductions. As municipalization extended it included sanitation, water supply, electricity, tramways, refuse disposal and a modest degree of housing.[2] These activities made the municipalities employers on a considerable scale, drawing them into the problems of labour relations, especially in the case of the tramways. The total current expenditure by Scottish local authorities rose from about 9 million pounds in 1893 to just short of 20 millions in 1914.

11 The Shared Experience

In spite of the important differences between Scottish cities, they had a range of experiences and consequent challenges in common. Cities on the new scale needed sanitation, water supply, housing, education, health provision, poor relief and policing. Each such requirement was a distinct problem both in itself and in its local manifestation, though there were, of course, links between them. The manner in which each was perceived and acted upon, though having a degree of local uniqueness, also derived from the prevailing Scottish pattern of class and wealth and the general relationships between the classes in terms of power and sympathy. These relationships were much affected by Scottish ideas and ideals, arising both from religion and rationalism, themselves in increasing conflict from the mid-century. Before, therefore, the welfare responses to the social problems of urbanization can be understood, account must be taken of the pattern of class. The cities arose from and functioned without the matrix of the country-

[1]See chapter 4, section 10 below; chapter 12, section 8 below.
[2]See chapter 6, section 5 below.

side, where class in some senses had always been strong, and continued to be so. Our agenda, then, is to consider the countryside as the complement of the cities, before turning to the national pattern of class and power.

3

The Rural and the Highland Scot

1 The Farming Responses

The countryside of Victorian Scotland, like its cities, produced a
number of distinct responses to industrialization. There were the
fertile arable areas where improvements initiated by landowners
and their tenants, especially in the period of the wars against
France, from 1793 to 1815, had so greatly raised the yield. Much of
this land of high potential lay in the east in the Lothians south of the
Forth, and northward through Fife, Strathtay and Strathmore. In
the south there was the Merse of Berwick and westward there were
the rich dairylands of Galloway. It was in these curiously dispersed
areas that intensive agriculture in Scotland produced a characteristic way of life that was closest to that of the midland, eastern and
southern shires of England. At the other extreme stood the Highlands and Islands – an area of remoteness and cultural distinctiveness, where pastoralism was typical, but was combined
with the small holdings of the clansmen, held on precarious tenure
and cultivated with the unreliable potato. This was a terrain that
had no real potential for increased wealth, and indeed could not
sustain its traditional population as the effects of industrialization
penetrated even such a remote setting. There were the southern
uplands and the borders, where arable and hill land made for a
mixed regional economy, with an infusion of industry based on
wool. There was, too, the north-east, with its distinctive mixture of
crofters, small tenants and cattle raising. Finally there was the
central belt of Scotland where the food needs of the cities, especially
Glasgow and its satellites, and Edinburgh, created a demand for
market-garden produce. This was an area of only moderately good
land that had traditionally been backward, but which responded to
the adjacent growth of population and industry, taking advantage
of city demand for market-gardening products.

2 The Landed Magnates

The landowners of Scotland as a class were in an even more powerful position than those of England. Their inheritances were preserved by an even stricter law of entail dating from 1685. In 1878 some 68 persons owned nearly half the land of Scotland, and some 580 owned three-quarters of it. At the head of the landed interest stood the mighty magnates, heads of the houses of Argyll, Bute, Atholl, Buccleuch and Sutherland, owning immense tracts of Scotland, successful practitioners of the art of land acquisition. The Scotland of Adam Smith, Ramsay, Burns and Scott, where the Enlightenment and the presbyterian religion had met, was largely the creation of the descendants of that class of men who in the sixteenth century had seized the opportunity presented by the disendowment of the medieval church and the consequent change in the mode of land tenure. The introduction of the feuing system and the activation of the land market made it possible for a new rural middle class to acquire and hold land. These men included great and small lairds and even modest husbandmen who inserted themselves between the king and nobility at the top of society and the peasantry at the bottom. The means by which this had been done had been largely forgotten by 1832. But from the 1880s the moral justification of the landholding pattern was being called into question, partly because a new concentration of landed wealth in the hands of relatively few families had gone a long way.[1] Rents took traditionally one-third of the gross product: down at least to the 1850s it was the incomes of the tenant farmers that varied, as against a considerable constancy of landowner's rental income and labourers' wages, though the latter were at a modest and often near-subsistence level.

Much of Scottish society and its culture could be read from its landscape and the buildings it contained. The landlord of the intensive arable of the Lowlands by 1832 and increasingly thereafter presided over an open scene, gracious and restful to the eye, with ordered fields and spaced-out farms. The great houses, many of which were built in Regency and Georgian times. owed a good deal to the Adam brothers and their successors, projected the civilizing ideals of the classical world. The country house was the focal point of the scene, as well as of wealth and authority. The farmsteads of the tenants were spaced out over the estate. The villages and small

[1]See chapter 4, section 12 below.

towns lay placidly and usefully where the roads and the hedges that defined them met.

The Highlands had a very different landscape, one of powerful and disordered forms of hill and mountain in the background and rocks and crags nearby, unsubdued by man. The black houses of the Highlanders, for all their primitiveness, contained the characteristic culture of the Gael, with his pipes and his poetry.[2] The home of his chief and the centre of his blood loyalty had traditionally been a stronghold gaunt against the sky standing against marauding neighbours and intrusive government. Some of the chiefs, amid their Highlands and Islands, had been remote from the high culture of Europe, but others, perhaps the majority, had been able to avoid cultural isolation from the late Middle Ages onward if not earlier: Dr Johnson in his tour of 1773 found a good deal to impress him. There were among the great ones like the Duke of Argyll chiefs who were major territorial magnates with wide cultural and political contacts, in effect being regional princelings.

The intensive arable regions and the Highlands provided contrasting paradigms of rural change. One was based upon a continuous ability by the farmers, in response to market demand, and under the discipline of the landowner and his manager, to improve yields. The other was characterized by the tragic dispossession of many of the clansmen and their expulsion overseas. This was partly, in the short term, the result of the remoteness, greed and insensitivity of Highland chiefs and landlords. But there was also the long-term circumstance that much of the land of the Highlands was harsh and unyielding to human effort, and no amount of new farming technique could prevail against it, freeing it from recurrent famine.

3 The Arable Areas

In the high-yield arable areas there was striking change. But there was also much continuity, such that in spite of continuous improvement of cultivation, the radical effect of the railways, and the rise and fall of rents, these parts of Scotland were in many respects not all that different in 1900 from their condition and social structure of 1832. The elements of continuity rested upon the fact that, in a fundamental sense, changes in farming method, so important in

[2]See chapter 8, section 6 below.

one respect, were not of a kind radically to remake the life of the farm labourer either in the fields or in the villages. The horse was the great source of traction power, and though it was hauling a few machines by 1900, these were unsophisticated, and were limited by the ratio between the strength of the horse and the weight and subsidence into the soil of the gear to be pulled. For the carriage of soil, clay and muck, and of the produce, the four or two-wheeled lorry or cart, drawn by horses, was the only means. The laying of drains was a matter of earth removal by human muscle, together with ditching and other tasks. An agriculture based upon horse and human power, even though advanced of its kind, must remain labour intensive. Thus the half-yearly feeing (hiring) fairs for humans, together with horse fairs continued to be important elements of country life. So too was the unmarried farm labourer: in Angus, Perthshire, Aberdeenshire, North Fife and (for girls) East Lothian, farm workers lived a distinctive kind of life in the 'bothies', dormitory structures which produced a kind of sub-culture with its lore and folk songs, especially the 'bothy ballads' of Aberdeenshire. This kind of homelessness, together with other circumstances, meant that marriage was delayed, and often was not entered into at all: in 1871 in Angus, of men and women between 25 and 29 years of age, just over half (52.7 per cent) were married (in 1961 the figure was 75.5 per cent). The sanctions of society and the Kirk sought to limit or even suppress sexual indulgence, but against this there was from Burns's day to Edwardian times a pretty universal bawdy folk culture, together with much seemingly precocious and promiscuous sexual experience. Bawdy songs could help to relieve sexual tension, especially through laughter (the Scots tended to accuse English bawdry of prurience, of being inclined to 'snirtle in its sleeve').

To all basic aspects of rural life the pattern of ownership and tenancy of land was basic. Large parts of these broad farming areas were owned by hereditary estates: the landlord–tenant farmer–farm labourer relationship were typical, as in so much of England. This meant, of course, very strong social differences. Indeed, this was a hierarchic society, which the taxation of inheritance after 1894 had not greatly affected 20 years later. It was an important element in Edinburgh's grip on Scottish banking, for the Bank of Scotland and the Royal were bankers to these men. It was the target of the Liberals in their assault on the landowning class. Such Liberals were prepared to concede nothing to the argument that this structure of ownership was basic to the levels of productivity achieved by such regions, not to mention the pattern of social coherence, held together by the landowners or heritors as the dominant figures in the local communities. The large and well run estates, though hierarchic and paying low money wages, where deference was strong and there was little moving with the times in terms of the assertion of working-class aims and potential, seem to have provided a mode of life for farm, estate and indoor workers that gave rise to no great protest, and was, indeed, accepted by most of them as being the natural order of things. On the other hand there were cases of landowners destroying cottages in order to push labourers off the land. In the north-east, society was more open and less deferential than in much of rural Scotland, for there the possibility of becoming a small landowner was a real one. This societal pattern was fundamental to the outlook of Scottish landed aristocrats, like Lords Dalhousie, Aberdeen, Napier and Minto when as proconsuls of the Empire they pondered on the necessary conditions for the improvement of backward agrarian societies.

These intensive arable regions supported numerous parishes and villages. The dominie and the minister were the dispensers of learning and admonition, and the local doctor attended to bodily ills. It must not be assumed, however, that the schoolmaster, the preacher and the doctor were always the douce apologists for the prevailing pattern of society, for they could comment critically upon an ungenerous poor law. In this, however, they might be muted by the presence of itinerant Irish labourers, seasonal workers in the fields, who were necessary but sometimes troublesome to the parish authorities. Each village had its minor elite of small craftsmen, especially the blacksmith, the wheelwright and cart builder, so important for the production and maintenance of the rolling stock of the community.

The family economy of the villager was to a large degree self-sustaining. There were long working hours shared by all able-bodied members of the family at peak seasons, and low wages, relieved to some degree by perquisites such as cottages and small plots of land. Its members provided their own fuel of wood or peat, carried the water supply from the burn or well, and walked from place to place. The traditional converters of scraps into the food which varied the cereal diet were pigs and poultry; an essential supplier of scraps as well as food was the potato grown in the villager's small plot, or the produce of the fields too small to be taken to market. There was little entertainment, and in most cases few books, except the Bible. Churchgoing was general, for the authority of God and the minister were not to be denied: thus the church was the focal point of village life.

Yet this seemingly self-perpetuating mode of living was subject to the forces of change. The fact that improvement, including better crop rotations, could redeem a farming economy of which, in most of the eighteenth century, nearly half the produce was weeds, inevitably brought a new pattern. The continuous improvement through the nineteenth century meant that the fears expressed by landowners that the repeal of the Corn Laws in 1846 would submerge them under foreign grain were falsified. But the golden age of Scottish agriculture that followed repeal required ever greater intensity of cultivation. This both raised the population of these parts of Scotland, and at the same time confirmed the pattern of economic and social relations on which it rested. Even the coming of the railways, so great a change in some respects, served to deepen further this pattern of arable society.

The railways, together with the steamship, did in the 1870s produce a threat to the system, carrying to British markets cheap American cereals, thus lowering prices, rents and wages. But there was a positive response. The arable areas had always produced fat cattle and sheep for urban markets: this trend to livestock was accelerated from the 1870s. This adaptation by the farmers carried their regions through the difficulties of the 1870s and 80s to the recovery of the 90s. In very general terms Scottish agricultural wages were far behind those of England in 1832 and remained significantly lower until the 1870s; by the end of that decade they were only slightly less than those of the English.

4 The Highland Experience

Against this pattern of continuous improvement combined with a not greatly altered lifestyle, may be placed the experience of the Highlands. There great changes took place between 1832 and 1914, namely depopulation and the liquidation of the old way of life. The Highlands had been a society of clans headed by their chiefs, bound together by an almost mystical tradition based on blood kinship and a communal ownership of the land, though under the authority of the chief. The final defeat of the Highland host at Culloden in April 1746 had been followed by a harsh pacification by the Hanoverian monarchy, an action approved by the Lowlanders, though it would have been even more repressive but for the Duke of Argyll, head of clan Campbell, and his friends. The clans were disarmed, Fort Augustus was built along the Great Glen to join Fort William, the road system was developed, and the attempt to replace the Gaelic language with English, begun before the '45, was carried further. Highland regiments became an important element of the armies of the Empire, and in the economy of the Highlands. There was reasonable prosperity during the Napoleonic wars, based upon high food prices, kelp and the fisheries, but these faded with the peace after 1815.

Meanwhile the forces of population growth had been released in the Highlands, the principal element of which had been the introduction of the potato from about the 1780s. Holdings became ever smaller as subdivision took place to accommodate new families.

From 1815 the clan chiefs had found their rent rolls shrinking rapidly, for the clansmen, so near to subsistence, and so vulnerable to food crisis, could not pay. Under the law of Scotland the chiefs owned the land; of this there had never been any legal question; indeed from the later Middle Ages the chiefs believed that in all senses they were proprietors. On these assumptions they operated throughout. There were strong bidders for the land in the form of flock masters, largely from the Lowlands, who saw the future of the Highlands in the form of sheep raising in place of the traditional cattle economy, with oats and barley as auxiliaries. The sheep were not, of course, an innovation, for the sheep economy, using the hardy Cheviot breed to replace the lower-yield Highland stock, had been progressing step by step with the potato, especially after 1800. Many of the chiefs, in the face of their failing rent rolls, sold out: a new kind of commercially minded landed proprietor appeared, with no sense of the traditional social bonds of the Highlands. The expulsion of the population in favour of sheep runs could proceed apace. These things were happening about the time that Sir Walter Scott was making of the Highlands one of the first and most powerful sources of the European romantic movement.

The first phase of the clearances, for sheep runs, dispersing the Highlanders to their coastal lands, to Glasgow and beyond the seas to the United States and Canada, had taken place before 1832. The most painful had been in the northern Highlands: probably between one half to two thirds of the population of Caithness, Sutherland, Ross and Inverness had been dispersed. Evictions had been used to accelerate the process: there are heartrending tales of brutal actions by the agents of the landlords. There were other devices to oust the Highlander, including the restriction or denial of grazing rights, the only basis for a cash crop. A broken people formed new societies in Nova Scotia and elsewhere, restoring their pride and remembering a lost heritage.

But the suffering was not yet over. In 1836–7 the potato faltered as the blight attacked it; in 1846 it collapsed. The Highlands, like Ireland, were deprived of their basic food. The following year was little better. The potato had proved to be a false support. It was now the turn of the western coastal area and the Islands to suffer: the old society of North-West Scotland was at an end. The government, in addition to bringing in emergency food supplies, made some effort to find a development policy for the longer term, including schemes for roads and harbours and help for the fisheries. But there was no way in which the old society could be restored: reduction of numbers by emigration was the only solution. A further wave of evacuation, the largest over so short a time, now occurred. The Highlanders, largely destitute, moved to the industrial lowlands and by emigrant ship to Australia, New Zealand, Canada and the United States. The Highland Emigration Society formed in London in 1852 was very active. But it could not prevent very bad conditions on the emigrant ships: the memory of eviction was climaxed by the fearful experience of a fortnight or more at sea in overcrowded and filthy conditions. Naked evictions largely stopped from 1855, but emigration, though less, did not cease. That there was brutality in the clearances, there can be no doubt, but part of the problem at least was the inability of the landlords to solve the problem of resettlement. Some of them entrusted too much to their agents and so partially insulated themselves from what was going on.

5 The Highlanders' Protest

For some 30 years the Highlander passed from general public consciousness. By the 1880s, however, his condition once again forced itself upon public and official attention. In the meantime, however, the struggle between landlord and the tenant had continued, the principal scene being the West Highlands and the adjacent islands. In these coastal and island districts those of the people who had survived earlier emigration were now confined to small areas of land, often inferior, while adjacent to them were large tracts reserved for sheep and deer.

The landlords' case was that the population was still greatly in excess of what the land could reasonably support. The crofters' case was that the landowners had deliberately crowded them and debased their condition in order to demonstrate the need for yet more emigration. They further believed that if land were made available to them they could work it efficiently and so provide the basis for the preservation of their way of life and the raising of their living standards. The Duke of Argyll as a great landowner was a leading advocate that low-level small-unit farming, with its vulnerability to subsistence crises, should yield place to an improved, capitalized agriculture with a smaller population and a higher standard of living. This view implied the landlord–tenant system, with the discipline of rents and removal. The crofters, partly inspired by the example of their counterparts in Ireland, would have none of this: for them both justice and efficiency demanded that in their part of Scotland at least there should be small holdings for all, owned by the occupier (or at least with minimal rental and maximum security of tenure), to be cultivated as he saw fit.

The differences between the crofters and their landlords were irreduceable. They were compounded on the landowners' side by a sense of righteousness in resisting threats and intimidations. This was further confirmed by the delegation of wide powers to their factors and agents, who were often their only source of information about the lives and actions of the tenants. The crofters, for their part, had so great an accumulation of grievances, past and present, that they could see no justification at all for the existence of the landlord or his agent. Moreover before 1884/5 the parliamentary franchise was such that the crofter was not only not represented in parliament, he was misrepresented, the Highland seats being held by the landlords. Teaching in Highland schools was done in English; ordinarily the crofters with their native Gaelic spoke one language and their landlords another.[3]

There had been rumbles of crofter resistance through the 50s and 60s; in the 1870s it increased. In the years 1881, 2 and 3 there were severe winters, bad fishing and poor crops. Resentment, indeed desperation broke out in the island of Skye, in what became known as the Battle of the Braes. Hundreds of crofters and their

[3]See chapter 8, section 6 below.

womenfolk hurled stones at the police who were trying to enforce evictions. The presence of the press at the Braes and at the subsequent trial drew attention to the fact that the crofters were effectively, by force, denying the law access to more and more parts of the Highlands.

The government, faced with the prospect of coercion, as in Ireland, opted for inquiry: in February 1883 as demanded by the crofters it set up a Royal Commission. Lord Napier, a lowland landowner, who had experience of land reform in India, was its chairman. It recommended not the total liquidation of landlordism as some crofters and their intellectual supporters demanded, but a fundamental reduction in its power, to be enacted by statute. A group of landowners, now throughly alarmed, tried to get their fellows to agree to a programme of voluntary concession in order to forestall legislation, but this proved impossible. This was in spite of the fact that while Napier and later parliament were deliberating, the agitation was growing stronger and stronger. Meeting the Commission, together with the publication of its Report, greatly increased the crofters' confidence. In 1883 the Highland Land League (on the Irish model) was set up, a frightening prospect. Disturbances extended to become the 'Crofters' War'; this was accompanied by a rent strike.

In June 1886 came the long-awaited Crofters' Act. It conceded much of the crofters' claims, as well as putting the government on a trend toward the guardianship of the Highlands and Islands. Security of tenure was granted, together with rent control and the right of compensation for improvements made. Broadly this solution was the same as that applied in Ireland. The crofters had gained a notable victory. They had done so by finally entering upon the perilous course of a direct challenge to the law. They were not given the land outright, as some had demanded, but they had found a kind of security within the limitations of the land available to them. Their main disappointment with the Act was that it did not oblige the land from which they had been cleared to be returned to crofting use. In 1897 the Congested Districts Board was set up, also following Irish precedent. It was to buy up farms and estates for the enlargement of existing holdings and the creation of new ones. It did what it could with inadequate funds.

The 80s and 90s also saw a governmental programme to stimulate the Highland economy, just as had been the case a century earlier. There were Treasury grants for the West Highland

Railway and for a road building programme, accompanied by further encouragement to emigration. The growth aspect, intended to propitiate the Scottish Land League, found a good deal of support in Glasgow.

The English played no great part in the Highland Clearances, which were effectively over by the mid 1850s anyway, though they could perhaps be regarded as a cause of them in the sense of providing a demand for Highland resources especially as serving as a market for wool. After the mid-century the wealthy English could be regarded as impacting on Highland life, led by the Queen and the Prince Consort, by indulging in tourism, seeking hunting and fishing facilities especially for deer stalking, and acquiring shooting properties. These intrusive activities provided Highland employment, but required a show of deference on the part of the Highlander often strongly but secretly resented. The Highlander was undoubtedly to some degree both romanticized and domesticated, as well as being militarized. The tartan became a social vogue, Highland servants graced London houses and the Highland regiments paraded proudly in the capital.

4

Class, Power and Politics

1 The Changing Configuration of Power

The great forces of change that operated on Scotland after 1832
meant that a contest for power must ensue. The traditional social
and class structure based upon the ownership of land had carried
with it the idea that a Scottish lord, Lowland as well as Highland,
was a lord of men as well as of land, though the idea persisted longer
in the Highlands. The landed lord had now to yield place to a new
and much more complex configuration in which the men of industry and commerce, followed by those of labour, made their successive challenges for power. This took place in a series of steps in the
form of extensions of the franchise, whereby successive bands of
men, lower and lower down the income scale, were granted the vote
and admitted to parliament.

In any given phase the politics of Scotland consisted of increasingly organized political parties, each with a powerful caucus,
manipulating or persuading the voters in the numbers and social
configuration in which they then stood. In simple terms, the first
such enlargement of the franchise, taking place in 1832, in Scotland
as in England, admitted the middle-class men of business for the
first time (previously there were less than 5,000 voters in the whole
of Scotland); the second of 1868 brought in the skilled artisans, and
that of 1884 admitted many farm workers, crofters, miners and less
skilled men. At the same time the working classes were increasingly
asserting themselves by supporting moves for further franchise
extension, and through their trade unions gaining greater power of
industrial action. In a very general sense Scotland shared with
England this political evolution. But it had strongly distinctive
Scottish aspects, both in class and in trade union terms.

The power of the new industrial and commercial order of men

over labour was at first virtually unchallenged; it was not to remain so. But just as labour asserted itself against its employers through the formation of trade unions, so the employers inevitably demanded access to parliament, and once achieved, used this to exercise pressure on governments in matters of trade union law, as well as of commerce and industry. They could also collaborate in their dealings with the unions. The middle classes, of whom these men were the most dynamic part, but which also included the professions (especially the lawyers), had gained the vote and entry into parliament in 1832 partly by their own exertions, but with working-class support.

In the four paradigmatic cities of Scotland, together with the lesser, often satellite towns, the newly agglomerated labour forces also gradually achieved group consciousness, demanding a share in political power. The manner and degree to which they asserted themselves largely reflected the economic base of their respective regions.

2 The Landlords, Power and the Enlightenment

In the countryside and in the Highlands the landlords and the clan chiefs also responded to the new economy and society, but they could not retain their traditional political control of the nation. The lairds of the arable lands continued to be of some political importance right down to 1914, though by then as minor participants in power rather than as the dominant element. In their countryside however their authority continued undiminished, resting as it did upon a confirming and deepening of a farming way of life based upon intensive use of labour. The Highland chiefs, by contrast, abandoned the ancient past with its control of large bodies of men. By turning to extensive rather than intensive land use, expelling most of their men in favour of sheep and deer, they ceased to count for much in the nation's affairs. But by the same token they had generated in the Highlands and Islands an open class hostility that reached the length of physical resistance to the law.

A necessary preliminary to understanding the evolving pattern of power and class in Scotland in Victoria's time lies in the Scotland of the Age of Enlightenment. Out of the Scottish landed class in the later eighteenth century had come a powerful intellectual component, namely the lawyer landowners like Lord Kames (1696–1782) who were eager agricultural improvers and reclaimers of land.

They were men of great breadth of mind, concerned themselves not only with the principles of natural justice as they related to the stages of development of societies, but with the links between property rights and economic development in the form of improved husbandry. Their conjectures converged with those of the academic philosophers, especially perhaps Adam Smith (1723–1790, father of political economy) and John Millar (1735–1801, father of sociology). In Edinburgh and Glasgow there was much debate on the nature of societal processes, especially those that had generated contemporary 'civil society'. Millar in his *Origin of Ranks* pondered explicitly upon the way in which the advanced economy of his day (the commercial society) had ordered itself into classes or 'ranks'. So, too, did Smith.

But Smith and most of his philosophic contemporaries had not challenged the class pattern as it rested upon private property, chiefly in land. Indeed, for him, because the right to hold property was the means of combining freedom, social discipline and economic growth, the state had a responsibility to protect it and its owners against the 'jealous'. It was on this position from well before 1832 that the Moderates, the men of property and intellect, especially in Edinburgh, rested their view of class and power.[1] In so doing they were assisted by the careerism of many of Edinburgh's lawyers. The challenge to this attitude came from the Evangelicals, men imbued with a zeal for good causes that stemmed from a much more strenuous view of religion and the social responsibilities it imposed on the more fortunate. But they did not go so far as to challenge property. In the latter they themselves shared, though they did so perhaps to a lesser degree than did the Moderates.

3 The Church and the Pattern of Class

Long before the 1830s the religious history of Scotland had profoundly reflected class behaviour. Many of landed nobility and lairds had inclined toward the Episcopalian church, in communion with the Anglican Church of England. In spite of being the heritors in many Scottish parishes claiming the right under the Patronage Act of 1712 to appoint ministers to the Presbyterian churches of Scotland many of these landed men continued their Episcopalian allegiance. This English affinity was further reflected in their

[1]See chapter 7, section 2 below.

sending their sons to the English public schools and to Oxford and Cambridge, thus breaking their sons' cultural ties with Scotland in their formative years. Whatever the effects of broadening of mind that this may have brought, it diminished the true Scottishness of the nobility and lairds, leaving schooling and universities with little benefit from this order of society, and making the educational system unresponsive to the idea of a distinctive Scottish culture.

Many of the landlords did however continue in the Church of Scotland. In it they were largely of the Moderate party as opposed to the Evangelicals. The landlords, or heritors, had long insisted it was their right to choose the minister for the parish kirk: in this scheme of things, approved by the Moderates, the landowners would have control of the principal access to the minds of the people, namely the pulpit.

By 1832 the fight between Moderates and Evangelicals over patronage had become the surface manifestation of new and complex differences of group, class and status that were rooted in the gradual emergence of a challenge to landed rule by the industrial middle class and the lesser producers and traders. Against the Moderates the Evangelicals brought all the zeal of the Covenanting past. But the patronage debate, because of its basis in religious belief, and because of its long and complex history, did not bear a simple relationship to class. Some congregations preferred to have their minister chosen for them in order to avoid the quarrels and divisions of deciding themselves.

4 Tory and Whig

There was, however, a second configuration of attitudes, namely those of Tory and Whig, both of which were based in the landed lords and lairds. Scotland throughout the Enlightenment, and indeed down to 1832, had been ruled by the Tories, wielding patronage in a different sense. The most notorious of the 'managers' of Scotland had been Henry Dundas (1742–1811), who, in order to retain the loyalty of Scottish landed families, had dealt out favours with a lavish hand, including public office and appointments in the East India Company. Thus by the manipulation of a tiny franchise Scotland had been kept strictly loyal to the Tory interest, which included Sir Walter Scott with his romanticizing of the Scottish past. But an increasing section of the Scottish intelligentsia was by the 1830s moving in a Whig direction, seeking an end to a corrupt regime and its replacement with one that could think and act in terms of society, and which would reflect an understanding of the principles that governed it. The young men associated with the *Edinburgh Review* (f. 1802) were the intellectual spearhead of the Whig-Radical challenge. They were joined by those men of business in Edinburgh, Glasgow and elsewhere who sufficiently resented the old oligarchy, and some of whom wished to see public policy given some basis in principle. Just as one aspect of middle-class protest culminated within the church in the patronage issue, so the second one did so over the Reform Bill of 1832. But again there was no simple class correlation: Evangelicals and Whigs and Radicals were far from forming a coherent group, though the Moderates and the Tories were closer to doing so. The Scottish Whigs and Radicals were successful in the 1832 Act; the formerly excluded middle class could now participate in parliament by the extension of the voting population to some 65,000. In 1833 the Burgh Reform Act meant that Scottish urban government was taken away from lax and self-indulgent civic oligarchies and restructured.

The Whig victory of 1832 proved a lasting one in Scotland. Those who had carried it obtained power in the parliamentary seats and in the town councils. As Whiggery passed into Liberalism from the mid century Scotland remained true to the cause: Gladstone could count on Scotland, as could his successor as leader of the Liberals and Prime Minister, the Scotsman Lord Rosebery of Dalmeny.

5 The Working-Class Response: Chartism

In 1832 the working classes had no formal place in politics, though indeed the demonstrations of that year showed they had great informal power. In church matters some congregations took direct action against the heritors and their nominated ministers, sometimes to the extent of barring the door of the kirk. But in spite of working-class effort and hope in the reform movement, it was followed by their exclusion from the extended parliamentary franchise in 1832, with consequent bitterness.

One response to this denial of political participation was Chartism. In it elements of the working and middle classes came together in an attempt to make parliament representative of the nation through adult male suffrage. Scottish Chartism shared with that of England the basic difficulty of division of opinion both on the tactics to be used, and the kind of renovatory programme the new democratic parliament should adopt. Though there could be a kind of truce over policy, it was always a matter of concern for thinking men how a democratic legislature would behave. In the shorter run the question of tactics, namely whether to rely on moral force, or whether to use at least the threat of physical force, was also divisive. This was so not only on moral grounds; it also held the prospect of escalating violence as authority fought back, thus raising the spectre of the French Revolution.

In practical terms the movement had to establish itself, organize, and find support. Working-class leaders recognized that the help of middle-class radicals was necessary. In a sense Chartism started in Scotland, for national organization of a kind was achieved there a year earlier than in England: the Scottish stronghold in Glasgow was better organized then any other Chartist centre in Britain. But this did not mean that Scotland was in the van of aggressive demands. On the contrary, it was in the main against physical violence and was fundamentally reformist. It stood for persuasion through education, and so was long-term in its perspective. It saw the petition to parliament as the proper weapon, rather than threats or the disruption of the meetings of the other contemporary move-ment, the Anti-Corn-Law League. It envisaged and formed Chart-ist Schools, co-operative stores and temperance societies. Perhaps most striking was the religious idiom: by 1841 there were some 20 Christian Chartist Churches, together with itinerant Chartist preachers, in sign of dissatisfaction with the attitude of the church to political and social reform. The leading Scottish churchman among the Chartists was the Reverend Patrick Brewster of Paisley, impelled to radicalism by a genuine sympathy for the poor, espe-cially the new poor among the handloom weavers.

As in so many matters there was an Edinburgh–Glasgow rivalry of personalities and leadership. Glasgow won, partly because of its size, together with its ring of satellite towns to which it sent mission-aries. Feargus O'Connor, the leader of the physical force element in British Chartism, was bitter about this Glasgow leadership and its douceness, referring, in contemptuous reference to its Presby-terian roots, to the 'saints' of the 'Glasgow Chartist Synod'. In a sense he was justified, for the shopocracy and skilled artisans who provided the leadership were sadly uncharismatic. O'Connor in praising the cotton spinner strikers of 1837 was heightening the contrast between them and the feeble reformism of the Chartist leaders.

It might have been expected that Scottish Chartism, so highly moral, might have borne some relationship to the stresses in the Church of Scotland leading to the Disruption of 1843. This appears not to have happened: the two 'movements' seem to have been largely independent of each other. Some Chartist support among the working classes came from men who flatly rejected the traditional claim of the Church of Scotland parish minister to access to the home in order to check family well-being and church attendance, and to catechize the children. Many Chartists from characteristically working-class backgrounds were not greatly interested in the internal affairs of the Established Church: among such the handloom weavers were prominent.

Scottish Chartism had an effective life of little more than four years, from 1838 to 1842. It did not then collapse, but gradually faded, elements of it, including Chartist churches, persisting to the 1850s. Indeed there was a final, nostalgic festival of Chartism in Dundee in the 1870s. A good many of the more active emigrated: among them was Allan Pinkerton (1819–84) who was to provide the United States with its celebrated detective and strike-breaking agency. Chartism had served as a kind of national safety valve, generating a level of protest that was, in spite of the nervousness of the authorities, containable with no great difficulty. It was also an educative experience of great importance in working-class circles. Newspapers (the *Scottish Patriot*, the *True Scotsman*, the *Perthshire Chronicle*, the *John O'Groats Journal*) were produced that stimulated reading and debate on public affairs, especially among artisans. There was an understanding among the editors of such papers that it was necessary, as a preliminary to political participation, as the *Scottish Patriot* put it, to form 'a character for the people which they have never before possessed – making them intelligent by instruction, and moral by inculcating the principles of total abstinence'. There were few real martyrs of Chartism; no one in Scotland paid with his life.

6 The Corn Law

In a sense resistance to the demands of the poor law could provide a common interest linking landowners and industrialists. Not so with the corn law. In pre-industrial times most of the community, being largely agrarian, could sympathize with a heavy tariff on foreign corn, at least at times of good harvests, thus maintaining prices against the threat of foreign competitors. But with the growth of the industrial sector, both industrialists and their workers could take a different view of the matter, demanding the cheapest grain whatever its source. This created a dilemma for many working-class Chartists, who wanted cheap food, but who suspected that the industrialists were interested in keeping down their wage bills by thus lowering the cost of living. There were fierce arguments among the Scottish Chartists as to the correct attitude toward the Anti-Corn-Law League, ranging all the way from joint action to disrupting the League's meetings. Repeal of the Corn Law came in 1846: by this time the landowner and farmers of the intensive arable regions of Scotland and brought their fields to levels of productivity that secured them against cheaper foreign grain: their parts of Scotland fully shared in the golden age of British agriculture from the 1840s to the 1870s or 80s.

7 Reformism

Meanwhile those who had found the franchise of 1832 so inadequate had, by the mid 1850s, recovered from the defeat of Chartism, and were once more pressing for parliamentary reform. But Scottish Liberalism, emerging, as in England, from the confusion of parties that had followed the Tory repeal of the Corn Laws, was confronted with the same split as had bedevilled reformism since early in the century, namely that arising from the wide range of liberalism merging into radicalism. A good many of the leading Scottish landowning families among the Liberals, including the Argylls, were Whigs. Such men wanted to see some degree of social amelioration, and some modest further participation in politics by worthy men somewhat lower down on the property scale than the 1832 £10 household franchise. But they wished also to see a continuance of a real bond between master and men, and not a confrontation. Urban radicalism, by contrast, had produced men of the working class and of the middle middle class (including the 'shopocracy'), who wanted to go much further in the extension of political rights. Beyond this there was an important general difference between working-class radicals and those of the middle class. The former wished more far-reaching action than the latter over the Factory Acts and labour legislation. Scottish Liberalism had thus three faces or emphases, one a mixture of paternalism and mild franchise extension, one pressing for a much greater sharing of the vote but little else, and the third wanting to add to the vote a specific programme in favour of the working classes.

A large and active proportion of Liberals also became deeply imbued with the exotic evils of autocracy on the continent, especially in Catholic countries: thus were Mazzini and Garibaldi of Italy and Kossuth of Hungary much admired, and invited as exiles to lecture to Scottish urban audiences. The great emphasis of middle-class urban radicals being upon freedom and the right to participate in the political process, they were vague as to what should be done by a more representative parliament in the remaking of continental societies. They rested their case on the view that the people, thus embodied in parliament, would act with wisdom and fairness. Radicals of all shades could thus become very impatient with the Whigs whom they regarded as willing to temporize over the franchise and other matters whenever Tory resistance was met. The landowning, and indeed urban, Whigs, for their part, were worried whether the radicals of the various shades understood the complexity and possible perversity of the forces they were seeking to release. As for the population generally, because this was an age of very limited entertainment, before the advent of organized sport, politics were a matter of great interest, much discussed. This general involvement was further strengthened by the prospect of taking a direct hand through an extension of the vote.

This came in 1868. The successful and careful artisan found himself on the electoral role, which now rose to 230,606, but the suffrage was still subject to a residential qualification. The new franchise was to make possible the election of Alexander McDonald the miners' leader from Lanarkshire to the House of Commons, a powerful voice for the unions, though sitting as a Liberal.[2]

Though the Act of 1832 had brought in Scotland the triumph of the Whigs over the Tories (the latter renaming themselves the Conservatives) the manipulation of voters had not ceased: nor did it do so under the Act of 1868. Both parties, given an open ballot, coerced tenants and employees to vote according to their masters' will. The Ballot Act of 1872 put an end to such paternalistic power: Scotsmen could now vote without fear of reprisals of varying degrees of subtlety and severity.

[2]See chapter 5, section 1 below.

8 The Churches and Society

The caution and temporizing characteristic of Scottish Chartism found no echo in the Kirk: whereas the moderates of Scottish Chartism won, the Moderates of the church did not. Religious conviction caused the greatest fissure in Scottish society and culture of the nineteenth century.[3] The Disruption must be given its place in the puzzling sequence of events that marked Scottish attitudes arising from class and power.

The church in its long preoccupation with the patronage question, especially since 1833, had relegated its social responsibilities to a second rank of consideration just when it was necessary to think and act more vigorously over these. But when, after 1843, there were two great Presbyterian churches, the 'old' church and the Free Church, a new configuration prevailed, with far-reaching implications for social attitudes and actions. The churches entered upon a competition which though divisive was invigorating. The structure of the Poor Law and of education, both deeply rooted in the class structure, were to be profoundly affected by the new duality.[4]

The churches, in spite of the schism of 1843, continued to be a very powerful element in the pattern of class and power. Indeed the Disruption, in a curious way and in some senses, had renewed the strength of religion, releasing the eager energies of the new Church, though it took the 'auld Kirk' a decade or so to recover its confidence. But even the new church was largely an affair of the middle classes and the better-off artisans. Of this many ministers and elders were painfully aware, but they were unable to find a way of bringing about social unity in religion, embracing the unskilled working classes.

The two churches shared a great emphasis on the Sabbath, keeping Sunday clear both of work and of secular entertainment. Though the great days of Sabbatarian obsession had been in the 1840s and 50s, with bitter controversy over the running of the Edinburgh–Glasgow trains on Sundays, the idea and practice of a holy day was still dominant in the 60s. As in so many matters it was a member of the middle class who launched the attack on the middle-class values that regulated Sunday life. Norman McLeod

---

[3]See chapter 7, section 2 below.
[4]See chapter 6, section 3 and 6 below.

(1812–72) minister of the Barony Church in Glasgow, let out his 'blast' in 1865 against the suppression of working-class entertainment by the locking up of the city's parks on Sunday, the only real day of relaxation for labour. McLeod condemned his fellow bourgeoisie for keeping the bulk of the population 'kennelled up in their wretched abodes'.

And yet many Scottish working-class families accepted the idea of decorum, of a special day on which one changed from working clothes in order to attend church, and in which to try to lift the mind above the commonplaces of life. Indeed the idea of the Sabbath was a means whereby many mothers could hold their families to the path of respectability. There was the difficulty, however, that many of the churches in the cities were financed by pew rents, which meant that much of the seating, and certainly the best of it, was pre-empted. McLeod and others of the clergy were deeply concerned about the class nature of worship, but could find no effective solution.

Some historians of Scotland have sought to integrate the Disruption into a philosophy of historical materialism, tracing the economic role and status of the participants, and arguing, in general, that the seceders were largely of the aspiring middle middle class to whom the established church, under Moderate dominance, had refused to give full scope. There would appear to be some truth in this view. In the case of the collapse of Calvinist theology 40 or 50 years later it is much more difficult to assign this kind of interpretation. There would appear to be a strong case for arguing that the change had its roots in intellectual and spiritual questioning, more or less independent of social class. On the other hand it can hardly be doubted that it was the thought processes generated by an industrializing and science-using society that brought the change in intellectual mode.

9 Later Scottish Liberalism

As with religion, political philosophy and allegiance could not be static. By the late 1870s the peak of Scottish Liberalism as an adjunct of English Liberalism was approaching. It was given added strength by the second Reform Act of 1868. Disraeli tried to revive Tory fortunes in Scotland, and the Scots indeed followed the gladiatorial contests between him and Gladstone with eager fascination, debating the Treaty of Berlin, the Bulgarian atrocities, the intentions of Turkey and Russia and the British occupation of Egypt. But the incubus of the landlord connection was too great for the Scottish Tory party. In 1879 Mr Gladstone made his celebrated progress through south-eastern Scotland with his Midlothian campaign, setting the seal on Scottish Liberal allegiance. But in 1886 he introduced his Home Rule Bill for Ireland, splitting Scottish Liberalism.

Midlothian was the first 'whistle stop' election campaign: Mr Gladstone took politics to the people in a new way, haranguing local Scottish crowds from train windows and vast civic gatherings in public halls. Because of his parentage he felt much at home in Scotland. He was triumphantly returned: he retained the seat until 1895. In 1885 some 2,500 delegates attended a Scottish National Demonstration in the Edinburgh Corn Exchange in honour of Mr Gladstone; he reciprocated by providing a splendid masonry pediment to embody the remains of the city's ancient 'mercat croce', and from which royal proclamations were to be read to the populace. The old liberal condemnation of foreign autocrats still had great power in Scotland. Mr Gladstone, in spite of being a High Anglican, became almost a cult figure; engravings of his eagle-like head lowering down from the wall of many a humble Scottish home to the terror of the children.

But Mr Gladstone's party, though still dominant in Scotland, was not so popular as he was. The endemic conflict between Whig and Radical continued. The party machinery was largely controlled by the Whig element of the east centred upon Edinburgh, provoking radical resentment in the west centred upon Glasgow. The Scottish radical Liberals asserted themselves in 1885 by setting up the National Liberal Federation of Scotland. It adopted a Chamberlain-type programme of·reform of parliamentary procedure and of the House of Lords, together with that of local government; the control of the land by the great owners was to be ended by altering the tenure and ownership system, and the Church of Scotland was to be disestablished. But it could not convert the Liberal Party.

Whereas the second Reform Act of 1868 had helped the Liberals, the third, that of 1884, greatly expanding the male franchise (to 560,580), did not. It complicated the picture by increasing the aspirations of the working classes to have their own party. Indeed the demonstrations in favour of an extended franchise in 1884 were the last to be focused on the older Liberalism of Free Trade and

Reform of the Constitution. The 200,000 people who converged on Glasgow Green, bearing their countless portraits of Mr Gladstone, were unwittingly celebrating the end of an age for the old Liberalism: thereafter began the long search for the new, which could come to terms with the welfare needs of the new age. This indeed was what the National Liberal Federation of Scotland was moving toward.

The Liberals had not been sympathetic to the emergence of a Scottish demand that Westminster be more responsive to Scottish identity and interests. Indeed Scottish Liberal support was taken for granted. The Liberal representation of Scotland began to fall to carpet-baggers. The election of H.H. Asquith for Fife in 1886 was an example of Scottish seats being filled by English barristers: resentment of this contributed to the rise of the Scottish Labour Party. The Crofters received a good deal of sympathy in Scotland generally, creating a dilemma for the Liberals. Being enfranchised in 1884, they chose their own five 'Crofters' MPs'. To concede too much to them was to alienate the Scottish landowning Whigs. The eighth Duke of Argyll, so long the greatest Scottish noble Liberal luminary, abandoned the party. Others of his class followed so that Scottish landed Whiggery at last faded away.

To all these difficulties was added the greatest of all, that of Ireland. Gladstone, driven by the belief that 'my mission is to pacify Ireland', split his northern bastion of Scottish Liberals. The seceders formed the Liberal-Unionist Party, the chief object of which was to fight Home Rule in any form. The General Election of 1885 returned 17 Scottish Liberal-Unionists. Their success was greatest in Glasgow, where it received support from anti-Catholic feeling and Orangemen organizations. For all this, however, the slimming of the Liberal Party by the defections of Whigs and Unionists meant that in the longer run it could become more coherent.

10 Local Government and Municipalization

At the humbler level of local government the later 1880s and the 1890s brought further changes inimical to the landed interest. In 1889, one year later than in England, County Councils were set up in Scotland, elected by ratepayers, taking over a wide range of functions in which landed men had formerly been prominent through patronage, including the important one of appointing the justices of the peace. There had long been confusions of functions and quarrels of jurisdiction between the police commissions and the town councils: the Burgh Police Act of 1892 greatly strengthened the framework of local government by removing these anomalies. At the same time local government was assuming a new range of functions, increasingly providing public utilities in the form of water, gas, electricity, tramways, libraries, art galleries and other services. Municipalism could bring together the business class who regarded it as an exercise in the managerial provision of an efficient set of services, and socialists who wanted collective action on ideological grounds.[5] The churchmen too gave support to the 'civic gospel'. A further aspect of municipalization was the provision of new civic buildings worthy of the newly developing pride in the city, and necessary to house its growing army of local civil servants. When Glasgow's splendid City Chambers were opened in 1889 there were, in addition to the civic procession and the Masonic procession no less than 25,000 representatives of other bodies. Down to the 1890s civic affairs were not seen in party terms; Liberals and Conservatives co-operated in a single effort of good government.

11 Labour and Liberals

Meanwhile two new foci of political debate and action had asserted themselves, namely labour politics and the Liberal-Unionist Party. In the first of these Keir Hardie (1856–1915) played a leading part. His childhood had been dominated by his bastardy, poverty, poor education, and working in the mines from the age of 10; he had learned his politics as a union organizer in the hard school of conflict between his Ayrshire miners and their colliery-owner employers. In 1892 he became the first real labour member of the British parliament, elected for the English constituency of South West-Ham, London. The cloth cap had arrived at Westminster: from beneath it came the uncompromising accent of the Lanarkshire coalfield of Hardie's upbringing.

Like so many of the Scottish working-class Chartists of a generation earlier his motivation and ideas contained powerful moral and religious overtones, together with the aspirations of Robert Burns for the brotherhood of men 'the world o'er'. There was neither the

[5]See chapter 2, section 10 above

analysis nor the bitterness of Marx in Hardie, but a strong redemptive urge. Through him as much as anyone this approach to politics and policy entered deep into English as well as Scottish labour consciousness: socialism, for Hardie, was the industrial expression of Christianity. In this he was not alone: just as there had been Scottish Chartist churches in the 1830s and 40s now in the 1890s there were Labour Churches and Socialist Sunday Schools. However far the Scottish working classes had removed themselves from organized religion in terms of church attendance, the long hold of religion on them through their forebears survived in this transmuted form. This did not mean, however, that labour was condemned to feebleness, either industrially or politically.

By the mid 1880s the politically conscious part of the Scottish working class had begun to query their alliance with the Liberals. The loss of the landed Whigs and the Unionists, though it made Scottish Liberalism more homogeneous, did not generate a radicalism within the Party that could reinvigorate the Labour affiliation. At the same time socialist ideas of the Keir Hardie kind were gaining ground in Scotland. Under Hardie's influence the Scottish Labour Party was begun in 1888, but it achieved little. In 1893, at Bradford, with a considerable impetus from Hardie, the Independent Labour Party was founded. In 1894 it absorbed the Scottish Labour Party, though with Hardie's agreement. Of the 'big four' of the ILP, namely Hardie, Ramsay MacDonald, Bruce Glasier and Philip Snowden, the first three were Scots. The Scottish Trade Union Congress came into being in 1897; the Scottish Workers' Parliamentary Election Committee followed in 1900, sponsored by the Scottish TUC and ILP. Thus was Labour increasingly finding an organized identity both politically and industrially.

But Labour were not yet ready with an effective challenge to the two older Parties. In spite of the extension of the franchise in 1884, it was Liberals and Tories who still commanded voting support. By the election of 1895 there was an effective alliance between the Conservatives and the Liberal Unionists. Together, in the General Election of that year, they routed the Liberals in Britain as a whole. Even in Scotland the Conservatives with their allies staged a remarkable recovery, winning 33 of the 72 seats.

To this the Liberal Unionists contributed a good deal. They had acquired the support of both the leading newspapers, the *Scotsman* and the *Glasgow Herald*. Their rise was the first manifestation in Scotland of a new alignment of politics. They provided a new voice and an organization among the industrial middle classes, placing emphasis on the retention of Ireland (and gaining Orangemen support thereby). But in spite of the success of 1895 the Liberal Unionists were unable to attract any sustained mass support. Nor did they produce a figure of major stature.

An element of the Liberal Party, led by Lord Rosebery, raised the banner of Liberal imperialism, urging on the nation the importance of its role in world affairs and in the empire. In his native Scotland Rosebery found but a weak response to this uplifting vision: it was not to be the basis for a new Liberal philosophy. The Liberal Party in Scotland and indeed in England, finding the Gladstonian philosophy of the minimal state inappropriate as welfare problems increased and as Britain's dominance on the high seas was threatened, was in search of a new identity. The temperance movement and other 'faddisms' were insufficient for the purpose. When the Boer War came in 1899 the Liberals were in great disarray, with Rosebery in favour in fighting, and his fellow Scot Sir Henry Campbell Bannerman strongly hostile.

12 The Land: the Crofting Question

A new form of radicalism arose in the 1880s and 90s. This had to do with the land, both rural and urban. The urban Liberal-Radicals had long been hostile to the landed interest. Now they found a new focus and new allies. The American, Henry George, toured Scotland in the 1880s. Having seen land appropriated by individuals on a massive scale in his own country, providing the basis of great unearned fortunes, he started the Single Tax Movement. It urged governments to tax the unearned increment on land that arose from the efforts of the entire society and not of the owner. Indeed George would have made such taxes the basis of the fiscal system. His ideas were eagerly taken up in Scotland. The Highlanders,[6] the critics of the lowland magnates and the urban radicals of Glasgow all seized upon them. The historical means whereby the great families had acquired their lands were called in question from platforms and in pamphlets. The concessions made to tenants in Ireland were pointed to. The new idea of nationalization of the land and the old one of endowing peasant proprietors converged: Michael Davitt, the Irish leader, toured Scotland urging radical reform of the land laws.

[6]See chapter 3, section 5 above.

Many Liberals, now that their Party was disembarrassing itself of its Whig landlord element, could turn upon the landed class as a source of revenue to pay for welfare and armaments. The landed men, indeed, were regarded as a kind of crock of gold, that would finance budgetary expenditure without encumbering industry with taxes, and without adverse effects. For the zealots an operation on the land provided a universal panacea, capable of saving British commerce from destruction, directing the social revolution already begun away from the strife of class, solving the labour problem by making higher wages possible by relieving the industrialist of taxes, and, finally, lifting Ireland from a prostrate to a proud position.

In all this there was an obvious 'socialist' element, urging the return to the people of their rightful inheritance in the land. To it a good many of the Scottish working class and their leaders were attracted. But there was a dilemma. The Single Tax idea, though it would remove one source of inequity, namely that associated with the land, would not, in spite of the claims made, touch the now basic source of conflict, namely that between industrial capital and the labour force. Just as with the Anti-Corn-Law League in the 30s and 40s, so with the Single Tax in the 80s and 90s, working-class leaders were invited by middle-class radicals to join them in a second great attack on the landed men. Understandably, Scottish labour leaders though accepting the principle, stood back politically.

The Single Tax Movement in Scotland never achieved the potency of the Anti-Corn-Law League. Working-class reserve was reinforced by distrust of the simplistic reasoning that came from the land reformers. There were a number of 'Land' candidates in Glasgow in the election of 1885, but they failed miserably. The Scottish Land Restoration Union was formed in Glasgow in 1892: its members gained a brief majority in Glasgow City Council and attracted the support of 7 town councils and 55 other assessing authorities to approach parliament to grant powers to make land values the basis of local taxation. But Glasgow's attempt to give a national lead failed. Even the claim that 12 men owned one quarter of Scotland, and the labelling of landowners as drones with no useful function, wholly given over to hunting, fishing, balls, flirtations, racing and gambling, did not avail. Nor did the alliterative injection of both rational and religious notes, calling for 'a revolution of the brain, not the barricades . . . a revolution in which Radicalism and Religion join' would carry the day. And yet all this effort did bear fruit, especially in Harcourt's Death Duties of 1894. These, in spite of the protests of Scottish magnates like Rosebery, began the process of slowly and over the generations taxing the agrarian landlords out of existence, though those who owned and speculated in urban land could largely evade its impact. In the meantime, however, Scottish arable agriculture, with its land-lord–tenant system, showed a high level of adaptability to the flood of cheap cereals from North America.

13 The Political Parties in 1900

By 1900 Scotland had four political parties, though Liberal–Unionism was to fade and the Labour Party was still in embryo.

The Liberals, who had for so long dominated the picture, were fumbling for a policy that would reconcile their old market-oriented philosophic basis with new needs, especially those of welfare. The early acceptance of liberalism by the Scots after 1832 had owed much to revulsion against the generations of corrupt political management by the Tories both nationally and in the Scottish cities; this became linked with the notion that the Tories had sold Scottish independence. In these senses it could be said that Liberalism began as a national reaction to the Tory abuse of power.

But there was an older and deeper level of feeling, namely that of religion. Presbyterianism had at its historical basis a powerful democratic element, whereby the equality of men before God was asserted, and which held that every man was entitled to his voice, and that wisdom might be found in anyone.[7] This notion was however qualified by the idea that wisdom had to be carefully trained and directed. The wonderful ideal of universal education was linked with the belief that by proper instruction a Godly society could be created: thus, though every man was entitled to his voice, it would be a right-speaking voice. In short the Godly society was at base a conforming society, militating against individual judgement and responsibility outside a governing paradigm of thought and behaviour. This view within Presbyterianism was of course hostile to decisions imposed from outside, as reflected in the attitude toward Episcopacy and especially, to the principle of patronage. The Disruption had aided Liberalism over much of Scotland: the United Presbyterian Church (f. 1847) was waggishly referred to as

[7] See chapter 7, section 1 below.

the Liberal Party at prayer. This perspective had been reinforced from the mid nineteenth century by abhorrence of tyrannical action abroad. The free market economics of Adam Smith, and the bitter fight against the Corn Laws had provided an appropriate economic philosophy for individualism. As Evangelicalism gained strength these elements of attitude were reinforced, especially as Evangelicalism adopted improving causes, particularly temperance seen as basic to the individual's sense of responsibility. To all of this was added intellectual support in the universities and from the newspapers. Among working men Liberalism, over at least two generations, appeared to be their best hope. Thus it was that Liberalism, a set of disparate fragments in 1832, could consolidate itself, become the majority party in Scotland, and hold this position. In so doing it was able to contain the endemic differences between its radical and Whig elements. But by the later 1880s Liberal dominance was threatened by an alliance of Tories and Liberal-Unionists. Moreover there was a confusion of factions within the Liberal Party. Home Rule for Ireland and other matters brought the Liberal percentage of voting support in Scotland down from 70.3 per cent in 1874 to 55.2 per cent in 1886; in 1900 it was 51.2 per cent.

The Tories, for their part, found it very difficult to make an appeal to the Scottish electorate as it expanded under the successive Reform Acts. Though their reputation for corruption could recede with time, something more positive was needed in order to overcome the hostility to the landed upper classes, the basis of the Party. In the Highlands the Tory cause was virtually destroyed by the clearances and by the dominance there of the Free Church. The lowland farming areas were the only hope. Many Tory landlords after 1832 sought to add additional sympathetic voters by the purchase of property for this purpose. As for the farm workers, enfranchised in 1884, it would appear that a sufficient number of these at least were prepared to vote for their masters as to secure a substantial number of country seats. In a sense there seems to have been an acceptance of a Burkean social bond in the Scottish arable countryside.

In the cities the Tories found life very hard, at least until the later 1880s. The attempt, under Disraeli, to appeal in Scotland as in England to a 'Conservative working class', had no great success. Among the magnates of the West there was the beginning of the emergence of an industrial Conservatism. The great William Beardmore (1856–1936), though he declined a Conservative candidature, gave his blessing to the Party: he was attracted by the Fair Trade agitation (for tariffs to equalize those of foreign nations). Moreover for many heads of engineering and ship-building firms by the later nineteenth century the imperial connection was becoming more important than free trade. Thus it was that Tory fortunes in Scotland were improving as 1900 approached.

The Liberal Unionists Party could never hope to become the government: its principal role seen in retrospect was to provide a bridge over which middle-class man could pass from Liberalism to Toryism without suffering any sense of betrayal, feeling that Joseph Chamberlain with his mixture of imperialism, mild eco-nomic management based on protection, and welfarism, was a truer heir to Liberalism than was Rosebery who, though an impe-rialist, was also a Gladstonian Liberal in many ways.

Scotland could always produce more than its share of men who would instinctively stand against authority and passively received opinion, who would compulsively question things as they stood, challenging their warrant and proposing something else. This gen-erated a middle-class critique of society that certainly took the landed interest as one target, but which could also condemn privi-leges and abuses at its own level of society. But the limitations on improvement imposed by the harsh realism of political economy was a severe constraint on middle-class radical critique. For this reason throughout most of the nineteenth century it side-stepped the problems of equity and welfare (commending the latter to the philanthropists). This had left as available options, programmes based on hostility to power and privilege, namely the extension of the franchise, the reform of local government, the resistance to patronage, the attack on landowning, the disestablishment of the church and the condemnation of foreign tyrannies.

The challenges for the more radical men on the labour side was how to get free of Liberal tutelage, how to convince the unions of the need for working-class policies proposed and fought for by a working-class party, and to this end how to find a structure wider than the ILP.

5

The Scottish Working Classes

1 Trade Unions and Politics

The Scottish urban workers in the course of the nineteenth century formed themselves into a new source of power, both industrially and politically, but the pattern was a complex one reflecting both industrial and city-region differences.

In 1832 there had been a good deal of urban working-class support for the Scottish Reform Act, but the same sense of betrayal as in England manifested itself thereafter. The Factory Act of the following year was a gain, especially for the cotton workers of Glasgow, though in spite of the new inspectorate the mill owners and their managers could find ways of evading its provisions. Unfortunately also the Scottish factory inspectorate turned out to be the weakest in Britain, being inefficient, lackadaisical and employer-oriented. In 1836-7 there was crisis in the cotton industry: markets collapsed and the spinners became militant in the face of wage cuts. Moreover the employers were introducing new machines on the Lancashire model. There was a bitter strike lasting for three months. The strikers were, as always, vulnerable to employers' pressure, especially the bringing in of substitute, ununionized Irish labour, which the spinners had been fighting since 1800. The police and the army were used to protect non-unionists. The spinners, however, had their weapons, giving rise to charges of intimidation and violence. They could chose which of the employers on which to concentrate their attack, usually those with the full order books. The strike of 1836-7 failed; it may, indeed, have been provoked by the employers to bring about a confrontation they could win. In 1838 after a much publicized trial the five leaders were convicted: they were held prisoners in the hulks in the Thames until, following public agitation, they were pardoned in August 1840. Sheriff Alison, author of a *History of the French Revolution*, the great spokesman for law and order, presented Scottish unionism to the world as dominated by violence. So ended the only real piece of industrial radicalism in Glasgow in the nineteenth century.

The spinners largely controlled entry to their trade by the employment of sons and brothers as 'piecers'. But it was the supervisors who set the piece rates and could send back yarn as unsatisfactory, thus reducing earnings. The unions did not fight the introduction of improved machinery as such, but demanded a larger share of the gains in good times and less of the losses when things were bad. Moreover the reverses suffered by the workers when a strike failed could often be recouped by sanction-backed bargaining at plant level. The legal aspect was complicated by the fact that in 1810 the Lord Advocate when approached by the masters had held that the Combination Laws did not apply in Scotland.

In spite of the spinners' defeat of 1836–7 it was in Glasgow in 1838 that the British Chartist movement was launched: the Birmingham radicals chose the city for the purpose. But its militance was muted; it relied instead on moral force.[1] The years 1842–3 produced a good deal of generalized industrial unrest. The textiles industries were in severe difficulties with the most dramatic of these manifesting itself in Paisley when the once prosperous industry of shawl-making was severely hit. It was the desperate conditions revealed in Paisley that demonstrated the hopeless inadequacy of the old Scottish poor law. The Dundee linen workers, partly in reaction to the introduction of power looms in the later 1830s, held a major strike in 1842, but were defeated by the Baxters and other masters.

The most sustained industrial action was to come from the Scottish coal miners. They were neither urban nor rural, but a distinctive culture. In 1842 there was much unrest in the coalfields, with the colliery owners having even more powerful weapons against their workers than did the cotton masters. They governed not only the mines, but also the workers' villages: they controlled employment, housing (the colliers lived in 'rows' as tenants at the will of their employers) and retail trade (through the truck system). Most important of all in times of conflict they had at call the magistracy and hence the police and the military. The colliers

[1]See chapter 4, section 5 above.

sought counter-weapons both through unionization and by control of entry to their trade by an apprenticeship system that would promote artisan status and ensure employment for their own kin. It was the ironmasters, who controlled so much of the coal mining of Lanarkshire, who were the harshest masters, using every weapon to hand, especially the Irish, to subdue their colliers. These included the sponsoring of sectarian fighting among the colliers by bringing in both Roman Catholic Irish and Ulstermen, the latter with their Orange Order and protestant churches. In spite of all, the miners in this endless running fight could have their victories. In 1877, for example, those of the West of Scotland, after strikes and lockouts, defeated the proprietors, both on wages and cottage rents. In the same year there occurred the fearful underground explosion at Blantyre Colliery killing 207 miners, conveying briefly to the nation the dangers of the miner's lives.

This was the setting in which Alexander McDonald (1821-81) came to prominence, starting from the Lanarkshire coalfield. In 1856 he was appealing unsuccessfully for an abandonment of miners' parochialism by the setting up of a Mineworkers Federation on a British basis. In 1874, having been President of the Miners National Association since 1863, and Chairman of the TUC Parliamentary Committee, he became the first MP to be elected largely by the miners in Britain, sitting for Stafford Borough as a Liberal. The satirists made great play with his Lanarkshire accent and his way of enlivening his Commons speeches by spitting on the floor of the House. McDonald tried to heal the breach between Protestant and Catholic colliers, to form a respectable unionism, confronting the ironmaster-coalowners with dignity and strength, working within legality, though trying to make the law less repressive by parliamentary action. He had much to do with the removal of employers' abuses by the introduction of check-weighers who could ensure that the miners were paid for the coal they raised without specious deductions; he helped to bring better safety precautions and ventilation as well as the shortening of the hours of labour and the lessening of victimization of trade union activists. His tombstone records that he 'spent his life fighting to improve the condition of the miners'. But McDonald was no class warrior, being without a socialist vision. He had paid his way at Glasgow University in his 20s by working extra long hours at the most dangerous seams; he continued to save his money, investing it in mining shares. Indeed he became a considerable man of property, owning and living in the fourteen-roomed mansion of Wellhall (with five servants) a mile from Blantyre Colliery. He quarrelled with other miners' leaders, including the young Keir Hardie who had a different social vision. In general, however, the Scottish unions were in a feeble state at the mid-century.

The Edinburgh Trades Council was formed in 1853, but a much more real and continuous counterpart was begun in Glasgow in 1858. These bodies were intended to make union action more effective by working on a regional rather than an industry-by-industry basis. There was however an intense concern for the autonomy of the various unions; this was related to the fact that so many unions were of a craft nature, small, localized and jealous of their independence of organization and action. The Trades Council principle, together with union autonomy dominated by the craftsmen, made Scottish unionism ineffectual (though the local threat of the Trades Council principle seemed to many employers to be greater than organization on an industry basis). The parliamentary enfranchisement of 1868, enjoyed by many of these men, excluded the unskilled.

In each trade the unions had their problems. The building boom of the early 70s damaged organization in the building trades by weakening the distinction between the skilled and unskilled workers, and the contraction of the economy in the later 1870s further reduced union membership. The jute workers of Dundee had no effective union organization until the 1870s. In shipbuilding the employers cherished their foremen and their cadre of skilled men, creating an element of loyalty that impeded unionism at these important levels. Lower down the scale the riveters and boilermakers established their unions on a tight craft basis. At the bottom in every branch of industry the unskilled labourers had no collective defences.

Meanwhile the miners had continued to be the best-integrated element of the Scottish labour force, an uneasy part of the polity, never very far from open class warfare, with the employers refusing recognition to their unions. In the 1880s Keir Hardie as the leader of the Ayrshire miners challenged the Scottish collier owners for union recognition.[2] He was more belligerent than Alexander McDonald had been, seeing class solidarity as essential. Indeed he quarrelled bitterly with McDonald over this. In spite of his

[2]See chapter 4, section 11 above.

powerful moralism he was no simple-minded class warrior, but sought working-class advance where he could find it. His role as a founder and chairman of the Independent Labour Party stemmed from this perspective. It was accompanied, as with the working-class Chartists, with the hope of attracting intellectual and some general middle-class support. While Hardie was the miners' hero they could not become really militant, even though he urged the ending of the Lib–Lab alliance of the miners to which McDonald had subscribed, and the gaining of direct Labour representation in parliament. But it was the miners, in their long and bitter struggle with the colliery owners, chiefly the ironmasters of Lanarkshire, who provided the driving force for Scottish labour action.

Scottish labour organization thus presents a curious picture during Victoria's reign. After the hectic militancy of the spinners in the mid 1830s no real challenge to the prevailing order came, though there was a good deal of labour organization and resistance at the level of the firm. The miners, though they could fight their strikes with great tenacity, were not, as a body, radicalized. The building trades workers, with so many individualist masons, bricklayers, painters and plumbers, could find little real unity. In shipbuilding the employers continued to ensure the loyalty of their cadres of foremen and skilled workers by special treatment.

On a city-region basis too there were inhibiting factors. In Dundee the female-dominated jute labour force in spite of valiant efforts could not really challenge the power of the jute masters. In Aberdeen the mix of employments and the resilience of the local employers in adjusting to changing markets helped to lower tension. In Edinburgh with so little of the labour force engaged in the basic industries, and so much of it providing services of one kind or another, there could be no strong unionism. Finally, in Glasgow, where heavy industry was becoming increasingly dominant so that militancy might have been expected, it failed to appear on any threatening scale after the 1830s. Glasgow unionists held onto their autonomy and their funds, refusing to pool these for a larger cause; too much of their outlook was narrow and sectarian and indeed, toward the Irish, racist. Beatrice Webb in 1892 found the Glasgow working-men's leaders uninspired and without enthusiasm. And yet the elements of working-class power were growing, providing necessary preliminaries for Red Clyde after 1914.

2 The Working Life

Down to the 1840s Scottish industrial class life was dominated by the cotton industry and by coal. Thereafter a kind of hierarchy of employments increasingly asserted itself. At the top were the engineering trades, culminating in shipbuilding, marine engineering and locomotive construction, with their high proportion of skilled men, able to organize in craft unions, and to enjoy a rising standard of life. The coal miners, in spite of their many trials, came next as a major category. Among them pit managers and foremen did well, and the general level of wages was high relative to most industrial employments other than the engineering trades. Textiles, especially the cotton industry, could produce moderately good wages in the upper echelons, but the largely female labour force was less fortunate. There is a descent through the unskilled labour force to the casual and ultimately semi-unemployable. The increasing rise and complexity of industry, trade and government made necessary a growing army of clerks. The police, too, came from the working classes, as did the army. Any verdict on Scottish working-class life must take account of the great differences prevailing both in the demands of the various tasks and their rewards.

The building of ships, large and small for peace and war, became an increasingly complex business. Engines became more efficient through an increasing grasp of steam power. Standards of comfort and indeed luxury at sea rose for those who could afford them; even for the steerage passenger a new virtuosity of ventilation and heating systems had to be developed as the liners, especially on the Atlantic, grew in size. This meant that a great range of skills went into the building of ships, including highly developed finishing trades of a splendid craft standard. Good workmanship and the effort at self-improvement were rewarded by 1900 and no doubt before; it was common practice to recruit under-foremen and foremen from among the men, provided that such men had attended night classes.

It was the great hulls, with their ribs, plates and rivets that dominated the shipyards, together with the engines and transmissions to power them. Work on the exterior of the hulls was done without shelter, in the open air. A shipbuilder with a full order book would drive his workers hard to meet delivery dates, using the discipline of the foreman. There was no question of canteens or other such amenities and in the machine shops there was noise, heat and danger. But there was also a sense of fulfilment. The creation of marvellous levels of engineering skill on Clydeside such as to earn the admiration of the world was a local achievement, not dependent to any great degree on borrowing from elsewhere. The craftsman could build his self-esteem around his skill and the marvellous products to which he contributed. There could certainly be contests with management: there was an engineering lockout on the Clyde in 1897 in which the unions and the Clyde Shipbuilders and Engineers Association confronted one another. But employers, foremen and workers could share a sense of achievement. At a launching the workmen, though sharply separated by a platform and bunting from their bosses and distinguished guests who had just partaken of a lunch of some indulgence, could look on with real satisfaction as the ship that was their creation took to the water.

Much the same atmosphere existed in the large engineering works both mechanical and civil. Here skills were at their highest peak, with a corresponding tradition of craft unionism, carefully defining and protecting particular skills. Though standardization of parts was making some progress, most jobs of any importance had a uniqueness that was a joint challenge to management, designers and engineers. There are splendid photographs of locomotive works showing the men who made the marvellous engines, from apprentice boys to foremen and management. Was this a scene of class tension or fraternal co-operation, or was it one thing at one time and something else at another?

Heavy engineering in its many aspects had a similar effect on the male outlook and hence upon family life as did shipbuilding. Men working under such conditions, as a facet of their mixture of self-assurance and dissatisfaction with their relations with their employers, could develop an assertive, not to say aggressive view of themselves. At the family level father was king of the home, with special treatment at meals and in other ways. The mother, if she was to hold her family together and promote its interests, had to accept this pattern, keeping the peace and conserving the money. The younger men often asserted themselves through drinking and general machismo, creating a thriving market for brewers and distillers, and great activity in the casualty wards of the Infirmaries on Saturday nights.

The life of a collier was full of dirt, lung disease and disasters in the form of asphyxiation, roof collapse, flooding and explosion, all of which had to be faced in the darkness and confinement of the coal measures. To these must be added the near-starvation of strikes and lockouts, together with the open hostility between Scots and Ulster Protestants and Irish Roman Catholics. There was, too, the isolation of the mining communities, confirmed both by the miners' own exclusiveness and the unwillingness of others, for example farmers' daughters, to associate with them. Thus could develop very close communities, bonded together by the fight against the dangers of the seams and the demands and manipulations of the employers. The bonds were all the tighter because of the work dangers of the men, and the shared fears of the women day by day and when they stood together at the pit-head when the seams had entrapped their men folk. The men took pride in their skills, for though most of them were heavily manual, the knowledge of the rocks and of the coal measures, of shoring timbers and the behaviour of underground waters was hard-won and cherished. It was such skills, together with the desire for security of employment, that made them aspire to artisan status, regulated by an apprenticeship intake. A further form of solidarity arising from shared experience lay in the fact that in the mining communities most colliers and their families lived in the same basic house type, usually of one room.

But behind all this, in the first half of the century at least, there was a nostalgia for the country life and a poetic tradition often prompting long walks in the fields that were fast being overlaid with bings from coal and iron workings. Inevitably such traditions faded, to be replaced in the harshest coalfields as in Lanarkshire by drunken 'fuddles' that all too soon became their own tradition, leading to violence, much of it fuelled by anti-Irish ethnic conflict. Some places produced in the 1860s 'Free Miners' Clubs with an anti-Catholic and semi-Masonic basis. A divisive tradition arose, namely the myth among the older population of miners of the 'freeborn collier' of some remote past, who had been destroyed by the incoming Irish.

Yet within this picture there could be strong contrasts. Coatbridge may perhaps be taken as the extreme of badness and the village of Larkhall as its opposite. Coatbridge between 1831 and 1871 exploded from a population of 2,000 to 22,000. It was a place of dreadful overcrowding, filth, disease, drunkenness, violence and prostitution, a kind of frontier town in which civil society scarcely existed. The Scottish and Irish elements were almost equally balanced: in 1861 44 per cent of Coatbridge colliers were Irish. This was the kingdom ruled over by families like the Bairds of Gartsherrie. Larkhall presented a very different picture. Only 17 per cent of its miners were Irish. There were a good many owner-occupied cottages, purchased by savings through the building societies. The markets supplied were those of Glasgow's houses and workshops rather than the great ironworks, so that employment and wages were more stable. The rural traditions of the place could survive much longer in the absence of the pressures and hostilities of Coatbridge. This was the atmosphere in which Alexander McDonald was formed, as was Robert Smillie.

Between these extremes there were many gradations. In Dunbartonshire the colliery owners in exploiting a new coalfield set up two adjacent villages: Croy for the Catholics and Twechar for the Ulster Protestants. On the face of it in the light of Irish history, to separate the elements was sensible. But it tempted the coal-masters to use sectarianism as a divisive control. In Croy it was the priest who was called in times of disturbance, not the police. More-over he would enforce temperance on much of his flock. In the Mid-lothian coalfield the old social bond of landed paternalism could survive much longer: the 1840s saw a Tory social movement of amelioration based upon humanitarian social reform. But, as in the collieries of Fife, paternalistic employers were often surprised and made indignant by the emergence of unionism with its demands for higher wages. Thus the provision of a village school, a reading room or other amenity could avail little when it became a question of trying to get wages down in so labour-intensive an industry when faced with falling coal prices.

The cotton masters in the first half of the century had been major employers, very conscious that their industry combined a high level of price competitiveness with labour intensity, making them very sensitive to wage claims and demands for the improvement of con-ditions of work. The spinning mills were places of noise and high temperatures, kept so in order to lessen thread breakages: the weaving sheds were even noisier; in both kinds of mill the tempo of work was pushed near the limit of tolerance. The prevalence of women made unionism difficult, but nevertheless the workers through combination could often get a better deal at plant level. Though the cotton industry was much reduced from the 1860s, it remained important, attracting the attention of the factory inspec-tors. One of these in the 1890s reported that one weakness of Scottish cotton production compared with that of Lancashire was that Scottish women refused to manage the number of looms that was customary in the English mills. The Scottish near monopoly of the jute industry however continued, its workers living in their 'platties', their bodies impregnated with the smells of whale oil and jute fibre, and the tenor of their lives set by the factories.

The fisheries provided a hard-earned living for both men and women. The men faced the dangers and heavy toil of the sea in a way made safer but more intense as steam replaced sail and as the more costly boats had to be made to pay. By the 1880s the fisher lassies were following the herring fleets from port to port, living a harsh life gutting and packing the catch into the barrels of their employers, the curers.

At the bottom of the workforce was the labourer, doing those jobs that required muscle, but just that degree of intelligence and flexibility that animal power could not be used, lifting, carrying, holding, pushing, shovelling, stoking, cleaning out, filling and emptying materials and wastes. The unskilled and casual man was without status and without union protection, at the mercy of the foreman for his job and for the effort required of him. So too politically: they were passed over by the extensions of the franchise in 1868 and 1884. One of the great users of casual labour was the chemical industry, centred upon Glasgow, Irvine and Rutherglen. By the 1890s some 85 per cent of those employed in it in Scotland were Irish. Indeed one of the first places incoming young Irishmen went to was a chemical works, moving to similarly low-paid employment elsewhere, thus keeping labouring wages down. The docks were another focus of casual labour.

The casualization of so much of the urban labour force became, in a sense, worse in the later nineteenth century. By then the number of employments involved had greatly increased. To general and building labourers had been added porters, watchmen, pedlars, newspaper sellers, messengers, cart and cab drivers, together with the lowest levels of skills like boxmaking and the sewing of sacks. Down to the 1860s or so it was possible for the middle classes and some of the more skilled to see the cause of casual labour in the moral failure of those who were not fit for anything else, and whose self-inflicted limitations were made worse by drink, bad health and ageing. But it was gradually becoming apparent to the less sanctimonious and more realistic observers that the system depended upon a wide range of dead-end jobs that brought their own debilitation. The school system had failed over the bottom range of society; low incomes among parents meant absenteeism among their children as they entered casual labour on a part-time basis as child street-traders, sewing sacks, or other such occupations. There was thus a running battle between compulsory schooling and early earning. The labour market in general was overhung by this element; the children committed to it had their chances in life limited from the outset.

At the other end of the working-class scale was the labour aristocracy of skilled men. They were jealous of their skills and of the favourable wage differentials these produced, carefully protected by trade union action. Many of them had adopted ideas of thrift and self-improvement and self-realization. Though these were certainly middle-class virtues, their adoption by working-class families was not an act of imitation, but arose from their own needs and aspirations.

It was the hope of many an artisan family that one or more of its sons should achieve the respectability associated with being a clerk. Such a status, relying on literacy and a minor element of numeracy, was work by brain rather than by hand, and could provide an escape from the limitations of working-class life and housing by moving to a clerks' suburb. On the demand side, as the century passed there was an increasing need for those who could keep account in offices of what was happening in works and warehouses, and who could supply a new range of retailing services. The improvement in education after the 1872 Act helped to enlarge the number of those qualified for clerkdom. The effect was to insert a new order of men into the pattern of labour relations. Down to the end of the century there was little unionism among them, for there was a strong tendency to share the ethos of their employers, together with efforts at self and mutual improvement. And yet there was an important element from the world of clerks in the early ILP.

Whereas young men could avoid industrial employment by becoming clerks, the equivalent escape for girls was domestic service. This indeed became by the 1880s the largest employment for women, remaining so until challenged by the needs of expanding retail trade for shop girls. At the bottom end of the scale where a lower middle-class family employed only one servant there could be harsh treatment for the skivvy. But in Edinburgh's New Town and in Glasgow's West End, where the household employed a number of servants, life could be less demanding. The girls in service, like the clerks, usually did not question the outlook that was held by their employing betters.

Finally there was that other offspring of the working class, the police force. To it there was a fair amount of Highland recruitment. The police, of course, were dedicated to law and order, and by the later nineteenth century had made the cities safe to a degree not known since they began their great expansion a century earlier.

6

The Welfare and Education of the People

1 The Challenges of Welfare

In 1832 the only agency for public welfare was the church: this role it combined with the custodianship of social conscience. The two came together in the moral duty which the church had always sought to place upon its members to help those in need through the giving of charity and the provision of personal and communal support. As the cities grew they attracted increasing numbers in need of help, as well as demoralizing or debilitating many already there. Even for the able-bodied the shadows of want and disease lengthened and shortened with the trade cycle. The Kirk was increasingly finding it difficult to discharge its traditional responsibilities. At the same time the Kirk was itself weakened as its urban coverage of churches in the cities proved less and less adequate. Moreover it had adopted in the new conditions a moralizing philosophy of poverty, namely that those in need were likely to be the victims of their own failings, and that there was grave social danger in exempting them from the consequences: this idea was strengthened by the new political economy. It led to thinking in terms of the 'deserving' and the 'undeserving' poor. In a sense the most serious of all these adverse circumstances was that many of the working classes, not surprisingly, were becoming indifferent to the church and some, indeed, hostile.

The Kirk made real efforts to meet these new challenges, both by extending and adjusting its coverage of parish churches and by re-activating the sense of social responsibility among its better-off members: in this Dr Thomas Chalmers was a leading figure. But two trends inevitably asserted themselves, namely toward the secularization of welfare services and the adoption of an element of control and uniformity through a central governmental authority.

At the level of thought also there was change: the idea gradually gained ground among the middle classes that it was not safe or right to continue to think of the welfare problem as concerning only those at the bottom of society.

Each of the four principal city-regions produced its characteristic welfare challenge and response, as did the rural and Highland areas. But there was also a general, shared agenda. Its principal items were the poor, health (including water supply and sanitation) and housing: education too had a strong welfare aspect. These were the great social matters to which Scotland had to respond. Though of course related, each had its distinctive, and Scottish, history of ameliorative campaigning.

Scotland was not, of course, autonomous in regulating the elements of its welfare system: as with so many aspects of Scottish life, welfare was governed by Acts of the Westminster parliament. This meant that, though there could be a degree of solicitude for Scottish views, the legislation was subject to the atmospherics of a parliament that was English in outlook and imperial in its scope and pre-occupations. In a sense it is fair to regard Scottish welfare provision in the nineteenth century as being, even more than that of the English, mean, grudging and censorious. On the other hand it is as well to view what was done in the light of criteria that are wider in time and space. No society has ever set as a preliminary condition for industrialization the maintenance of levels of welfare: all have proceeded on the assumpton that economic growth is the source of general prosperity and hence of welfare and that to impede growth by welfare taxation and excessive regulation is to diminish welfare itself by limiting the quantum of wealth from which it comes. To this belief most of the entrepreneurial middle classes and their extensions warmly subscribed.

2 The Heroes and Heroines of Amelioration

It is right for certain purposes to think of the basic trends and needs of society as generating, in an impersonal way, a range of welfare responses. But this is to lose sight of an essential element, namely the dynamic of individual conscience and action. Men and women of zeal amounting sometimes to obsession were required to drag their society into action. They, like the entrepreneurs, came from the middle classes. They were imbued with the evangelical spirit which required them to aid their less fortunate fellows. With this, of course, went an element of self-fulfilment, for the philanthropic urge in its absolute form, free of selfish impurities, is difficult to locate, or even in philosophical terms to conceive of. The Scottish philanthropists were as intriguing a lot as were to be found anywhere. It was they who took up the cause of so many who could so easily fall outside the net of the Poor Law and who had special needs; the orphans and street arabs, the vagrants, the prostitutes, the alcoholics, the feckless, those wavering on the border of insanity or those who had passed beyond it. Moreover it was the philanthropists who were the driving force behind the legislation in the main areas of welfare, forcing the state itself to intervene.

A few names give the flavour of this driven and driving band. There was John Ure (1824–1901) an example of the civic politician who took it as his life mission to promote effective action against Glasgow's living conditions and death rate: with him may be joined the name of Provost Blackie (1806–73) whose vigour in promoting the Improvement Commission to clear the slums of central Glasgow cost him his position as Lord Provost. John Dunlop (1789–1868) fought a life-long battle against drink: he founded the Scottish Band of Hope. Dr W.P. Alison (1790–1859) campaigned for a more humane Poor Law, perceiving that poverty was so often the result of poor health, and that both were related to low or unstable incomes. Sheriff John Wood of Peebles and David Stowe of Glasgow (1793–1864) opened schools in Edinburgh and Glasgow embodying new educational ideas. William Quarrier (1829–1903) set up near Glasgow his homes for orphan boys on the village principle. William Mitchell vice-chairman of the Glasgow School Board, as well as founding a Home for Infirm Children and creating other facilities for children, was largely responsible through his staff of uniformed attendance officers for both enforcing compulsory school attendance and helping the less fortunate families to meet its requirements. Though the women were usually in secondary roles to the men, there was among them Beatrice Clugston (1827–88), who saw the need for post-hospital care and founded two convalescent homes. At a lonely and often humiliating level there was Bailie James Moir (1806–80) whose untiring persistence, amid much scoffing and sneering, brought public urinals to Glasgow in the 1860s: in so doing he began the attack on the filth and indecency of the city's streets, stairs and closes, making the latter at least a degree more tolerable as courting places for the young. These were the men and women who in their various ways took up causes that lay outside official provision. Moreover they were forever seeking out social casualties and causes that lay outside the official provision, a kind of philanthropic watch-committee.

The strong streak of individualism among the philanthropists meant that there was a lack of co-ordination of effort. In 1868 the Edinburgh Association for Improving the Condition of the Poor was founded in an attempt to bring a degree of order into such activities in the city: a similar organization was set up in Aberdeen in 1870 and in Glasgow in 1874. All these bodies were intended to conduct 'careful investigation' of the needs of all applicants for charity. They eventually merged, joining the Charity Organization Society founded in England in 1869. Out of this activity was to emerge the professional social worker.

3 The Poor Law

It was, however, the Poor Law that constituted the principal recourse for those who could not support themselves. Its essence and the divisions of opinion concerning it are perhaps best conveyed by the debate between two Tories, Drs Chalmers and Alison in the 1840s. Chalmers was the great protagonist of the spirit of the traditional Scottish Poor Law and the general social philosophy of which it was a part. His mind was formed in the atmosphere of the rural parish where those in need of help were relatively few and where a good deal of the old social bond between classes still survived. He believed that in accord with the old Scottish rule there should be no provision for the able-bodied based upon taxation enforceable at law, but that there should be a vigorous revival of the social responsibilities of the middle-class members of the Kirk, together with self-reliance and mutual help among the working classes. All this should be augmented by a programme of church building and school founding in the working-class areas. Thus, in a sense Chalmers's view was harsh, but its emphasis lay not on harshness but on a combination of independence of spirit and mutual aid between and within classes. Chalmers indeed believed that his experiment in St John's Parish in Glasgow between 1819 and 1822 proved that this approach could be made to work.

Alison, on the other hand, argued this programme to be hopelessly anachronistic. The new industrial forces were too vast and too crushing on a large section of the population for Chalmers's programme to meet their needs. The realities of poverty and pauperism should be faced, namely that a large part of the population was caught in a trap in which low incomes and unemployment were debilitating, producing ill health and psychological collapse which closed the circle of poverty in which they found themselves. Alison proposed that the middle classes should tax themselves to make available a reasonable Poor Law system, and that this should include provision for the able-bodied who were out of employment because there were no jobs. This High Tory and Episcopalian, in his day the 'father of the medical profession in Scotland', using a perspective derived from clinical experience, was more realistic than Chalmers the divine. Participants in the Poor Law debate divided roughly between these two points of view.

The Disruption of 1843 rendered the Church of Scotland less able than ever to carry out its old welfare and educational functions. With the Church split asunder, the old Poor Law based upon the parish as run by the Kirk Session was no longer viable. Even before the Disruption a Royal Commission to study the Poor Law had been appointed: it reported in 1844, basing itself upon a comprehensive survey which gives a marvellous snapshot of the social problems of the Scotland of the time. The resulting Poor Law Act of 1845, though retaining the parish as the administrative unit, set up Parochial Boards with some elected ratepayers. It also set up in Edinburgh a Board of Supervision which, though not elective, was to be representative of the regions of Scotland. The Board was not an assertive body, but tended to adopt a responsive attitude to the parishes. But it did set out minimum standards of care, as well as requiring each parish to appoint a paid official as parochial inspector of the poor. It soon became the recipient of complaints and appeals. The Act stated in general that adequate funds should be raised for the non-able-bodied poor; over the years more and more parishes abandoned the various informal formulae the Act made available and adopted legal assessments, that is to say enforced a tax.

The great legal difference between the Scottish and English systems remained, namely that the Scots able-bodied were to continue to be unrelieved. But the Board of Supervision over the years quietly campaigned for the parishes to relieve the 'occasional poor', so that Board and parishes together moved some distance away from a fundamental principle of the Act. Alison's perspective was gaining ground, not through legislative triumph but by pragmatic adaptation to reality, though it can be argued that the Alisonian spirit had not conquered the Chalmerian one in respect of relief to the able-bodied right down to 1914.

The system continued to contain much harshness. Provision was minimal and subject to severe tests. It was uneven over Scotland. The Act authorized the building of Poor Houses. This could involve combining parishes in order to meet the costs: large parochial areas came into being in the cities. Poor House schools were required by the Act where no other suitable facility was available. So too was medical relief. By these means the Poor Law became involved in education and health. By 1866 Scotland had 66 Poor Houses with a capacity of 12,000. But outdoor payments continued to be the most general form of relief. Indeed Scotland was never to develop a Poor House System or Work House tradition of the English kind; the Act though it brought the Poor House to Scotland did not make it so important an element in working-class life. The Parochial Boards were unwilling to shoulder the burden of debt involved in building a large Poor House; the Board of Supervision, only slowly gaining power, could not force Boards into action. Thus, by historical accident, Scotland learned before England that it was impossible under industrialization to discipline a significant proportion of the working population within the confines of Poor Houses, in a society in which the spirit of democracy was growing. The Scots' sense of economy brought them earlier to the principle that it is cheaper to keep people in their own homes than in residential institutions. Always the counter-ideas of a more severe Chalmerian kind were in contention with moves toward a more generous system. Moreover there was always the hope that philanthropy would bear much of the burden of poverty, thus relieving the Poor Law assessment.

The Board of Supervision continued its task of humanizing the Poor Law within the limits of contemporary acceptability until it was wound up in 1894. The Local Government (Scotland) Act of that year set up the Local Government Board which took over responsibility for the Poor Law. Although between 1845 and 1894 the differences between the English and Scottish Poor Laws had been steadily eroded, the systems remained administratively distinct.

4 Health Care

The growth of the cities threatened the health of people of all classes.

Early death, illness and accident and the failure to achieve a reasonable level of physical and mental performance haunted the working classes; through infectious diseases the entrepreneurs, even though they moved their homes further and further from the centres of infection, could also be threatened, as in the cholera and typhoid and typhus epidemics. The threats to working-class health extended all the way from the immediate environment of the debased parts of the cities (pollution of land, water and air, the disposal of human wastes, water shortage), to housing (with its sometimes fearful over-crowding, lack of ventilation and sanitation), to diet (inadequate both in quantity and in variety), finally to incomes (better earnings were of course the key to escape from the worst conditions). Family incomes could be threatened by capitulation to fecklessness and drink, reducing the effectiveness of such sums as could be earned.

How was this syndrome to be broken? Some philanthropists and reformers started with the drink question. The working classes were to be weaned from this temptation by a mixture of exhortation and the control of licences and hours of public houses. The major piece of temperance legislation in Victoria's reign was the Public House (Forbes Mackenzie) Act of 1853, based on the controls adopted in Edinburgh under its Lord Provost Duncan McLaren (1800–86), a determined enemy of the drink trade. The Act strictly limited licensing hours, giving the magistrates strong powers of supervision. All the major cities also had their Police Acts which could further regulate working-class alcohol consumption. Such Acts could embody the device of 'local option': for example Glasgow in 1890 was empowered to allow its wards to exclude pubs from their areas. Bodies like the Band of Hope tried to inculcate the children with the evils of drink. But though there is much to be said for such devices as immediate actions, they did not touch the basic problem of why alcohol was such a temptation. Working-class organizations had concerned themselves with temperance even earlier than the middle-class philanthropists: it was indeed a standing concern among artisan organizations for mutual improvement.

A fundamental attack on the health problem was called for. It had three components. The first was infrastructural – the need to undertake the great capital works that would provide water and sanitation on the scale required. These were the means whereby the greatest advance in health could be made. Secondly there was the provision of health facilities in the form of infirmaries (hospitals), dispensaries and clinics. This aspect lay mainly with the philanthropists as fund raisers and managers and the medical experts as practitioners. Thirdly there was housing.

Sanitation and water supply were problematic enough; they called for corporate civic action; they involved urban politics, especially in terms of finance: each city had to make its own response. Glasgow set a splendid example for Britain with its Loch Katrine water scheme, opened in 1859, bringing a plenitude of pure water to the city over a distance of some 50 miles. But it took a good many years to connect up the standpipes in courts and closes, and to carry the supply into working-class houses.

Sewage disposal, made even more pressing by the new inflow of water, was an even more difficult matter. The Police Acts could be used in an attempt to enforce standards of cleanliness (watering, sweeping and cleansing of closes, emptying of middens, disinfecting of premises). But this could avail little with no adequate sewage system. Glasgow's sewage traditionally went, untreated, into the Clyde: its foulness was a threat and an embarrassment. In 1867 Sir Joseph Bazalgette, who had built so much of London's sewage system, advocated pumping the sewage to a distant outfall in the Clyde estuary or on the Ayrshire coast, but this was prohibitively expensive. In 1888 the Company that was to build the subway, in order to obtain the necessary powers from the city, undertook to remodel the sewage system in the centre of the city; this was done. The overall system had consisted of some 40 miles in 1850 and was 100 miles by 1890. But still the sewage was discharged raw; the Clyde, like other British rivers, was an open sewer. It remained so until 1890 when the building of treatment stations was begun first at Dalmarnock then at Dalmuir and Shieldhall. So it was that throughout Victoria's reign the sewage problem had continued largely unsolved.

In this Glasgow did not differ greatly from the other major cities of Britain: the ratepayers were, in general, unwilling to meet the costs of evacuating their cities. Moreover Scottish medical opinion was sharply divided. The majority Scottish view, as opposed to the English, favoured the contagion theory (believing that fevers passed by contact between persons, their clothes and other effects), though conceding to the miasma theory (favoured by Edwin Chadwick) that a contributing factor lay in noxious gases arising from rubbish, wastes and excreta. The contagion theory, of course, greatly weakened the case of those who wanted an improved sanitation and sewage system. Even James Burn Russell, Glasgow's great Medical

Officer of Health, favoured the earth closet, and so did not see a water-borne sanitation system as important.

Health care presented a different set of problems. It had two aspects, namely doctoring and hospital facilities and their various auxiliaries, and the inspection of homes, food, shops and sanitation, together with the gathering of statistical data that would allow doctors, anxious to understand the interaction between their profession and society generally, to do so.

The provision of facilities had always been the concern of the medical profession and the philanthropists, and so it remained. The infirmaries were financed by charitable appeal. As teaching hospitals they became the centre of power and prestige in the Scottish medical profession. But in 1832 they were severally limited in a number of ways. They had to shed their responsibilities for fever patients, for lunatics and for the chronically ill: as the provision of Poor Houses extended this became possible. Secondly, they needed a class of professional nurses. This came from the 1880s as training and residences were made available, attracting young women of character and dedication.

As for the available therapies, a distinction must be made between the surgical and the medicinal aspect. In Victoria's reign the surgeons made real progress, with the Scottish hospitals making striking contributions. In Glasgow Royal Infirmary in the 1860s Joseph Lister (1827–1912) developed his system of antiseptic surgery; by the 1880s it had been routinized in Scotland's hospitals. In the 1890s William Macewen (1848–1924), Lister's pupil and successor, went a stage further with aseptic surgery, putting the world's doctors into white coats. Earlier, in 1847 at Edinburgh, Sir James Y. Simpson (1811–70) had developed and popularized the technique of anaesthetics in childbirth. Simpson had to fight the view that God had ordained that childbirth should be painful: this he countered with a reference to the Lord putting Adam to sleep before extracting the rib that was to become Eve. Fortunately the Queen, who kept on having babies, took to anaesthetics under her Aberdonian *accoucheur*, Sir James Clark. With a combination of anaesthetics and greatly reduced infection the surgeons could advance their general techniques enormously. In 1895 Glasgow men, with Kelvin at their head, took up X-rays: in 1896 John Macintyre achieved at the royal Infirmary the 'first X-ray cinematograph ever taken'. All this, however, had no parallel on the side of medicine. So too with lunacy: though Scottish doctors earnestly sought a theory to guide their treatment of mental illness, none was available.

The other great line of attack lay through the Medical Officers of Health. Their great priority at the outset was to prevent or deal with fever epidemics. To this end they used two techniques. They undertook inspection of drains, middens, and indeed all the cleanliness requirements embodied in the Police Acts of their respective cities, together with the inspection of the milk supply and the abbatoirs. Secondly they tried to establish a scientific basis for health policy through the gathering of data and the development of medical and social theory to explain it and to suggest remedies. Edinburgh had the first Scottish Medical Officer of Health in 1862, Dr Henry Littlejohn (1826–1914). He was a dedicated and forward-looking man who became Medical Officer of the Scottish Board of Health set up under the Public Health (Scotland) Act of 1867. Glasgow produced two notable MOH's, Dr William Tennant Gairdner (1824–1907), appointed in 1863, and his successor James Burn Russell (1837–1904), appointed in 1872 and continuing in office until 1898 when he, like Littlejohn, became Medical Officer of the Scottish Board of Health. Gairdner's pioneering efforts at data collection were a good deal opposed both as intrusions into privacy and as likely to create embarrassment for landlords and property owners; the police too were resentful of this encroachment. In the cholera epidemic of 1866, Gairdner, through the Sanitary Visitation Movement, revived in a secular form Chalmers idea of middle-class visitations of the working classes, urging on them cleanliness of persons and of homes. Russell created the public health service in Glasgow, making the Sanitary Department efficient and effective. Some 200,000 people were added to Glasgow's population during his period, many of them poor. Russell was inevitably driven on from the prevalence of infection to housing and overcrowding: he was the author in 1888 of a classic paper, 'Life in One Room'. He introduced the system of 'ticketed houses', whereby there was nailed over the door a 'ticket' which stated the number of adults and children legally entitled to live there. The sudden spot checks of his inspectors were resented, but this was perhaps softened by becoming the object of working-class jokes.

Indeed the attitude of the working classes toward what was being done for and to them by the middle classes was an important aspect. Down to the 1880s they were largely passive acceptors. Indeed almost every Glasgow medical man knew of cases in which parents of a family of 10, 12 or 14 children had lost all but one or two, and had

come to think that this was in the ordinary course of God's provi-
dence, or was simply inevitable misfortune. The infant mortality
rate (children under one year) for Scotland indeed gave some warrant to this attitude: in the period 1855-9 the official figure (probably
an under-registration) stood at 118 per thousand and in 1895-9 had
risen to 130. Glasgow's figures were a good deal worse. Indeed it was
here that the great loss of human life lay. The crude death rate for
Glasgow had, over this period, however, declined from 29.6 to 22.7.
From the 1880s working-class fatalism and docility was lessening.
The working classes were finding in increased industrial and political power new forms of articulateness: they could make their way
onto School Boards and Boards of Poor Law Guardians. Moreover
the surgical and nursing revolutions meant a notable improvement
in what could be provided.

5 Housing

By and large the Scottish medical profession was not radicalized by
what it saw in the slums. A number were indeed very conscious of the
links between low working-class incomes and poor housing and bad
diet, as Alison had been. Many with working-class practices worked
devotedly to repair the damage to individuals so far as this was possible, though this was not the path to wealth and prestige in their
profession. To have gone further would have required a political
programme involving a substantial redistribution of incomes, and
indeed a different concept of society. Even a concerted attack on the
housing default through a subsidy paid for by taxation was too
radical a proposal to be seriously enterained. For indeed the cost
would have been very great.

The result was that the supply of houses was, by and large, left to
the market. It failed to respond adequately at the unskilled working-
class end. Landlordism down to the 1850s and beyond operated by
the subdivision of old premises ('making down') and the inbuilding
of open spaces, generating a dense mass of humans in the central and
eastern parts of the cities. Where there was building for low earners it
was minimal, with the only amenities being a fireplace and a
chimney. When building regulations came, from the late 1860s,
these meant that the building of even such houses was reduced in
favour of more sub-division, over-building and in-filling. The ever
rising cost of urban land compounded the problem. As the railways
thrust their way into the centre of the cities they cleared large areas of

packed housing, causing the occupants to move to the diminished supply. The result was almost incredible densities. In parts of Glasgow the census of 1861 showed that 226,723 'houses' consisted of one apartment (of which nearly 8,000 were windowless): this meant that almost one-third of Scotland's people were living in dwellings of one room. Many more lived in 'a room and kitchen'.

The data collected by the Medical Officers of Health showed how close was the connection between bad housing and bad health. In the 1860s in the old parts of Glasgow the people lived 1,000 to the acre: the houses were packed so closely that tenants could shake hands with one another from their windows; air and daylight could hardly enter, for in Bridgegate, Saltmarket, High Street and Trongate the tenements were separated by only five to six feet. These same narrow passageways were used as the only drains. Intermixed with all this were fetid industrial processes such as slaughter-houses, foundries, tanneries, chemical works, as well as docks and gasworks where the unskilled could find employment. This was the nadir of debasement and overcrowding. It must be remembered, however, that so many of the incomers from Ireland and the Highlands had known only primitive homes in conditions of rural deprivation and so had low housing expectations.

The Medical Officers of Health struggled to limit densities and to enforce standards of cleanliness. The philanthropists made efforts to improve the supply, within the limits of the charity principle. James Begg of Edinburgh (1808–83) urged that 'The most important physical remedy for the woes of man is a comfortable and wholesome dwelling'. But the voluntarist principle was a limited one. It sought to provide 'model' dwellings that could be built cheaply: careful economy of construction plus an educative programme for the occupants might, it was hoped, close the gap between the costs of such provision and the lower working-class incomes. But experience showed that the scope for such a programme was limited. The encouragement of savings banks and building societies did indeed help respectable families, usually with a skilled breadwinner, to improve their position, but this still left the poorer families without a solution.

Thirdly, there was communal action. In this Glasgow, with its Improvement Act of 1866, took the lead, though only after bitter controversy. The Commissioners were to buy property especially in the decaying core of the city, clear it, and then sell the land for new building at a higher standard. In the longer run from the 1890s the scheme had considerable success, with the City doing its own building. In this way much of the very worst of Glasgow's housing was cleared, though the Commissioners were criticized, like their counterparts elsewhere because the new housing was delayed, and when it came was much less than had been removed. Meanwhile, however, the growth of the population had continued relentlessly. Edinburgh obtained its Improvement Act in 1875, under which 3,250 dwellings were to be acquired and cleared; the Leith Improvement Scheme came in 1880.

A Royal Commission on Housing sat in 1885: its members perceived that in Scotland as in England the fundamental problem was low and unstable incomes among the unskilled. In 1888 the Presbytery of Glasgow appointed a Commission to report on the housing of the poor in relation to their social condition. By this time Edinburgh had outstripped Glasgow in improvement, thus helping to incite a new effort. The Glasgow Commission in 1891, found that the very worst conditions of 20 years earlier had gone. By 1885 52 per cent of those who died had been enrolled as members of Friendly Societies. There had been much tenement building in areas like Partick, Shettleston and Bridgeton Cross for the housing of artisans, clerks, and other families that had won their struggle for respectability: to this limited degree the housing problem was solving itself on market principles.

In most cases Scottish working-class families were tenants rather than owners. Few workmen thought of themselves as property owners, being partly conditioned by prevailing circumstances. The tenement system in its classic form as in Glasgow largely precluded owner-occupier status for the worker: the tenements were owned by small tradesmen, provision dealers, widows, small savers and investors of all kinds, and were managed for them by firms of factors. In a sense the skilled and the unskilled were in the same situation. They shared the same neighbourhoods; there were blocks of good tenements alongside bad, so that there were no 'ghettos' in Glasgow. Much of the housing was on yearly lets, which meant a mass moving in May when the population changed houses, causing a fever of flitting among the women and adding to the trials of the school attendance officers and to the factors in pursuit of rent arrears. The yearly lets were for houses over £10 rent per year: lower down the scale were the 'monthly' houses, carrying a certain amount of stigma. The result was that the building societies did not achieve success in Scotland as they did in England.

But the situation at the bottom of the social and income scale was still very bad in the 1890s. Glasgow still had some 36,000 one-apartment houses, with 60,000 of two apartments; of these 70,000 were ticketed. It was here that the Presbytery of Glasgow Commission concentrated its scrutiny. It divided the people there into three categories: (1) the industrious and well-behaved, though very poor; (2) the dissolute and drunken, many of whom work but waste their wages; (3) the criminal population and the waifs and strays. The first category, able in the same block as the second and third to maintain their houses scrupulously clean, comfortable and wholesome, roused the sympathy of the Commissioners; the others did not. Thus was reflected the classic policy dilemma of rigour or relief.

Those who took the side of the apparently feckless, like the socialist Bruce Glasier (1859–1920), pointed out how the conditions of work for many men were so abominable that any sort of housing was better: as he put it: 'Moulders coming from a fiery atmosphere, literally black with dust and laden with mineral gases, soon lose their natural perception of cleanliness and domestic health. Dock labourers, exposed to wet and cold, and begrimed with manifold dusts, will be apt to esteem even the poorest hovels pleasant and refreshing after a long day's or night's toil'. Glasier was clear in his mind on the question of subsidized housing chargeable to the rates: 'I think it is the very first duty of the Corporation to undertake it.' Though the Corporation did indeed enter upon house building in 1890s, it was for policemen and other civic servants, together with a few families who would be a credit to the new flats: subsidy was not envisaged.

6 Education

In elementary education, as with the Poor Law, the church by 1832 was losing its capacity to perform its function adequately. It did indeed make considerable efforts to repair the gaps now obvious in the old parish provision. Its Education Committee (f. 1824) had by 1865 set up 214 'Assembly Schools'; there were also 120 new 'Sessional Schools'. The Disruption of 1843, however, created a new situation – the Free Kirk began at once to set up its own schools. By this means Scottish elementary education was both fragmented and stimulated. There were now three principal educational bodies, the old Kirk, the new Kirk and the Roman Catholic Church.

The advent of the Free Church both greatly increased the facilities and activated educational thought and provision. Yet, in spite of this, the need for schooling was outrunning the supply of schools both in quantity and quality. Moreover Scotland, with so long a tradition of unified education under its national church, was uneasy with the new pattern. With both the Church and education thus split, the unity of Scottish culture was damaged, making it difficult to maintain a distinctive Scottish educational tradition; this opened the door to the Anglicizers. James Begg in 1850 was indignant that 'We are sinking in our national position every year, and simply living on the credit of the past. Had we the means of universal education, we might expect soon to rise again on the scale of nations . . . the Parliament of England despising us, our natural guardians joining in the oppression.' But though a majority of thinking people in Scotland believed that a unified Scottish system was essential to stop the educational decline, the contentious nature of religion stood in the way. On the other hand the hold of religion on education was beginning to slip: by the Education Act of 1861 Scottish school teachers were no longer required to subscribe to the Westminster Confession of Faith or be communicants of the Church of Scotland.

In 1866 the government responded to misgivings by setting up the Argyll Commission, under the eighth Duke of Argyll, a Scottish Whig grandee of wide interests. It found that of 500,000 children needing education 200,000 received it under efficient conditions, 200,000 were at schools of doubtful merit with no inspection, and 90,000 were attending no school at all. Even so, however, it would appear that there were 14 per cent more Scottish than English children at school. Scotland shared with Germany, Holland, Switzerland and the Scandinavian countries the lowest rates of adult illiteracy at between 10 and 20 per cent. Under pressure from Scotland the government was anxious to proceed with legislation: after two abortive bills the outcome was the Scottish Education Act of 1872.

It is one of the great landmarks. It was a much more comprehensive measure than its English counterpart of 1870. Under it the Scottish tradition of a unified system was resumed, but now under secular aegis. The new School Boards took over at a stroke the schools of the old and new churches. All three Presbyterian churches could agree on religious education, namely some 45 minutes per day using as its basis the Shorter Catechism, in sharp contrast to continued bitter denominational feuding in England. Moreover the system taken over by the Scottish School Boards was sufficiently comprehensive to make compulsory attendance possible almost at once: this took 10 years in England. This was adopted for all children from 5 to 13 years. Parents were not to be permitted to plead poverty in keeping their children from school: those who could not afford to send their children to school were made entitled to assistance from the Poor Law. The School Attendance Committee and its officers set vigorously about the task of bringing the children in, hailing defaulting parents before them. Where there were gaps in the provision the Boards set about filling them. The building programme produced schools of a splendour previously unknown. Within 27 years of the Act the payment of fees was wholly abandoned; elementary education had become both compulsory and free. Within a decade or so Scotland could claim once more a place in the forefront of national education systems. Her school population of some 500,000 had by 1908 reached almost a million.

There were, however, unsatisfactory aspects. Though a special Scottish Education Committee was set up, it was located in London, thus exposing the system to Anglicizing influences. Indeed the two most powerful educators, Sir Henry Craik and A. Craig Sellar, the men chiefly responsible for implementing the Education Act of 1872, though Scotsmen, were sympathetic to English ideas. As against this the local Boards had a large degree of independence of action. The great aim after 1872 was to achieve 'unification of effort' in the interests of 'efficiency': thus a uniform goodness was to be preferred to the previous mix of the excellent and the awful. The closely controlled national pattern of education that resulted gave Scotland one of the most centrally organized systems in the world. Because of the great demand for places there was for a generation or so a good deal of overcrowding of classes, with as one account put it, the teacher shouting like a drover at 70 pupils. Moreover because a certain percentage of passes was required of the teacher there was a tendency to learning by rote, with emphasis on exactness, rather than on inquiry and thought. Because of the system of inspection it was necessary to cram even the less responsive child lest the inspector light upon him or her. Thus it became apparent that even on the new scale of provision education for the new age presented appalling problems. It is hardly surprising that elements reminiscent of the factory system crept in. And yet the achievement was remarkable.

On the side of schoolmastering and teaching method the Scots had already made a large contribution. Andrew Bell (1753–1832), born in St Andrews, developed the 'monitorial system', whereby selected older pupils could teach and supervise the younger. Out of it was to come the pupil-teacher system of training. Bell was a figure celebrated throughout Britain and was buried with great ceremony in Westminster Abbey in 1832. It is not surprising that his initiative should be Scottish, arising as it did from the challenge to economize on teachers. Sheriff John Wood developed the monitorial system further, and David Stowe in 1836 founded the first Scottish Teachers' Training College. The latter two men however differed, representing conflicting educational theories. Wood, though he believed in the need to understand the child, encouraged fierce competition in the classroom, reinforced with strict discipline. Stowe, on the other hand, stressed the need for a bond of sympathy and understanding between teacher and pupil, with no corporal punishment and no giving of prizes. It was the Wood view that prevailed in Scotland, reinforced indeed by demands of the 1872 Act to process so many children.

The Scottish Act, unlike the English, also made some provision for secondary education. Previously there had been a range of grammar schools and burgh or parish schools where boys were prepared for the universities of Scotland. There was also a number of boarding establishments ('hospitals') that had been founded by charity. The Commissioners on Endowed Schools (Scotland) of 1872 insisted that they take in more pupils. These were largely from the middle classes, leading to such schools being socially pre-empted. The most prestigious were in Edinburgh, including George Heriot's and the Merchant Company's Schools.

After the Act and subsequent legislation some School Boards undertook the management of a range of secondary schools, designated 'higher class schools' or 'higher grade schools'; some of these were the old grammar schools, such as Edinburgh and Glasgow High Schools, Aberdeen New Grammar School and Perth Academy. The 'hospitals' were revamped mainly as day schools: their endowments were reorganized, and on the basis of these they maintained their independence. The middle class continued to be the chief beneficiaries under the bursary system and subsidized fees. A few of the hospitals, like Fettes, became 'public schools' on the English model. Around the mid century there had appeared other schools of the English kind, like Merchiston, Loretto and Trinity College, Glenalmond: these went their independent way. Scotch secondary education was thus strongly divided on class lines, confirming the advantages of middle-class children.

The mass of the workers did not aspire to secondary education for their children, though there was an important element that did. The government view was that because secondary education was so largely middle class, fees should be paid. But as elementary education became more effective humble parents asked for more.

The weakness of secondary education before and indeed after 1872 affected the universities. The old parochial schools system had meant that students went to the universities very young, aged 14 or 15, thus requiring that the universities hold junior classes. Local schoolmasters 'brought on' the 'lads o' pairts' who had impressed them favourably, often providing something close to private tuition. This practice stood in the way of the development of a proper secondary system. On the other hand by 1872 the ratio of those at university was five times as high in Scotland as in England: the Scottish universities were open to all, from all levels of society, without entrance qualification. The Scottish student had a difficult existence, struggling along on a bursary or modest family support, living in lodgings in the town: his was a life very different from that of the Oxford or Cambridge undergraduate. Indeed many promising men overstrained themselves, dying early. But this was the way to a profession or even to political power. The Scottish student took the MA in Arts, where philosophy was queen, and then might take specialized training for the ministry, medicine or the law.

7 Middle-class Surveillance; Crime

Much of the debate over social amelioration went on among the middle classes, over the heads of the workers. The Charity Organization Society, in its rationalizing efforts and with its distinction between the deserving and the undeserving poor, was certainly an affair of the middle classes. It was under their aegis that the police enforced the law and the Medical Officers of Health carried out their inspections. The Scottish National Society for the Prevention of Cruelty to Children, founded in 1884, with its inspectors powerful in the localities, was also a middle-class initiative, reaching into working-class families largely on the basis of neighbours' reports. In two aspects, however, there was inter-class collaboration, namely in the temperance movement and in school attendance as enforced by the elective School Boards in which the artisan class played an important role after 1872.

The dominant aspect of crime in the 1830s lay in offences against property: of the crimes brought before the High Court in Edinburgh in 1830 no less than 93 per cent were against property and only 7 per cent against the person. Much of this was against local tradesmen and fellow members of the working classes, committed much more frequently in winter when food and money were scarce. In 1900 crimes against property were still by far the largest category, at about 84 per cent.

7

Religion, Morals and Social Responsibility

1 The Centrality of Religion

Religion, though related to class and power in Victorian Scotland,[1] cannot be merely subordinated to these elements. It was a central theme, with its own powerful identity and a baffling complexity. It came from a remote but still compelling past: it had seized hold of the minds of Scotsmen in a highly distinctive way from the Scottish reformation of 1560, long before industrialization came, and was to be one of the most complex reactions of Scotsmen to the new way of life. For those who took their religion seriously, the cultivation of the soul and its preparation for the life after death was the most important business in life.

The compulsions, convictions and controversies of religion were especially strong among the middle orders of society which contained the bringers of change. For the respectable Scottish artisans the Presbyterian religion became a support in raising themselves above the degradations of the cities. Even among the less skilled and the labourers, though so many of them had by the mid-century ceased to attend church and had escaped from the Shorter Catechism, the pattern of Presbyterian belief and its moralism remained strong. Kipling celebrated this in a poem entitled 'McAndrew's Hymn':

> From coupler flange to spindle guide
>   I see thy hand, O god –
> Predestination in the stride
>   O' yon connectin'-rod.

In the countryside the Kirk had a more continuous life, though

[1] See chapter 4, section 3 & 8 above.

controversy was no less bitter there in the first half of the nineteenth century. The Highlands produced their own distinctive religious response: there a new piety, strongly Calvinistic, arose in the 1830s.

Scottish religious doctrine owed much to what was brought from Geneva in 1555 by John Knox, based upon Calvinism, and was embodied in the Westminster Confession of Faith ratified by the Scots Parliament in 1643. It did not quietly fade away as the new economy and society asserted themselves from the industrial revolution onward, and as they widened the field of human thought and perception in terms both of science and theology. On the contrary, the old questions assumed a new urgency as church order and the faith itself were, step by step, called into question.

Central to all this was the Calvinistic belief in predestination and the doctrine of the elect. It asserted that God had inscrutably chosen from the beginning of time these who should 'sit on His right hand', and those who should be damned to eternal exclusion, and indeed to hell's fires. This set of notions became increasingly tough after Knox; indeed much that was fundamental to Scottish religious consciousness was post-Knox; he himself was not a Presbyterian. The significance in Victoria's time of such a set of beliefs, so closely related to the individual and his fate, is very difficult to judge, involving as it does the psychological problem of living out one's life not knowing whether or not one was numbered among the elect. It may be that success in business would engender confidence in one's status with God, thus generating further success in a cumulative way. The tombs in Glasgow's Necropolis and the absence of self-doubt in men like William Beardmore suggest that some people at least, if they did not know they were of the elect, were pretty confident that it could hardly be otherwise.

Presbyterianism further asserted that God watched over His creation, and would intervene in response to contrition and prayer to mitigate the consequences of individual and national stupidity and selfishness, as well as of the calamities of nature, thus suspending the laws of causality on which emergent science insisted. The church was of divine origin, with Christ as its head. The Bible was the inspired word of God, the foundation of all Christian belief: it was not to be questioned, but was to be accepted as the literal truth. Scottish life was overshadowed by the ferocities of the Old Testament rather than the healing of the New. God would be vastly affronted if the Sabbath were not kept holy. In broad terms the old ideas on these matters of doctrine, though called in question, survived in Scotland almost intact until industrial maturity, down to the 1870s and 80s.

It was largely the influence of Presbyterianism that made the Scots regard all the issues of life in the broadest and most morally abstract terms. It was this, for example, that caused the Scots to take the initiative in the British agitation against slavery between 1833 and the American Civil War. The slave question could be regarded in simple terms of good and evil, as well as having an appeal deriving from universalist ideas about the brotherhood of mankind, rooted in the teaching of the churches. The Glasgow and Edinburgh Emancipation Societies were the British spearhead.

The manse, of whatever denomination, was a source of social and intellectual leaders. It raised men and women in an atmosphere of education and duty. The homes of the ministers of the Established Church were independent because of the tiends (tithes) and the glebe. These, though they were a form of endowment of the Church, did not pertain to the family of the clergy, so that each new generation of the young was obliged to face the world again, just as was the case with the other churches. Behind such men and women was a home that had inculcated the confidence of being in God's care, with a reciprocal responsibility to Him.

In principle the Kirk session of the Presbyterian Churches was democratic, controlled by the body of the lay members, with their influence extending upward to presbyteries, synods and The General Assembly. The basis of Presbyterianism was thus intended to be democratic. This was indeed the reality in many cases. But there was often a tendency for oligarchy to emerge, with the elders becoming a virtually self-perpetuating group, normally selecting their successors.

2 Orthodoxy, Church and State; the Disruption

The continuance of older ideas on doctrine was helped by the fact that Scottish Presbyterianism had for some time before 1832 directed its intense controversial energies not to fundamental theology, but to church government. The Church of Scotland, unlike the Anglican or the Roman Catholic, had permitted little latitude of belief: all her ministers dispensed the same minutely detailed creed based on the Westminster Confession and dinned into the young by the Shorter Catechism. The Scotch intellect, running free in so many other directions in the Enlightenment and after, did not directly challenge the nature of religious belief. The ministers, with the constant threat of deposition confronting them, dared not allow speculation to confront orthodoxy. Thus was generated a marvellous uniformity of faith that was not to be questioned, at least openly. This meant that the whole force of Scottish religious disputatiousness in the early nineteenth century was confined to the realm of church government. But then it could be bitter and divisive.

The 'Ten Years Conflict' beginning in 1833 and culminating in the Disruption of 1843 had its origin in the legal sense in legislation of Queen Anne's time, namely the Toleration Act and the Patronage Act, both of 1712. Under the first the parliament at Westminster had imposed upon Presbyterian-dominated Scotland the right of freedom of worship for the defeated Episcopalians. Thus could Scotland continue through Victoria's reign to contain a significant Episcopalian minority, along with other tolerated groups. The second Act was an attempt to solve a conflict within the Church of Scotland itself: each church together with its presbytery was to 'call' its minister by agreement between the heritors (the landlords) and the elders of the congregation. What was to happen if they disagreed, as increasingly occurred among a literate population with an individualist religion, was left ambiguous. A good many heritors (some of whom were absentees), insisted that in such a situation their choice should prevail. Indeed church patronage had become an important element in the secular politics of Scotland. Conflicts inevitably arose, fuelled by much self-righteous appeal to absolute principle.

Inevitably the argument embraced the ancient contest for primacy between church and state. The non-intrusionists (the opponents of the heritors' claims) invoked the First Book of Discipline of 1560, drawn up by Knox and five others, which declared that 'it appertained unto the people and to every several congregation to elect their minister'. They asserted that in such a matter the state had no jurisdiction, so that the Patronage Act had no status. In this the Evangelicals were the most uncompromising. They reflected in part the changes that Scotland was undergoing, being to a considerable extent men of the growing lower middle class whose urge for recognition could make them intolerant and intractable. They challenged the Moderates, the cultured and undogmatic element, who preferred to accept the civil power rather than confront it,

especially as so many of them were comfortably placed in the prevailing order of things. Thus was Scotland moving, only one year
after the commotion of the first Reform Act, toward schism in its
most comprehensive institution and a bulwark of its culture, its
established church.

The Moderates, having been in control of the General Assembly
of the Church of Scotland for at least two generations, found to
their alarm in 1834 that the Evangelical ministers and brethren had
achieved a majority. The Evangelical hostility to Erastianism (the
subordination of the church to the state) could now fully express
itself. The predominately English government at Westminster in
the 1830s as in 1712 found itself confronted by Scottish differences
it did not fully understand, though it was unwilling to concede the
full claims of the Evangelicals. The latter pushed through the General Assembly of 1834 the 'Veto Act', which purported, in uncompromising terms, to give to congregations the absolute right of veto
of a minister presented to them by the heritors. Within months the
Veto Act was challenged in the Court of Session in Edinburgh: the
Court issued an Act of Declaration, decreeing in a test case that the
parish of Auchterarder was bound to accept the nominee of its
heritor, the Earl of Kinnoul. The Veto Act was thus pronounced by
the Scottish court *ultra vires* and the claim that the Church of
Scotland was an 'independent spiritual community' free of state
jurisdiction, was rejected. The House of Lords, in a somewhat
casual judgement, confirmed this view. Evangelical passions were
now fully aroused, aimed at the Scottish Moderates and the English
legislators. In 1842 the General Assembly drew up a 'Claim of
right', an intemperate document.

When the General Assembly met in St Andrew's Church in
Edinburgh on 18 May 1843 all was set for high drama. After a
sermon on the text 'let every man be fully persuaded in his own
mind', followed by prayer, a Protest by the Evangelicals against the
'disabilities under which the whole Church and its General
Assembly labour' was solemnly read. Then came the dramatic
moment. The reader of the Protest, Dr Welsh, laid it on the table,
bowed to the Marquis of Bute the Queen's representative, and,
accompanied by the greatest figure present, Dr Chalmers, together
with other leaders, walked into the street. Their followers, sitting
together to the left of the Moderator's chair, rose in a mass and filed
through the door, leaving half the church a blank; on the right hand
side, the Moderates and conciliators sat silent and bewildered. No

less than 470 out of the 1,200 Church of Scotland ministers had abandoned their 'whole privileges, emoluments, status and obligations'. The stream of clerics made its way to Tanfield Halls where they forthwith set up a rival Assembly and a new Church.

The Free Church, thus dramatically brought to birth, was an extraordinary phenomenon. Its members, including Chalmers (chosen as its first Moderator), believed it to be not a seceding body, but the true national church, the Church of Scotland, as well as being 'free'. It began at once the heroic task of duplicating all the undertakings and services provided by the Church it had left. The Free Church called upon its members to contribute generously in money terms: this they most notably did. Within a few years, in spite of the hostility of landowners who controlled so many sites, the Free Church had brought into being a duplication of church buildings and schools. This caused a great reinvigoration of Scottish religious life, for the Church of Scotland had also to respond to the new situation. The Free Church celebrated its differences with the Church of Scotland with the jingle:

> The wee Kirk, the Free Kirk,
> The Kirk wi'out the steeple;
>
> The auld Kirk, the cauld [cold] Kirk,
> The Kirk wi'out the people.

The Disruption meant that the Poor Law could no longer be left to the depleted Church of Scotland, and had to be put on a new and more adequate basis. The educational effort of the Free Church schools under Dr Candlish raised the qualification and payments of teachers. But there was undoubtedly a strain on manpower in the ministry and in school teaching in both churches as a result of duplicate and rival systems.

Against the undoubted stimulus of the Disruption must be placed the damage that it caused to Scottish culture on the one hand and to religious belief on the other. The Church, in spite of earlier secessions, had been the great unifying institution of the Scottish nation. There were soon two major churches in every city, town and village; they shared the Westminster Declaration of faith, but were in strong and often bitter rivalry. Education too was split. Instead of Scottish culture moving forward on the basis of the relatively relaxed perspective of the Moderates, it was now fissured and in some senses narrowed, so that it could the less effectively resist the Anglicizers or modernizers.

Not long after the Disruption came a danger much more threatening in the longer run than a dispute over church government: the nature of the faith itself was called in question. Anti-Calvinist feeling, together with literary criticism of the Bible and secular and scientific thought, began to assail both contestants, threatening their fundamental shared beliefs. Indeed, as if to anticipate this threat, two much earlier dispersed fragments, the Relief Church and the Secession Church, drew together in 1847 to form the United Presbyterian Church. This meant, in effect, that Presbyterianism in Scotland consisted of the Church of Scotland, the Free Church and the United Presbyterian Church. The Presbyterian religion was now a three-cornered affair, a weak basis on which to meet the new theological and cultural challenges. In 1874 the issue of 1843 was finally laid to rest: patronage was abolished by Act of Parliament. But the issue of the Disestablishment of the Church of Scotland rumbled on through the nineteenth century, kept alive by the Free Church.

3 The Urban Masses

A good many ministers and laymen, especially among the Evangelicals, had as early as the 1830s or even before, realized that the old church had been losing contact with the urbanized working classes. This involved both spiritual deprivation and the danger of civil unrest. In Glasgow the group of young men headed by William Collins the publisher and George Burns the shipowner had, in the early 1830s under the influence of Chalmers, launched a church extension movement. With the government refusing money, these philanthropists, with the support of Chalmers, Thomas Guthrie and Robert Candlish (the three great leaders of the Disruption) had formed in 1832 the Association for Promoting the Interests of the Church in Scotland, intended to supply churches in the newly populous areas of the Scottish towns for the 'unchurched masses'. Between 1835 and 1839 some 201 churches were built, costing about a quarter of a million pounds. Though a considerable number of skilled workers were thus attracted, the bulk of the urbanized masses remained unchurched. To them the formula of seat rents and pew places as a means of meeting costs had little appeal when set alongside daily survival. The formation of Bible Societies could do little to change this. The simple belief of middle-class sponsors that exposure to the Scriptures would console, reconcile and redeem the urban working classes rested on an ignorance of the conditions under which they lived, especially the more hard-pressed and less literate among them.

4 Revivalism

But there was another kind of religious manifestation, very different from the organized earnestness of the philanthropists. It came from the distant past. Emotional religious revivals great and small had punctuated the eighteenth century. The 'Cambuslang Wark' (Work) of 1742 was one of the most famous, bringing burning religious fervour to Lanarkshire and deeply affecting Thomas Gladstones, whose grandson was to become prime minister. These 'awakenings' were traditionally sacerdotal, centring round mass communion after highly charged preaching, sometimes by laymen, threatening damnation and offering in its place the possibility of felicity to the repentant. The 1840s saw revivals in Kilsyth and in Aberdeen where there were spectacular manifestations. The Kilsyth awakening was the last great sacramental one, and so may have been a turning point of a kind. Against this sort of emotional Evangelical appeal the Moderates of course turned their faces. All areas of Scotland seem to have been susceptible, making class or occupational explanations unconvincing. To this the Calvinist enigma of not knowing whether one was of the elect may have contributed. In 1859–60 there was yet another outburst, accompanied as in the past with 'strikings down' and cataleptic states.

In 1873–4 came a new kind of revivalism, that of the Americans Dwight L. Moody the evangelist and Ira David Sankey the singer and organist. They brought preaching, singing and uplift, together with happy conversion. Their success in Scotland was immense, in strong contrast with the theologically thorny diet of sermons from Scottish pulpits, bringing the hope that a return to a simple Biblical literalism and a casting away of the burden of sin would not only stop the decline of church attendance, but reinspire and reinvigorate the nation. Moody and Sankey did indeed have a profound effect on Scottish Protestantism (much greater indeed than in England), bringing a kind of religious populism that cut across theological refinement by its fundamentalist appeal. But it could not arrest the long-term trend toward secularism. Nor could

it reach far beyond the artisans, clerks and students. Rival claims
on mass emotion were being felt, especially politics with the extension of the franchise, and the rise of spectator sports especially
football.

5 Roman Catholicism and the Irish

Fragmented Scottish presbyterianism had not only to contend with
its own internal divisions, with the lost loyalty of the unskilled,
with the challenge to its theology and with the excitement of
awakenings: there was yet another problem. This was Roman
Catholicism. In 1829 had come the Catholic Emancipation Act. It
had met with stiff resistance in Scotland. Though it could be
claimed by the Evangelicals that the Church of Scotland was independent of the jurisdiction of the state, its spokesmen did not hesitate to proclaim who should have civil rights within the state. All
protestant churchmen denied the Pope's authority and condemned
transubstantiation and the Mass (and after 1870 papal infallibility)
as grievous errors; many Scotsmen associated the Papacy with continental tyrannies. But not all were prepared to deny to Catholics
their civil rights, for this would be an affront to liberty of conscience. The ministers of the Church of Scotland and most of their
congregations were against emancipation: its support came from
middle-class Whigs, together with an element of the dissenting
congregations of the day, the Relief and the United Secession
churches. The great mass of the petitioners against Catholic emancipation were of the uneducated lower classes, no doubt motivated
by fear and distrust of Irish labour, so often used by employers
to make effective unionism impossible. Thus the hostility to the
Catholics was greatest in the industrial west, fading toward Edinburgh and the East: this pattern was to persist throughout the century. A full Scottish referendum would have rejected the Catholic
claims: the parliament at Westminster however accepted them, as
it had those of the Episcopalians.

Scottish sectarianism did not cease with Catholic emancipation.
Instead it gained in virulence. The 'no popery' movement found a
new vigour: with it went anti-Irish feeling. Amid the confusions
and divisions of Presbyterianism anti-Romanism became a kind of
obverse religion, reassuring as a kind of fixed target of condemnation and abuse in a shifting scene. Though emancipated in 1829,
the Irish in Scotland did not gain their first real participation in

political power until the Reform act of 1884.

As for the fast-growing Irish Roman Catholic community, its priests were humble men of the same social background as their parishioners, without wealthy supporters, and free of the barrier of middle-class social status that encumbered the Presbyterian ministers. They kept their flocks firmly to the faith by church and by school. These hard-pressed priests worked with great energy; many died young from their exertions. Father Mathew, the great Irish crusader against drunkenness, visited Glasgow in 1842 to launch the Catholic Temperance Movement in Scotland. A high proportion of the Irish were churchgoers, for it was in their religion that they found identity and comfort, and in their priests that they found leadership and community. In their churches with their space, light and statues they found a world beyond the saloon and the shebeen. Catholic church architecture was indeed innovatory in a way that was perhaps surprising in an ancient church, serving a community so largely derived from the Irish peasantry, highly conservative in the Irish manner: there was much inventiveness in the development of neo-Gothic, neo-Byzantine, octagonal and other forms. In 1878 the Roman Catholic hierarchy was restored in Scotland, making the Church there complete; by this time there were probably some 300,000 Roman Catholics in the country. The Scottish hierarchy remained distinct from the English, with its own character and outlook. It was the Roman church that had a real place among the urban poor. But, like the Presbyterians, it had its tensions, deriving from differences between the continuing Scottish Catholic tradition and that of the Irish Catholic, low-income incomers. The Catholic Church was of course concerned with the movement for Irish Home Rule, so that for many of the Irish working class in Scotland religion and politics went together.

6 Foreign Missions

While the Scots were resisting Catholic claims at home they took their first missionary initiative abroad: in the very year of emancipation the Church of Scotland sent out its first missionary: Dr Alexander Duff, full of the zeal of an early apostle, sailed for Calcutta, where he was to become a magisterial figure. Foreign missions became, indeed, a major Scottish overseas activity, involving intimate contact with many distant societies and bringing a painful form of the challenge of culture clash.[2] The problem of converting the heathen became the more perplexing in the light of the divisions within Christianity and within even the Presbyterian faith: to this was added the scientific-secular challenge, together with Biblical criticism. These two matters posed the dilemma for missionaries of either retreating into a closed state of mind or risking the corrosion of the simple and literal kind of faith that was appropriate to the foreign mission fields, and which indeed had carried most missionaries there.

7 Fundamentalism in the Highlands

But much nearer to home there was work for the Church to do. Just before the Ten Years conflict some 40 churches had been built with public money in the destitute districts of the Highlands – the Parliamentary Churches. Their endowments were slender and their ministers lacked status. But there had been an extraordinary burst of activity by the Highland ministers, most of whom were intensely Evangelical. The quarrels between the Church of Scotland and the Free Church over sites was in 1849 referred to a Parliamentary Commission: it revealed a curious situation in many of the northern and Hebridean Free Church parishes. In them had arisen 'The Men', a set of zealots who, with the aid of sacramental gatherings, domineered over such ministers as there were, and who had set such fanatical standards of belief and conduct that in parishes with two or three thousand people only some 20 or 30 were allowed to take communion. Dancing and card playing were almost deadly sins and to use an umbrella was almost as bad. Thus could remote and introverted communities work to an extraordinary pitch the implications of Calvinist doctrine.

The Church Extension scheme became the Endowment scheme: some 100 further new churches in Highlands and Lowlands were the fruit of its efforts. The Free Church in the Highlands was, of course, the strongest element of Presbyterianism there. It was also the most intractable in Scotland. In the early 90s, as conversations developed for the reunification of the United Presbyterian Church and the Free Church, and as the Westminster Declaration of Faith was brought under discussion in the Free Church, feuding broke out within the latter: those who rejected reconciliation and who insisted on the full Declaration, mainly in the Highlands, formed in 1892 the Free Presbyterian Church, the 'Wee Frees'.

[2]See chapter 9, section 5 below.

8 The Return of Sound and Sight

While parts of the Highlands adopted a new austerity of religion, the Lowland Presbyterian Churches were reaching back into the past in search of a sense of form and beauty for their churches and their worship. The early church reformers after 1560 had seen the advantage of involving the congregation, having the Scottish Psalter printed at the expense of the General Assembly, but music in church was abandoned. The rise of ritualism in England no doubt played its part in bringing back the appeal of sight and sound: the Scots had begun to feel the need for an escape from barn-like buildings and austere services. Glasgow Cathedral acquired a splendid set of stained glass windows. In 1859 Dr Robert Lee of Old Greyfriars Church in Edinburgh, wherein the Covenant of 1638 had been signed, was called before the General Assembly of the Church of Scotland to justify what appeared to be a liturgy, augmented by a harmonium, the first musical instrument heard in a Scotch church since Knox's day. In 1864 the General Assembly decided that such innovations should not be put down. Thereafter they spread rapidly, with organs, tuneful singing, an order of service and stained glass. The Scottish middle class, especially in the wealthier parts of the cities, though it still required the preaching of the word in good measure, and continued to abhor images, by the 1870s wished to be sustained by the beauties of the senses.

9 The Crisis of Belief

The simultaneous reversion to pre-industrial religious primitivism over certain areas of the Highlands, and the Lowland search for beauty in worship, coincided with a growing crisis of belief. It was of a triple nature. One aspect derived from theology, one from natural science, chiefly geology and biology, and the third from the humanistic science of literary criticism as applied to the Bible.

The theological challenge came in the form of an attack on Calvinistic belief, especially the notion of predestination. By the 1870s all sections of Presbyterianism had turned away from this formerly central belief, except for the northern province of the Free Church, the irreconcilables of the Gaelic Presbyteries. The natural-science threat took the form of the challenge posed by evolutionary thinking to the Book of Genesis and the story of the Creation it contained. The Scottish geologists Hutton, Lyell and

Chambers saw in the record of the rocks an evolutionary process.[3] The stone-mason, crusading journalist, attacker of Highland grandees and intense Evangelical, Hugh Miller (1802–56), a self-taught man, rejected such ideas. His book *The Old Red Sandstone* of 1841 became a minor classic, attacking the evolutionary approach associated with Lamarck and others. The world was created in a moment of time, he insisted: 'There is no formation progression. . . . If fish rose into reptiles, it must have been by sudden transformation.' But Miller was placed under immense strain by the conflict between the science of his day and his Presbyterian faith: his mind lapsed into paranoia, fantasy and suicide. Miller was not alone in going through agonies in the attempt to reconcile belief and science. But the scientific debate could in a sense be set aside while worship went on in the old way.

The new German 'higher criticism' threatened the Bible itself. It applied textual and other tests of consistency and origins. The most dramatic incident in this challenge to old beliefs was the trial of William Robertson Smith (1846–94). He was a professor in the Free Church College in Aberdeen, a man with a strong scientific as well as theological background. The imp of perversity raised him up in the bosom of the Free Church. He wrote for the new edition of the *Encyclopaedia Britannica* the article on the Bible. In it he applied the new tests, taking the view that the Bible should no longer be simply seen without question as a Divine document, but should be subjected to the same kind of scrutiny as any other. To many Evangelicals this was not merely impiety, it was an attack on the very foundations of Christianity. In 1877 Smith was hailed before the Free Church Presbytery of Aberdeen; the General Assembly took up the matter. For some four years to 1881 controversy raged within the Free Church over Robertson Smith. He was finally condemned and dismissed from his chair, a kind of Scottish Spinoza. But the Free Church, unlike the Church of Scotland, had confronted the problem of reconciling a liberal view of freedom of conscience and of speech with the new scholarship that threatened to diminish the status of the Bible.

Robertson Smith was the victim of an irresolveable dilemma. If Smith had not been so treated the Free Church might well have had a major split: it was the concern of Principal Rainy, the other great figure in the drama, to prevent this. But there was a sequel. In 1892

[3]See chapter 8, section 7 below.

the Free Church passed a Declaratory Act which toned down the Westminster Confession of Faith, recognizing diversity of opinion; it was this that produced the 'Wee Frees'. But the disruption was a minor one: the old generation of 1843 had died away, leaving the main body of the Free Church ready for reconciliation rather than division. In 1900 the Free Church and the United Presbyterian Church merged in the United Free Church.

So it was that Biblical authority was allowed to recede into the background: Robertson Smith had no successor as martyr. The same was true of predestination. Moody and Sankey, with their emphasis on God's love and forgiveness, helped to push the harshness of Calvinism from people's minds. Evolutionary ideas from geology and biology were allowed to coexist with the Book of Genesis, without dramatic resolution. By the later nineteenth century there was a disposition to leave these divisive and threatening matters to time rather than to adjudication by trial or to resolution by agreed statement. By a temporizing tolerance church members were excused the need to make an exclusive choice. Only the northern parts of the Free Church refused to make this accommodation, clinging to the old faith in all senses.

10 The Social Gospel

While the Scottish churches were thus struggling with their doctrinal basis, the same changes that had posed such problems, namely applied science and technology and the industrialization they brought, were continuing to estrange much of the population from religion. In 1891 the churches collectively claimed that 73.6 per cent of the population were 'in affiliation' with one or other: the respective shares were Church of Scotland 28.5 per cent, Free Church 19.1 per cent, United Presbyterian Church 11.3 per cent, the Roman Catholic Church 8.8 per cent and others 5.7 per cent. These figures are more useful as a guide to distribution than as an indication of absolute size: 73.6 per cent seems an excessive claim. It is true that in middle-class areas the streets would be thronged on Sundays with churchgoers, with the frock coat and the lum hat the proper attire for males, but this masked what was happening at the bottom of the social scale.

A number of responses were tried. The Church of Scotland had showed its continuing concern for social data on a parish basis by its sponsorship of *The New Statistical Account of Scotland* completed by

1845. Attempts at church extension to working-class areas continued especially in the 1870s and 80s, together with the provision of 'free pews' and efforts to break down working-class inhibitions in terms of their dress. The lessening of austerity in worship, with the introduction of music, though it had its roots in the inner needs of the middle classes, might make church attendance more attractive generally. Then there was revivalism of the Moody and Sankey kind which could certainly have dramatic effects, if only in the shorter run. All of these, however, could not arrest the increasing 'Godlessness' of much of the lower income group, the semi and unskilled worker, leaving the churches far removed from much of the life of the nation.

At the same time a good many churchmen had by the 1880s come to appreciate that the alienation of the masses from religion had deep roots. One of the most important of these was the middle-class failure of conscience, largely ignoring the fearful extremes of poverty and wealth. So arose the social gospel, the idea that the churches could only renew themselves by a real intervention in the working of society. Moreover religion could only be real once a certain material level of living had been attained: thus the Alison view gained ground over that of Chalmers. In short evangelicalism began to take a secular turn within the churches.

It was the Free Church that was most affected by radical ideas and associated programmes. This trend was reinforced by the rise of Hegelian philosophy in the Scottish Universities in the 1880s, especially in Glasgow. There Edward Caird (1835–1908) as Professor of Moral Philosophy from 1866 to 1893 ran counter to the prevailing liberal-individualism, arguing that man was a social being and could only be effective when acting together in some societal sense. Socialism of various kinds was also gaining some ground, especially of a humanitarian and fraternal kind.

But the content of the social gospel proved as difficult to define as was the theological basis of Presbyterianism. It could run all the way from an extension of philanthropic, ameliorative action of an *ad hoc* kind, including the temperance movement, to a general programme for society. But it was out of the question under prevailing conditions to advocate a general redistribution of incomes. The next level of attack was housing. In 1858 the Rev. Dr James Begg had sought to stir the Free Church in the direction of housing and sanitary reform. The housing inquiry of the Presbytery of Glasgow reporting in 1891 was an indication of deep misgiving, but it could lead to little. As for education, the churches (apart from the Roman Catholic) abandoned their role to the School Boards in 1872. Whereas the churches had feared social disturbance or even revolution in the 1840s, by the 1890s the fear of socialism took the form of its potential for secularism.

8

The Intellect, the Arts and the Sciences

1 The Scottish Cast of Mind: the Manichean Tendency

Two great influences had worked upon the Scottish intellect before 1832. These were religious thought, namely in the Calvinist tradition, and the rationalism of the Scottish Enlightenment. At bottom these were irreconcilable. The more ancient of the two stemmed from a highly particular set of concepts concerning a divine order that regulated both the individual and his society. The newer idiom posited a world of causality that could be understood by man, and which was amenable to control, provided it was approached through reason and not an emotionalism that was ultimately based on fear of the unknown. There was, too, an element of Stoicism in Enlightenment thought, eschewing the easy comfort of reassuring mysticism, for though the Enlightenment implied an optimism for human betterment, in Scotland for most people this was tempered by the dourness of the religious tradition of Calvinism.

Victorian religious life in Scotland in its evangelical form, as a major part of its inheritance from its Knoxian church, was shot through with an almost Manichean distinction between good and evil. This left little room for the middle ground upon which real debate about human behaviour could take place, and where most of life resided. It reduced the question of behaviour to a simple addiction to the good or the bad, the former to prevail only through Christian atonement. This placed arguments for attempts at the controlled improvement of the society at a discount. Against it the rationalist and investigative perspective of the Enlightenment had to contend. There was also among the Evangelicals deep distrust of the polite Scottish learning of the Enlightenment, as being impregnated with a new materialism, made the more dangerous by its brilliance, threatening morals and religion with the pitfalls of scepticism leading to metaphysical anxiety and the unhappiness of rootlessness.

The Manichean dichotomy was also inimical to humour, thus gravely inhibiting artistic expression in all its forms. A life that was dedicated to duty and the soul, ruled by a code of unremitting solemnity, made very difficult open and uninhibited laughter, that great perspective setter. From this cultural repression there were two escapes. The Scottish peasant could find relief in the bawdy tradition in which Burns had excelled and which never lacked for exponents: so a kind of release could be generated in the tavern or the bothy. There was also that Scottish specialism, 'pawky' humour. This was a dry, sly, cynical affair, never far from the frailties of neighbours or colleagues.

The church in 1832 still embodied the notion of divine order and imbued it with powerful moral sanctions over the individual. It also claimed a jurisdiction over basic social institutions, of which marriage was the most important. Knox had entrusted the church with the instruction of the people, both sacred and secular. The church had long ago abandoned its claim to a theocracy, conceding a place to the secular state (though not as affecting its own affairs), but the Knoxian ideal of an organic order of things presided over by the church, at least in terms of beliefs and values, was still strong. Chalmers gave much thought to this. In a Scotland that had had no parliament since 1707 the General Assembly of the Church of Scotland had no rival as the voice of the nation.

But the split within the church after 1843 greatly inhibited it. The Evangelicals were the custodians of the older view of the church, intensely jealous of intrusions by the state. They asserted, often with obsessive conviction, a highly moralistic way of life and belief. They tended to regard the new rationalism in which Scottish philosophers had played so large a part as dangerously innovative. The Moderates, on the other hand, under the influence of the Enlightenment, were anxious to release the powers of intellect in the study of both the physical and social worlds. Down to 1833 they had been the dominant element in the church. Nor did they usually confront the church's theology, but sought rather to disentrammel themselves from it in order to see how far reasoning could be carried, seeking to keep the two exercises separate, not pressing them to the point of collision.

The senior intellectuals of Edinburgh, of which the landowning lawyers had been the core, had been the driving force of the Enlightenment, together with certain academics. They had been reinforced and succeeded by the eager young men who founded in

1802 the *Edinburgh Review*, assisted by the satirical Englishman, Sydney Smith. There were also youthful Tory *illuminati* in Edinburgh associated with *Blackwood's Magazine*, begun in 1817. Both of these journals had a national circulation among informed people in Scotland and England. Glasgow, for all its achievement in engineering and applied science, did not generate an intellectual class of the Edinburgh kind. But it did produce a Whig component. The great difference between the two cities was that whereas the Glasgow Whigs were largely a product of a rising commercial and industrial class, those of Edinburgh reflected landed wealth and the professions, especially the law. Thus Scottish Whiggery had by 1832 developed an economic base and an intellectual one, shared between its two major cities, but with different emphases.

A case can be made that the Evangelicals did much damage to Scottish intellectual and cultural life not only by impugning the use of the rational faculty, but by frowning upon the cultivation of the senses through the arts and thereby stultifying the exploration and expression of emotion. The Moderates on the other hand can be charged with seeking to carry Scotland away from old loyalties that were cohesive for the nation and sustaining to the individual, an essential component of Scottish life. It should be remembered that the Enlightenment with its cool reasoning could also be inhibitive on the imagination.

Sir Walter Scott and Lord Byron had introduced a third element into the Scottish mind and culture, namely that of romanticism. In their writings there was expressed in different degrees a yearning for contact with the past, for colour, for emotion, for piety, for heroic action, for idiosyncracy, for arbitrary power and for personal devotion. All these were elements that fitted ill with either the dourness of Calvinism or the cold rationality of the Enlightenment. So it was that though Scott was much read and honoured in Victorian Scotland, and Byron too admired, the romantic movement ran to seed on its native heath, unable to assert a creative identity against two forces more powerful than itself. The poets and musicians of the Continent were its heirs, especially in the Germanic lands and in France.

In all this the Scots were sharing with other societies the tensions inevitable in the extension of secular culture, closely related as this was to the process of industrialization. The Scots produced their own characteristic response. Those in whom an active and questioning mind collided with the older pieties, as in England and elsewhere, could suffer great stress. For some this struggle culminated in that Victorian dark night of the soul known as losing one's faith; for others religion was simply relegated, in a pragmatic sort of way, to the back of the mind. In Victoria's reign important areas of Scottish thought and expression could flourish, as in scientific inquiry and in applied science. Others, as in the arts, perhaps suffered a degree of stultification.

2 Culture and the Arts

The cultural expression of a people is difficult enough to describe: it is even harder to explain. In the case of Victorian Scotland as it passed through industrialization these difficulties are particularly acute. Literature and the drama may well have been damaged by repressive ideas stemming from religion. The same is true concerning musical expression. The church since the seventeenth century had made the spoken word primary in its own services in the form of sermons and Bible reading. But because of its stiff moralism, its stern rejection of religious imagery and its casting aside of all Popish celebrations and festivals, together with its dimly apprehended fear of the welling up of subconscious thoughts, it had inhibited the written word as a form of spontaneous human expression. Robert Louis Stevenson, though he could write so movingly of his beloved hills of home, was deeply unhappy in the dourness of Edinburgh life. By the exclusion of any form of musical instrument from divine service the church had greatly narrowed the musical experience of the common people as well as inhibiting music as a developing art. Until near the end of the century the 'precentor', the leader of the congregational singing, was a prominent figure in Scotch life: his pitch pipe was the only auxiliary to the human voice heard in most of the Scottish Presbyterian churches. Even hymn singing was not authorized in the Church of Scotland until 1864.[1] As to achievement in the visual arts, it would appear that the influence of the church was not directly a major inhibiting factor, though any circumstance that limits perception in any direction must damage it in all.

The church would thus seem to have cast a cloud over Victorian Scottish cultural expression. There is, on the other hand, the possibility that the Bible and the sermons based upon it, together

[1] See chapter 7, section 8 above.

with the Calvinist theology with its threat of hell for the non-elect, could make their own contributions to the imagination, though on the darker side, as with James Hogg's *The Private Memories and Confessions of a Justified Sinner* (1824) and Stevenson's *Dr Jekyll and Mr Hyde* (1886). The marvellous seventeenth-century English of the Bible could implant an intense imagery and a flowing cadence of words. These, together with the powerful dramas and heroes and villains of the Old Testament gave the imagination real scope. But it could not easily be released in expression: the church bore a large responsibility for a Scottish inhibition on revealing the inner self.

Could the other great strand, that of the Enlightenment, compensate by providing a release of the Scottish imagination and self-expression? On the contrary, it rejected mysticism, the Gothic, the cataclysmic event, the action of arbitrary forces. Moreover the Enlightenment, in expressing itself in science and technology, often had little time for the artistic. It was a masculine culture. The Scottish National Museum founded in the 1850s had its origins not in an interest in the cultural past, but in the development of science and technology.

But the influences stemming from the church and from the Enlightenment did not remain static. As the decades passed the church softened its theology and gradually readmitted music, ceremony and embellishment. It took much more time however for attitudes so deeply ingrained to change in the inner being of the Scots. At the same time the rationalist strand began to perceive that the natural world was not only causal but also beautiful. In this the splendour of the great engines made in the West of Scotland, with their rhythmic articulating members and the universal natural forces at work within them played their part. So too did the vast civil engineering structures culminating in the Forth Bridge, embodying science and daring in a skeleton of steel, a wonder of the world.

3 The Written Word

To the literature of the nineteenth century the Scottish contribution was notable, but uneven. In terms of timing, the literary efflorescence of which Sir Walter Scott was the greatest figure was fading (Scott died in 1832); there was then a lack of major writers for some 50 years until Robert Louis Stevenson in the 1880s. It has been charged that Scotland failed to match the Irish in literary achievement, being incapable of withstanding the influence of England, and suffering through much of the nineteenth century from a real but unacknowledged sense of national inferiority. Henry Cockburn in 1850, lamenting the drawing power of 'hungry London', charged it with having 'devoured my friends'. Behind all this there lay the problem of the nature and use of Scottish English: the difficulties this involved made it hard for Scotland to produce a literature that was organic to itself. Certainly there was a proliferation of imitators of Burns, with almost every village with its second Rabbie, too often writing at an abysmal level. In the 1890s came the 'Kailyard' (cabbage yard), school led by James Barrie. In the interval there were linking lesser figures. In terms of content the course of Scottish writing does not, on the face of it, seem to reflect any inner logic; at a deeper level it may perhaps be possible to detect characteristic Scottish influences at work.

Scott's success had depended in large measure on his poems and novels based upon the Scottish past both Highland and Lowland. Though a monarchist and a supporter of the union, he projected the tragedy of the '45 and the discontinuity it marked in Scottish life: his romanticism and nostalgia, so inconsistent with his acceptance of political reality, was to infuse Scottish letters throughout Victoria's reign: indeed the tension between the two was to become characteristic of Scottish life. To be fair to Scott as a historian, he interested himself in the newly formed historical publishing clubs, the Bannatyne in Edinburgh (1823) and the Maitland in Glasgow (1829), thus assisting in a new antiquarian and scholarly interest in Scottish history and language.

He was perhaps the first great case of the author as business man: in creating the historical novel he also gave great impetus to the three-volume work that was to dominate the middle-class market for some 70 years. It was Scott who discovered the novel as a source of wealth, status and cultural power. In spite of his romanticism, so powerful in its impact, the characters who triumphed in his novels were not those of extreme views and actions, but moderates. Scott's outlook was very different from that of Burns, for he rejected the womanizing, hard drinking, bawdy and rebellious posture of the underdog: Scott favoured a subservient poor, not prone to cry out for economic justice.

Scott helped to generate another long-lasting influence on Scottish letters. This was the dominance of Edinburgh, the seat of the traditional Scottish landed ruling class and the lawyers, like Scott himself, who serviced them. The *literati* of Edinburgh followed Scott in not interesting themselves in Glasgow and the industrial west. The great entrepreneurs, the projectors and swindlers, the hard-faced rejectors of organized labour, together with the working classes, indeed the new realities of the age, are all passed over. Glasgow could not itself repair the omission, for it was too much involved in projects, toil and bustle to produce literature. Victorian Scotland had no one like Mrs Gaskell (1810–65) who in the 1850s wrote of the industrial realities of Manchester, or Arnold Bennett (1867–1931) who in Edwardian times depicted the towns of the Potteries. Thus it was possible for Scottish literature either to live largely in a previous pre-industrial age, or to indulge in an unrealistic idyll as with the Kailyard school.

The long interval between Scott and Stevenson produced two interesting lesser lights. Both began publishing in the 1850s. There was R.M. Ballantyne (1825–94), one of the early writers of adventures for boys. His settings in the Canadian wilds for the trapper and the hunter, and in the tropics, often based on personal observation and experience, and the actions of his heroes in these contexts were so clean and upright in all respects as to be school prizes for generations: the best known was *The Coral Island* (1858). Ballantyne thus escaped from the Edinburgh-dominated literature of Scotland, opening up for boys worlds of imagination that were in the tradition of the great Scottish travellers like Mungo Park. Mrs Oliphant (1828–97), in contrast, placed her flow of novels in traditional douce Scottish rural settings and so thereby achieved an immense popularity in England.

With Stevenson Scottish literature assumed a new stature. He could play Scott's game based on the Scottish past, combining it with an adventurous verve that owed something to Ballantyne, as well as to his own travels around Scotland with his lighthouse-building father: so were written *Kidnapped* (1886), *The Black Arrow* (1888), *The Master of Ballantrae* (1889) and *Catriona* (1893). But perhaps the real depth of Stevenson lay in *The Strange Case of Dr Jekyll and Mr Hyde* (1886) and the unfinished potential masterpiece *Weir of Hermiston*. The first has become a classic among tales of terror, a variant on the theme of what might happen should a man play with dangerous knowledge, especially about his inner self wherein is hidden great power for evil. *Weir* is the tragedy of a man called to play the part of a Calvinistic God: he is a Scottish judge who must condemn his own son to death. Both Stevenson and Burns rebelled against the dour side of their Scottish upbringing: Burns's revolt took the form of populism and a yearning for freedom of the spirit, together with drink and womanizing: Stevenson's was a less radical rebellion, taking refuge in boyhood romances, children's poetry and the macabre.

The Kailyard school centred its tales on a rural Scotland in which the villagers or small town folk under their laird, their minister and the dominie (schoolmaster) lived virtuous and Godfearing lives, playing out their little comedies and tragedies in an atmosphere that was simple, with corruption held at bay by a fixed and stable setting. Of this idiom the great exponents were J.M. Barrie (1860–1937), Ian Maclaren, born John Watson (1850–1907) and S.R. Crockett (1860–1914). The urge to slow down the forces of change, indeed to go back, if only in imagination, to a simpler world, to find an emotional haven, was strong not only in Scotland and England but elsewhere. This gave the novels an enormous vogue, reinforced by the replacement of the Victorian three-decker with the six shilling novel. But the Kailyarders failed Scottish reality in two senses. Like Scott and those who followed him, they took no account of industrial reality at its epicentre, namely Glasgow and its region. Secondly within the rural setting they passed over the negative side of rural life – the small-mindedness, the self-satisfaction, the barrenness of thought, the obsessive gossiping, the deep class distinctions, the premature ageing and work-induced crippling. The inevitable reaction came with George Douglas Brown (1869–1902); in 1901 he published *The House with the Green Shutters*. In it are sharply and bitterly depicted the meanness and debasement that the Kailyarders had so largely set aside. Attracting less attention, but of considerable interest, were the peasant writers of the North-East, of whom William Alexander with his *Johnnie Gibb O' Gushetneuk* of 1871, perhaps the best of the kailyard novels though not the best known, was he most notable. Gibb and others, though they used standard English as a 'continuity', employed a true representation of Scots in reported speech and commentary.

In Scottish Victorian literature industrialization and the Enlightenment are both missing. One would scarcely know from it what was happening to the majority of Scots. The Enlightenment could hardly inspire literature, for literature did not view society in terms of logical constructs, but intuitively. But religion was certainly powerful, infusing Scottish literature with moralism (the evil are punished and the innocent kept safe), together with a view of man that sees him locked in his own convictions as with *Weir of Hermiston*, or the victim of his evil side as with Hyde, and yet, as in Barrie's *Dear Brutus* (1917) carrying his destiny within himself. Barrie's achievement went far beyond the kailyard, his *Peter Pan* of 1904, with its concern with identity and growing up having a staggering success and becoming a classic.

4 Drama and Music

It was on the drama and on music that the hand of the Kirk was most heavily felt. The Christian church had always entertained a profound distrust of the secular stage and its players as being destructive of religion and morality. Presbyterianism shared this view in full measure. It did not wish to see its charges carried from the written word as expressed in the Bible to the spoken and enacted word as presented by venal mortals. In consequence the Scottish Victorian contribution to the drama was slight.

As for music, Calvinism did not oppose its enjoyment as such, having no objection to it in the home or in concert halls. But its prohibition in church meant that a main line of development both for composers and participants was cut off. This meant that though there was a chair of music in Edinburgh from 1839, this innovation of the Moderates had little effect. Only after hymns and organs could gain ground from the 60s could Scottish music be invigorated. The gospel hymns and organ of Moody and Sankey accelerated this. Organs indeed became a component of great public buildings, as in Glasgow's Kelvingrove Art Galleries and Museum of 1892. But there were also losses. With the Presbyterian rediscovery of hymns, choirs, anthems and chants the old Scottish metrical psalms fell into relative disuse. Moreover as the musical standard rose there was a tendency for congregational participation to decline, leaving the service to the minister and the choir. From the 1870s choral music could begin to become part of Scottish life as in the north of England. The Scottish Orchestra was founded in 1891, with Herschel as its first conductor. Because of a lack of higher-training in Scotland there had to be a reliance on English and foreign conductors and organists. From the Celtic past the sound of the bagpipes was still heard in Scotland, though weakened as the Highlands emptied. In the Highland regiments, however, they thrived. As the pipes of war and of the sorrows of death they stiffened the thin red line and lamented the fallen.

5 Painting, Photography and Architecture

Two matters arise in considering Scottish Victorian painting. The first is general: why was it so difficult to find a guiding and stimulating national tradition; why did the Scots fail to match in the arts their achievements in science and technology? Was this a matter of the size of society: could some three to four million people generate artists with the necessary distinctive visual perception? Was it something to do with the problem of Scottish identity? Was it a question of lack of the proper kind of patronage: did Scottish life fail to provide a market for works of art such that they could represent a real and native tradition, breaking with imitation deriving from tastes acquired by the new Scottish leisured class as they travelled in France and Italy? Was the church an inhibiting force here as elsewhere? There seems to have been a measure of truth in all of these aspects.

The second circumstance is more specific, namely the powerful literary tradition that stemmed from Scott and Burns, and which impregnated so much of Scottish culture. David Wilkie (1785-1841), with his genre paintings with their characters and situations both familial and historical, was a kind of Scott on canvas. This was a strand that was to be prominent in British Victorian painting, but it was not such as could be built upon in terms of artistic exploration. Thomas Faed (1826-1900) was hailed in the *Encyclopaedia Americana* in 1886 as having 'done for Scottish Art what Robert Burns did for Scottish song'. His narrative sentimentality was shown to great effect in his 'Last of the Clan': he showed the people of the countryside and the Highlands with their own dignity, resigned to what fate might bring them. Scottish genre artists also excelled in patriotism: in the 1870s Lady Butler painted 'The Thin Red Line' and 'Scotland for Ever', the latter a head-on view of the Scots Greys in full charge at Waterloo, regarded in its day as a damn fine thing for a woman. Reproductions in the folksy and the military traditions appeared in many simple homes and in schools, with their messages of social morality and steadfastness based on story telling. Tory-Jacobite romanticism was also important, centring upon figures like Mary Queen of Scots and Bonnie Prince Charlie. So it was that from the 1830s to the 1860s Scottish painting, though it had its achievements, was without great native inspiration.

But there did develop thereafter a range of smaller masters working their way with vitality and variety toward a Scottish artistic expression. Some of these training in Scotland, like John Pettie (1839–93) and William Orchardson (1832–1910) were drawn to London in the 1860s and later, where they found a wider and readier market.

Between 1885 and into the earlier part of the new century Scotland did produce an artistic manifestation that was characteristically its own. This was the group known as the Glasgow School, or the 'Glasgow Boys' as they preferred to be known, including William McTaggart, W.Y. Macgregor, George Henry, E.A. Hornel, Joseph Crawhall and James Lavery, asserting itself in the 1880s. They owed a good deal to the French impressionists, challenging the tradition of Scottish painting with its literalist drawing and high finish, replacing these with a free and vigorous handling embodied in bold colours. The Glasgow School exercised its greatest influence on Scottish art in the Edwardian years. Before 1914, however, four painters, the Scottish Colourists, were preparing to supersede them: these were S.J. Peploe, J.D. Fergusson, Leslie Hunter and F.C.B. Cadell. They continued to exploit the new freedom, drawing upon the forms and palettes of Van Gogh, Gauguin, Cezanne, Whistler and others. The Dundee painter, George Dutch Davidson, was the most talented of the east-coast artists. As with Scottish writers, so with the Scottish artists of Victoria's reign: from neither would it have been possible to guess that they were formed in a society in which industrialization was the dominant experience.

Meanwhile photography had made its appearance, making possible both a new literalism and a new impressionism. Robert Adamson (1821–48), having acquired an interest in optics from Professor Brewster at St Andrews, set up a photographic studio in Edinburgh in 1843. He was joined by David Octavius Hill (1802–70) who photographed over 450 members of the seceding body of 1843 as preparation for a vast memorial painting of the epic scene. George Washington Wilson (1823–93) a crofter's son, moved from art to photography, becoming 'photographer to the Queen': by 1880 his firm in Aberdeen could claim to be the largest publisher of topographical views in Britain. These men gave

Scotland a notable place in the history of the new art that had stemmed from science.

The architects, unlike the writers and painters, could not ignore the needs of the new industrial age, but they did not wholly capitulate to it. Industrial and agrarian wealth opened new vistas for Scottish architects, builders and civil engineers. There was a demand on an altogether new scale for homes of varying degrees of stateliness in town and country. More important as architectural challenges were the factories, mills, warehouses, bridges, harbours, railway stations, hotels, banks, municipal buildings, churches and philanthrophic institutions. This demand was reflected in a steady increase in design and building to the 1850s; thereafter there was an even more rapid acceleration. But though this was a time of hectic change and challenge most architects opted for traditional styles, at least so far as externals were concerned. The neo-classical mode had made a great impact in Georgian Edinburgh and Glasgow, used by such as William Playfair, Robert Reid, James Milne and Thomas Hamilton, and could still produce fine buildings in early Victorian times. The romantic movement produced an important idiom, revived Gothic, though it was much varied by the architects, guided by their own tastes, by those of their patrons and by functional needs. Scottish Neo-Baronial asserted itself beginning with the rebuilding of Balmoral Castle by William Smith for Victoria and Albert in the 1850s. Cast iron and glass facades, the true harbingers of a new era, were given a pure and beautiful exemplification in Glasgow by John Baird, with his 'Gairdner's' (the Jamaica Street Warehouse). The neo-classical style achieved a new statement in the 1870s in the work of Alexander ('Greek') Thomson (1817-75) in Glasgow. One of the leading figures in the Art Nouveau movement, though without real recognition in Scotland in his lifetime, was Charles Rennie Mackintosh (1868-1928), whose masterpiece was the Glasgow School of Art (1897-9 and 1907-9).

6 The Gaelic Culture

There was one element of Scottish culture that came from a highly distinctive past. It lay in the Highlands. The Gaels had songs and poetry, their pipe music, their fiddlers, their dancing, especially the Reel, together with the *ceilidh*, a gathering usually round a homely hearth in which entertainment provided by those present mingled with conversation, both being enlivened by whisky. The Highland games re-emerged, an assertion of the Highland spirit, with competitive dancing, running and the throwing the hammer and the tossing of the caber (a 20-foot tree). This was the heritage of the Highlander, evolved from his life and language, but threatened by industrialization, anglicization and the clearances. There were some Scots who were aware of what was being lost. Among them was the eighth Duke of Argyll (1823–1900), who between 1862 and 1871 paid a wage to John Dewar, a woodsman on his estate, to wander about the Highlands gathering tales and oral traditions in the Gaelic.

But though threatened at its historical source, the culture of the Gaels was brought by Highlanders to the Scottish cities, with the result that Highland symbols were increasingly adopted by the Lowlanders. The Glasgow police, with its backbone of Highlanders, played an important part in this, especially concerning pipe music. In 1883 the Gaelic language achieved academic status with the founding in Edinburgh University of a chair of Celtic. It was the outcome of the convergence of scholarship, encouraged by European researches into Celtic culture, and the politicization of the people of the Highlands leading to the Crofters' War. The chair had two objectives, namely the study of Celtic comparative philology, and the provision of scholarly teaching of the vernacular to those who would pass their lives in the Celtic districts as clergymen, teachers, lawyers, physicians or indeed as landed proprietors. The influence of the Gaels could also reach the larger world: there was in the music of Greig (1843–1907) a ring of the Gaelic dialect in his harmonic language: Charles Rennie Mackintosh rediscovered the Gaelic tradition of design.

7 Science, Pure and Applied

In Scottish science the Enlightenment could rule, uninhibited by the influence of the Church. In part this was an accident of chronology. The sciences that were to offend the church were geology and botany and zoology as they moved toward a questioning of the Book of Genesis. In geology the Scots made an important contribution: James Hutton (1726–97) of Edinburgh was the first to see geology as a continuous process of earth formation: Charles Lyell (1797–1875) born near Kirriemuir, established in 1830–3 the validity of Huttonian ideas and pressed Darwin to publish his *Origin of Species* (1859). Meanwhile Robert Chambers (1802–71) had published in Edinburgh his *Vestiges of the Natural History of Creation* (1844) which suggested an evolutionary approach to the earth. But, for fear of charges of heterodoxy from the church, his authorship was kept secret until the twelfth edition of 1884: his instinct was sound, for his book created a huge fuss. But the church did not by this time have the strength or the procedures to attempt to contain the new ideas. As to botany and zoology their great impact via Darwin was even later, representing a gathering of forces that was to become irresistible. The Kirk could thus exert no restraining hand on Scottish science.

The latter had found its direction and its chief idioms in the second half of the eighteenth century. Two principal lines of development were present: through natural philosophy (physics), and medicine which led via chemistry to so many fields of inquiry. Chemistry was brought from Holland by Scotch pupils of Boerhaave of Leyden (1668-1738): it was seen as a new and powerful physical science, and not a mere adjunct to medicine. In this important sense Scotch development was continental, owing a good deal to the fact that Calvinism had linked Scotland to Holland, replacing French cultural influence with that of the Dutch. By 1832 Scotland had six established courses in chemistry of university rank. At the same time the physics of Galileo and Newton had energized Scottish philosophy in all its branches including the natural. On this firm basis the Scottish universities of the nineteenth century could become places of great scientific achievement.

Within Scottish science and medicine it is possible to detect a difference of general idiom between Edinburgh and Glasgow. The former had a strong Cartesian character, running in terms of pure theory, without great regard to practical tasks or applications. Glasgow professors like Joseph Black (1728-99) had begun early the tradition of linking the academic world with that of industry: his discoveries of latent heat and specific heat were forwarded by his effort to help the distillers to develop quality control. This linkage between the scientists and the industrialists became a feature of Glasgow, both in terms of its University and the Andersonian University, later the Royal College of Technology and later still Strathclyde University, with a real claim to being the world's first institute of technology. Glasgow doctors too, had a strong strain of practicality as they sought to cope with the victims of the industrial accident and civil violence that the city and its region produced.

The Glasgow–Edinburgh scientific dichotomy may perhaps be

exemplified in the two most illustrious names in Scottish and indeed British, Victorian science, namely William Thomson (1824–1907) later Lord Kelvin and James Clerk Maxwell (1831–79). Kelvin, though one of the authors of the laws of thermodynamics, was greatest as an applied scientist. He earned his knighthood for his work on underwater ocean cables: his income from his patents reached £5,000 per year, helping to pay for his yacht the *Lalla Rook*. He spent his life near the Clyde, that great hive of industry; there he sought to fuse science and technology, helping the west of Scotland to assert its world dominance in branches of engineering and applied science. By contrast, Clerk Maxwell's work had nothing of the practical, but was deeply philosophical, having to do with the fundamental nature of the physical world; it escaped from the mechanistic mental models then dominant. Maxwell's youthful paper 'On Faraday's lines of Force' was a first step toward a theory of electromagnetism, from which was to come the marvels of the radio and further developments. It is to be noted however, that both Kelvin and Clerk Maxwell had to go to Cambridge for their pure mathematics, for at Cambridge mathematics was free of practical considerations, thus achieving a virtuosity impossible in Scotland.

8 The Four Universities

The great engines of Scottish scientific and indeed intellectual achievement were her four ancient universities, three founded in the fifteenth century and one in the sixteenth. In them was fought in Victoria's reign a battle for modernization (or as its enemies regarded it, Anglicization). The traditionalists and neo-scholastics, with their strength in the chairs of divinity and classics, strongly resisted the introduction of new subjects, especially the costly and disturbing new physical sciences. Yet Scotland, with the aid of direct state intervention, did admit the new kind of learning and consolidated important schools of science, pure and applied, a generation or more before the three English universities did so. Roughly speaking the Scottish universities had achieved this by the 1870s; in England the real battle began in the 1880s and was not won until about 1900.

Natural philosophy and medicine had had an important place in the eighteenth century in the Scottish universities, as the name of Joseph Black testifies. But the professors in possession of the dominant traditional subjects, being largely dependent upon students' fees paid direct, were hostile to innovations. In Edinburgh the University until 1858 was the 'Town's College': this meant that it was poorer financially, but its professors were never able to dig in as they had done in Glasgow. So bad was the latter case that the Crown intervened directly by setting up Regius Chairs. The last of these in Glasgow was the Chair of Engineering, founded in 1840, the first in the world. It was to become enormously distinguished under its second incument William John McQuorn Rankine (1820–72) who held it from 1855 to 1872. Rankine involved himself deeply in the industries of the west, becoming founder President of the Institution of Engineers and Shipbuilders in Scotland. In scientific terms he became a world authority on heat engines. The other Regius Chairs had all been in the sciences, in medicine, chemistry, natural history and botany. But there was still much niggling resistance by the old Chairs. This prompted the government at Westminister to intervene much more comprehensively. It extended its purview to the Scottish Universities generally, for St Andrews was at a low ebb, and the two small colleges at Aberdeen were seriously sub-optimal. Under the Act of 1858 a new set of Commissioners was appointed: they supervised a restructuring over a period of seven years. St Andrews was revivified and a united Aberdeen University formed; Edinburgh University was taken out of the care of the town. In Glasgow the power of the traditionalists was severely limited. Indeed in all the Scottish universities there were set up Courts containing representative outsiders to administer the funds, and General Councils of Graduates. Thus did government remake the universities from outside. But even this was not enough. A second Act of 1889 was required, setting up a further set of Commissioners who further modernized the Universities between 1889 and 1900. Under them new Arts subjects received the status of Chairs including Modern History and French and German; Political Economy was raised to this standing. By 1914 Glasgow had three chairs of Engineering.

It has been charged that the two sets of Commissioners gravely damaged Scottish intellectual life, especially by their actions after 1889. The reforms are seen by some as a victory for those who wished to Anglicize Scottish institutions, destroying the native tradition of a broad philosophical training by promoting Honours Schools and a consequent premature specialization in the Universities, as well as destroying much of the democratic character of Scottish education. The reforms can, however, be seen as a considered and sympathetic compromise between the older Scottish values and the requirements of a society increasingly in need of scientific and technical knowledge. The democratic tradition was certainly preserved in terms of cost: whereas by 1900 it cost a student £200 to attend Cambridge for a year, in Scotland he paid some £15 fees and lived at home or in cheap lodgings.

Some further indication of the Scottish scientific achievement and its relation with the universities may be given. Thomas Thomson (1773–1852) first professor of Chemistry at Glasgow founded the 'Shuttle Street laboratories' in 1831: they have a claim to being the world's first scientific laboratories. Pupils of Thomson's started practical chemistry at Aberdeen shortly after. Chemistry at this time included heat, light, electricity and magnetism and a good deal of geology through mineralogy. Each of these was in due course to become its own specialism, with a Scottish stake in each. With each of them engineering was to make its connections. Not least important in so doing were the makers of scientific apparatus, to whom the investigators owed so much. But the crown of Glasgow achievement came with Kelvin. At the age of 22 he was appointed to the Chair of Natural Philosophy. By the 1870s he and Rankine had made Glasgow the leading centre of teaching and investigation in science and engineering in Britain. Not surprisingly, the new Japan, in its world search for best practice, turned to Glasgow for science and engineering. When the University moved to Gilmorehill in 1870 Thomson could abandon the turrets and cellars of the Old College for new and more worthy facilities. Archibald Barr (1855–1931) Professor of Engineering, invented the range finder, thus revolutionizing naval warfare: Admiral Togo credited it with the ability of the Japanese fleet in 1904 totally to destroy the Russian fleet. A harbinger of a new age in science appeared between 1894 and 1904, namely uranium and the atomic age: Frederic Soddy (1877–1956) was in 1903 appointed to a new lectureship in 'Physical Chemistry including Radio-Activity'. A new Glasgow school arose to rival Sir Joseph Thomson (1856–1940) at the Cavendish, Cambridge, and Ernest Rutherford (1871–1937) in Manchester, evolving the Displacement Law and Soddy's conception of the Isotope.

In Edinburgh too there were notable achievements. David Brewster (1781–1868), though he had earlier connections with St Andrews, may be taken as an exemplar of the Edinburgh scientific community of the mid-century. He based his researches on optics: he sought to improve the microscope and invented the kaleido-scope, as well as making contributions to the development of photography. He was also a scientific journalist and encyclopaedist, spreading knowledge through his many publications; Carlyle described him as 'a grand superficial man'. In 1859 he became Principal of Edinburgh University. As an ardent evangelical he believed in a 'holy alliance between science and religion': he was deeply involved in the Disruption of 1843. Another Edinburgh figure was Fleeming Jenkin (1833–85) first Professor of Engineering, appointed in 1868. Jenkin was a kind of polymath, writing on science speculative and applied, on literature and drama and on political economy. His particular engineering concerns were with ocean telegraphs, and with mechanical drawing, that is, the problem of how to represent three dimensional forms with the precision necessary for execution. The Department of Chemistry acquired new accommodation in 1884, described as 'palatial'. In 1886 Edinburgh held its International Exhibition of Industry, Science and Art.

There was, however, criticism of the Scottish professoriate of the later nineteenth century: William Robertson Nicoll, Scottish doyen of British nonconformist journalists and graduate of Aberdeen, was puritanically scathing, writing that 'The vast holiday, the majestic temper induced by the work, the fact that no effort is needed to keep the place or attract the students, the petty cliques which form among the professors, the induced sense of superiority to ordinary industrious beings, gradually corrupt the finest and noblest natures'. Nicoll perhaps took too little account of idealism in the Scottish universities, the university extension lectures and the Settlement movement, not to speak of the achievements of Kelvin, Paton, Henry Jones, Raleigh, Bradley and others.

9 Medicine

The Scottish medical schools had dominated the British scene until the first quarter of the century. Thereafter developments in London were an increasing challenge. This early predominance had been due to the giants of the Enlightenment, including Black, Cullen, and the Hunter brothers. It had been a prominent part of the Scottish Enlightenment, with a strong intellectual base. This intellectual aspect continued in both Edinburgh and Glasgow. But especially in the latter case it was reinforced by local conditions and the practical priorities these presented, together with working examples in plenty of almost all kinds of human ailments.[2]

The greatest joint contribution of Lister and Macewen lay in developing antiseptic and aseptic surgery respectively. The first of these stemmed from three sources. These were a practical need, namely to make surgery safer, from a theoretical insight, namely the 'germ theory' of Pasteur, and from pragmatic discovery, namely the effectiveness of certain chemicals in treating sewage. Lister moved from Edinburgh to Glasgow in 1860 and back again in 1869. On arrival at Glasgow Royal Infirmary from the comparatively healthy wards of Edinburgh, he found septic infection to be rampant: so was established a pressing priority. Macewen was a lifelong Glasgow man. It was out of Glasgow conditions that his further contributions came, namely a wide range of surgical techniques, including the lessening in children of the distorting effects of rickets. But it was in neurosurgery that he achieved his greatest triumphs. As surgeon to the Central Police Division of Glasgow, running a peace-time casualty clearing station, he learned how to distinguish between coma arising from intoxication, apoplexy or fracture of the base of the skull. This led on to his contributions to the surgery of the brain, and to an understanding of the relationships between the parts of brain and the performance of mind and body. So it was that in the cases of both Lister and Macewen the imperatives and opportunities of a major city, with its violence and ill health, served as an inspiration and a setter of priorities.

These Scottish doctors make a gallery of personalities of great interest. James Y. Simpson, the chubby, cheery pioneer of anaesthesia in childbirth, gaining his chair in midwifery at the age of 28, and an ardent Free Churchman, turned in his 50s to a deep pietism. Dr John Brown (1810–82), general practitioner, gained great celebrity as the author of *Rab and his Friends*. Joseph Bell, who taught Conan Doyle as a medical student in Edinburgh University between 1876 and 1881, often using the deductive method in his diagnoses, has been supposed by many to be the model for Sherlock Holmes, though it can also be argued that Holmes was a composite of the detached scientific brilliance of the great doctors of Edinburgh.

[2]See chapter 6, section 4 above.

10 The Study of Society

Not least among the Scottish intellectual achievements has been the study of society. Though the nineteenth century was not to equal the giants of the eighteenth (Hume, Smith, Millar) it was to produce some notable figures. But these were to make their mark in the latter park of the century. In the meantime the impetus of the Enlightenment in opening up understanding of society was largely lost. There appear to have been two reasons for this. The church as the somewhat grudging custodian of social welfare was not challenged in its ways by Adam Smith and the others: the Chalmerian view could continue to prevail at the level of ideas and indeed through the Poor Law Act of 1845. In the economic sphere the church did not call in question to any serious degree the market system and private property: these had become by 1832 the agreed basis of civil society. In the study of society the two strands of Scottish life, church and Enlightenment, were thus in alliance, dampening debate.

But there was not a total absence of challenge, especially on the social side. Alison, in his attack on Chalmers's view of the proper treatment of the poor,[3] spoke from the practical world of medicine, urging a new social and practical morality in conflict with that of the church. This was reinforced by the statisticians who demonstrated the seriousness of social need and the threats to health: Glasgow produced James Cleland, Charles R. Baird and others who sought a scientific basis for social improvement. It was the Medical Officers of Health, however, who pressed furthest on this front: James B. Russell, for example, produced an extraordinary list of studies, including his *Sanitation and Social Economics* (1889).

But no major Scottish figure made an impact on nineteenth-century social analysis until the 1870s and 80s. The first to do so was Edward Caird[4] in Glasgow University and later as Master of Balliol, he projected a form of idealism as opposed to individualism. Basing himself on Hegel, he argued that men and women realize themselves most fully as members of a community: the greatest happiness of society is promoted by a conscious governmental pursuit of communal objectives, including the assisting of social casualties. Young men were taught to aspire to the role of

[3]See chapter 6, section 3 above.
[4]See chapter 7, section 10 above.

Plato's guardians, a concept Jowett took up after Caird at Balliol. This outlook on society, coinciding in important aspects with the social ideas of Ruskin, and with those of the Christian socialists, had a profound effect on a good many young Scots, including William Smart, Professor of Political Economy from 1896 to 1915: out of it came the Settlement Movement in Glasgow in the late 1880s.

In anthropology Sir James G. Frazer (1854–1941), educated at Glasgow and Cambridge Universities, was a pioneer. He gave a new meaning to the study of early societies with his brilliantly titled *Golden Bough* of 1890. It won him instant and lasting fame. Frazer brought religious belief, like natural and social phenomena, within the realm of objective investigation; he believed that the origin of religion lay in the magic of primitive peoples, intended to propitiate nature seen as a personal force. His somewhat derogatory treatment of religious ritual might be sympathetically regarded in Scotland, especially among fundamentalist evangelicals, but the implications of his anthropology for belief in the supernatural was less appropriate.

Patrick Geddes (1854–1932) gave a new perspective to contemporary social interaction. He started not from general philosophical principles, but turned the trained observation of a biologist upon the state of Scottish urban society in Edinburgh and Dundee. This organic rationalism was, however infused with strong Scottish national feeling, together with Stevensonian romanticism. Geddes condemned the mindlessness with which urban life had formed itself and proliferated. He preached an understanding of urban forms and the experiences and nervous debility they generated. He was a great exponent of his own notion of planning, urging that cities could be understood in their evolution and so guided toward the promotion of a worthier life. But he probably made too great an emotional and working demand on his followers.

Geddes was at the other end of the economic and social process to that of the entrepreneurs, both in outlook and in timing. He did not concern himself with the viability and growth of the firm in dynamic and difficult markets; much less was he concerned with the articulated functioning of the economy. This meant that he could too easily treat culture and capitalism as opposites. Moreover he took matters up not when industrialization was accelerating, but when it had already remade the life of the cities. His mind was untramelled by any sense of the economic limitations of his programme of refashioning the whole of the urban-industrial environment. Curiously he centred his interests on Edinburgh, evocative of a romantic Scottish nationalism, ignoring Glasgow where the real problem of industrial-urban society lay. He hoped to make of his 'Outlook Tower' at the top of the Royal Mile the focus of a remaking of the city, its 'Tree of Life'. It was only with the insight and drive that come from economic innocence that it was possible for Geddes to generate a movement such as his, challenging both the accepted pattern of values and the fatalism or indifference it sponsored with respect to man's power to control his social fate. But Geddes urged that there should be no ill-considered meddling with the environment: action must be based upon understanding. Like others who came after, he was not able to reconcile urban evolution with its unpredictable organicism with planning and with planners. Yet Geddes can be regarded as one of the fathers of modern sociology, perhaps the creator of environmentalism, and the founding inspiration of a perspective in planning.

9

The Outward Impact: the Empire and Beyond

1 The Diaspora

The Scottish intellect was, of course, for export. It spread over the globe with the Scots of all levels of society and all regions as they sought greater opportunities abroad. The move to England was the largest, accelerated by the union of the crowns in 1603, of the parliaments in 1707, and of the economies thereafter. From the later eighteenth century the Scots penetrated everywhere overseas, accelerating in doing so in the nineteenth. They were to be found in the United States, in Canada, in the outback of Australia, on the South African veldt and the Argentinian pampas. To the east they played important roles in the European intrusions into India, China and Japan. Abroad the differences and disputes of the homeland were largely forgotten (except perhaps in church matters), the Scots being often bound together by a common feeling infused by nostalgia and idealization of the homeland. Masonic Lodges and St Andrews Societies helped to merge them as 'brither Scots'. The Masonic Order, very strong in Scotland, was carried abroad, with Scots Lodges in North America and round the Indian Ocean and the China Seas to Japan.

And yet, especially in the first half of the nineteenth century, ancient differences could manifest themselves, as when observers commented on the Highland Scot as a settler in North America: if isolated among his own kind he showed a traditional carelessness about cleanliness or planned and sustained work or saving for the future. However, once dispersed or intruded upon by higher achievers, he soon adapted and strove for economic self-improvement.

The classic case of success abroad was perhaps Andrew Carnegie (1835–1919) a blond wee mannie from Dunfermline, son of a weaver of table cloths, whose family was well respected in the district, who by a combination of ruthlessness and business genius was to become a steel magnate in America of unimaginable riches. He was always to remain, at bottom, a Scot, endowing the native town, and seeking out the ninth Earl of Elgin whose grandfather had been the local magnate of his well remembered youth, to be the chairman of his Carnegie Trust for the Universities of Scotland, and pronouncing on every possible occasion the philosophy of Samuel Smiles of Haddington.

There was a second sense in which Scots could differ from one another. This derived from Scottish radicalism. Many who left home for other parts of the world were men of independent, not to say intransigent, mind, carrying the ideas of Tom Paine and Robert Burns to the lands of recent settlement in North America and the Antipodes. William Lyon Mackenzie who led the rebellion in Upper Canada in 1837 was one such. Thus Scotland could export not only men on the make, working profitably within the prevailing system; it sent out also men on the break, challengers of iniquities and exploitations.

2 Proconsuls and Generals

At the other extreme were those Scotsmen of the landed nobility who went to the Empire and elsewhere to govern and negotiate, men like Dalhousie, Brisbane, McQuarrie, Aberdeen, Elgin and Minto. It was they who so often had to seek to contain the pressures that the radicals had generated. As landed men they naturally took an ordered, hierarchical view of society: this had to be accommodated to new realities in Canada, Australia and elsewhere, and to ancient ones in India.

Many of the Scots nobility, after perhaps having a little local schooling, were educated in the public schools and universities of England. Such men could be Anglicized in a way in which Scots ministers, lawyers, merchants and industrialists were not. Many, in spite of their lands, were hard up for cash. Elder sons could be excluded from the House of Commons once they succeeded their fathers if their titles included an English one; hence they could be in a weak position re politics and patronage at home. This left the diplomatic service, offering a career in exile and often long and arduous travel, and often, as in China, the danger of brigandage. The proconsul could thus live on the public purse, and be able to close down both town and country houses. Typically such men discharged their duties assiduously, though sometimes inflexibly. A striking example of a successful itinerant diplomat was the eighth Earl of Elgin (1811–63), representing the Crown in Jamaica, Canada, China and Japan and finally as Viceroy of India.

The sanctions at the disposal of Elgin and the others as diplomatists were of course the British navy and army. In the army, Scots leadership and valour in the ranks were prominent, celebrated on the Esplanade of Edinburgh Castle with its memorials of the heroes of India, Afghanistan and the war against Napoleon. These glories were celebrated in painting: the 'Thin Red Line' of the British Army was composed of Highlanders. The relief of Lucknow during the Indian mutiny was another Highland achievement, led by Sir Colin Campbell with the cry 'Forrard the Tartan!'.

3 The Scot in Canada

Though Canada was much too big a place for the Scots to engross it, they became indeed a major component of its life, reproducing there much of the value system of the homeland, and helping to set its distinctive British tone and identity as against the Americans. Canada is perhaps the best laboratory in which to see the Scot adjusting to new conditions, yet retaining his identity. It is an intriguing thought that so many of these emigré Scots, some of them effectively forced out of their native land, should be so conservative and loyalist, rejecting the attraction of Americanization and playing so large a part in keeping Canada British. It is hardly surprising that Victoria was deeply honoured as Queen, while Scots doctors, professors, engineers, lawyers, judges, historians, bankers and politicians provided the professional and ideological core of so many Canadian communities, and indeed of the country as a whole, especially perhaps in the populous parts of Ontario, the most prosperous province. When William Lyon Mackenzie (1795–1861), born in Dundee, attempted to set up a Canadian republic in 1837 it was another Scot, Sir Allan MacNab, who led the loyalists against him. But it was also MacNab who helped to generate the constitutional crisis of 1849 that the eighth Earl of Elgin courageously resolved. Scots were prominent among the Fathers of Confederation in 1867 and indeed dominated Canadian politics for a generation after, epitomized in Sir John A. Macdonald (1815–91) the Conservative leader, born in Glasgow, and in George Brown leader of the opposing party, the 'True Grits'. The Scots dominated every aspect of the commerce of British North America down to 1825; Montreal, their first great commercial stronghold, was joined by Toronto and Hamilton. In railway building, that titanic transcontinental undertaking, the giants were Donald A. Smith (1820–1914), later Lord Strathcona and Mount Royal, a Morayshire lad who became principal shareholder and Governor of the Hudson's Bay Company and with his cousin George Stephen, later Lord Mountstephen, builder of the Canadian Pacific Railway: their rivals were brother Scots William Mackenzie and Donald Mann, the driving force behind the Canadian Northern Railway. Thus it was that the Scots had a large part in running Canada: they controlled the fur trade, dominated the banking and insurance companies, were the formative influences in education from the elementary through the university, were paramount in the railway world and provided major political leadership. Down to 1900 the Canadian village outside Quebec typically had its leading Kirk and minister, its Scottish schoolmaster and its Scottish-derived editor and printer.

4 The Merchant Princes

The Scots had increasingly traded abroad in the eighteenth century, shifting their interests from the Baltic and the low countries to North America and the West Indies. They had certainly had much more than their share in the affairs of the East India Company, dating especially from the patronage of Henry Dundas. Their interests in India continued after the Mutiny and they were in the van in the penetration of China and Japan from the 1840s. Indeed the immense new opportunities within the Empire and beyond were eagerly seized by Scotsmen.

Glaswegians, already exploiting their westward access to North America, took up the potential offered by the steamship in the North Atlantic. Robert Napier, prince of marine engineers, had been pondering what might be done from the shipbuilding point of view; George Burns and David MacIver with their coastwise shipping interests had been doing the same. When Samuel Cunard from Halifax, Nova Scotia, approached them with a proposition involving a subsidy for carrying the mails, the interests of the four men converged in 1840 in the shipping company that was to become The Cunard Steam Ship Company, ruler of the North

Atlantic, and intruder into the Mediterranean. Napier's engines provided the reliability which rendered the penalty clauses for the late arrival of the mail to become virtually unnecessary. The control of Cunard was vested in the Cunard, Burns and MacIver families down to 1876, a classic case of continuity into a second and indeed a third generation. The ships were Clyde built, a powerful support to the local yards. A range of other, though lesser lines, plied from Glasgow, including Donaldsons. Thus could Scotland promote and benefit from the rapid carriage of the mails, goods and people (including the vast emigrant traffic from Europe), especially on the busiest of the sea lanes, that of the North Atlantic. But the management of Cunard's ships passed to Liverpool, with its more central location.

The ending of the East India Company's monopoly to India in 1812 saw Kirkman Finlay and Company of Glasgow and other Scotsmen like Sir John Gladstone seizing the new opportunities of the east. The opening of China after 1833 and of Japan from 1859 and of Africa in the 1870s called the Scots to the China Seas and the Indian Ocean. But they could not maintain a major role on the other side of the globe direct from Scotland: it was necessary to focus their enterprises on the world of big business centred upon London. So it was that a succession of young Scotsmen were drawn into the new imperial economy of the east. They were lads o' pairts, the products of good Scottish schools, but not university trained. They were often infused with evangelical zeal. They recruited large numbers of other Scots, typically through the links of kinship and family friendship. Cousinship was indeed recognized as a kind of family obligation, as well as providing the basis of loyalty and discipline, as other ethnic groups had discovered. It also meant that the patriarchs of these firms exercised a strong family patronage.

The most celebrated of the Scottish commercial firms was that of Jardine Matheson and Company begun in 1832 to trade to India and China and finally to Japan: it became the greatest of India and China agency houses, bill brokers and bankers. A dark aspect of its early years was the trade in opium from India to China, providing the means of payment for Chinese goods, especially tea and silk, but detonating the Opium Wars of 1840–42 between China and the Western Powers. Hugh Matheson entered Matheson and Co. of London, a firm with close links with Jardine Mathesons, and dominated it. He was from Edinburgh; he attended the University of Glasgow while serving in a counting house there. He was greatly attached to his house in Ross-shire. William Keswick (1834–1912), educated at Merchiston's Edinburgh, was a great nephew of William Jardine. He became very powerful in Jardine Matheson in the Far East and later assumed control of Matheson's in London, a dominating position which succeeding generations of Keswicks have maintained. It was William Keswick who opened the firm's No. 1 House in Yokohama in 1859. Perhaps the most intriguing associate of the firm was Thomas Glover (1838–1911), born in Fraserburgh, who helped to smuggle out of Japan in 1862 the six young samurai who were to play so important a part in the modern-ization of Japan, and who opened Japan's first coal mine at Takashima near Nagasaki, attracting its first modern labour force. A lesser house was that of Andrew Melrose of Edinburgh and his son William (1817–63) wholesale dealers in tea: it was an example of the innumerable lesser Scottish commercial houses. William, like other Scots in tempting situations, relied heavily on his moral earnestness to save him from the temptations of Canton, chiefly gambling and drink.

Thomas Sutherland (1834–1922) from Aberdeen became chair-man of the Peninsular and Oriental Steam Navigation Company (the P & O), before he was 40 and held that post for 40 years. It was he who in 1864, as the result of reading a series of articles in *Black-wood's Magazine* conceived the idea of founding a far-eastern bank. This development had been delayed by the dominance of the agency houses like Jardine Matheson, but was accelerated by the threat that British traders in India might seize the initiative. Thus inspired, Sutherland wrote the prospectus for the Shanghai and Hong Kong Banking Company (f.1865) and became its first Deputy Chairman. It rapidly established branches throughout Asia and in New York and London, becoming the major financial power in the Far East.

Charles Addis of Edinburgh (1861–1945) was another striking Scottish figure in the orient. His career began with the Hong Kong and Shanghai Bank in 1880. He became one of the most influential westerners in China. As a careful but nevertheless highly active investment banker he was one of the few who dominated matters behind the scenes in the great days of British commercial power in the East. Because he believed that China was one of the last unexploited fields for British capital, he inevitably became deeply involved in the politics of that vast but enfeebled empire, both as banker and as adviser to the Foreign Office. As the son of a Free

Church clergyman he held a deep evangelical faith. But though he had a strong idealistic streak he does not seem to have perceived the points of conflict between his mighty Bank and the Chinese people in the throes of the political disintegration of their country.

Another major Scottish initiative centred upon the Indian Ocean. This was that of William Mackinnon (1823–93), principal partner in Mackinnon and Company of Glasgow, and Mackinnon, Mackenzie and Company of Calcutta. From a base in Glasgow's cotton trade Mackinnon was the founder of the British India Steam Navigation Company, the Netherlands India Steam Navigation Company and the Queensland Steam Shipping Company, a director of the Suez Canal Company and chairman of the Imperial East Africa Company. Mackinnon was a giant of the imperial economy, his interests extending from India and Burma to Australia via the Straits Settlements to the Persian Gulf and East Africa. In 1888 the British India Company's office was moved from Glasgow to London, another recognition of the centripetal attraction of Britain's major business centre. But Mackinnon's ships continued to be supplied by Denny of Dumbarton and A. & J. Inglis of Glasgow. Mackinnon partly financed his uneconomic routes by mail and trooping contracts from the Indian government. In ringing the Indian Ocean with Scottish merchant houses he too used family and friendship. Like Matheson and Addis and other Scottish merchant princes he was a dedicated evangelical; his commitment to the Free Church was very real.

The Scots were among the most vigorous promoters of British business imperialism. But the benefits to Scotland diminished as the horizons broadened to embrace the world, while at the same time the focus narrowed, drawing so many of the great commercial decisions to London.

5 The Missionaries

One of Scotland's principal contributions to Empire lay in her missionary activity. In India, black Africa, the West Indies, the New Hebrides and in China the Scots were among the leaders of this form of European and American activity. That British home medical missions had their strongest centre in Edinburgh was due largely to the evangelical enthusiasm of some of its medical men, especially James Miller (1812–64) Professor of Surgery. Such men aspired to merge the cure of the body with the care of the soul, not only in Scotland but in the remoter parts of the world. Home missions were to feed and service those abroad. In missionary effort, culminating in the great name of David Livingstone (1813–73), the Scots not only attracted the attention of the western world, they also played a leading part in the cultural changes of these pre-modern societies.

The great impetus came from Presbyterian Evangelicalism, combined with a Scottish didactic drive. For in spite of the splits in the Church in Scotland its various elements each developed the urge to reach out to the rest of the world. The terrible earnestness of some missionaries carried dangers, including that of racism and cultural superiority. One Scottish missionary condemned Hinduism as 'a monstrous compound of error, impurity and tyranny'. Africa was seen by the missionaries and their societies as being in the grip of the bestialities of heathenism, deeply compounded by the avarice of the Arab slave trade. Though some missionaries could see certain values in the primitivism in which they found themselves, most thought in terms of promoting a new pattern of belief and a new kind of society. To these ends two aspects of Scottish life were to be brought to bear, namely education and medicine. Most nineteenth-century Scots missionaries, in their dedication, spent their lives in such a context, in their loneliness and frustration looking back longingly to Scottish homes and scenes.

It was Livingstone who provided a larger perspective for Scottish missionary effort in Africa. He concluded that heathenism and the slave trade had so debased African life that there could be no general acceptance of Christianity until African societies had escaped from this trap. The route lay through the replacement of slavery by legitimate trade and commerce, thus embarking African life on an upward cultural spiral. Only when a certain level had been attained would the African mind and soul be ripe for the reception of the beliefs and morality of Christianity. This process could be accelerated by the settlement of Scots farmers on the Shire Highlands in East Africa. By this difficult path Africa was to move to a form of European managerial economy (or 'colonialism') as a stage on the way to self-determination and Christianization. Thus Livingstone combined an economic development programme with Christian conversion. So was born the notion that Europe and especially Britain had a mission to civilize Africa. The fact that later missionaries did not find all the actions of traders helpful does not destroy Livingstone's vision.

Livingstone was not, of course, alone among Scots in dedicating his life to Africa. His wife's parents Robert (1795–1883) and Mary Moffat had preceded him. There was Mary Slessor of Calabar (1848–1915), born in Aberdeen, who had worked for 15 years as a mill girl in Dundee amid the din of machines and the insanitary overcrowding and malnutrition of the platties. She spent 28 years as a United Presbyterian missionary in Nigeria. The mission of which she was a member had gone out to Calabar in 1846 to fight a slow and bitter war on cruelty, superstition and magic. Mary Slessor arriving in 1876 found the people living under a primitive tyranny where life was cheap and where slavery was commonplace, and where a dead chief was accompanied to his grave by hundreds of slaves killed or buried alive with him. She earned the name of *Eka Kpukpro*, Mother of All the Tribes. Aberdeenshire was extraordinarily generous in its contribution to the mission fields, sending many men and women from its crofts, schools and university. Of the Aberdonian-Africans notable examples were Robert Laws (1851–1934) who helped to determine the development of modern Malawi, and Patrick Manson (b.1844), regarded by some as the father of tropical medicine.

In India too, the Scottish contribution was important, though of less relative weight than in black Africa. There the Free Church was especially active, the missionaries in India having 'come out' in 1843. Alexander Duff in Calcutta seems to have had as his programme for India a Christianization that would make possible the kind of society envisaged by Chalmers for Glasgow in his St John's Parish experiment and in his general social philosophy. John Wilson wrought in Bombay, seeing evangelization as an escape from a life of repressive superstition, including the caste system. The combined Scottish universities ran a mission in Kalimpong and Sikkim.

In Japan Scots' medical missions had some success. They produced a notable figure in Dr Henry Faulds who contributed a good deal to medical science under the Meiji, as well as defending the theory of evolution at the time of the trial of Robertson Smith. He was an inventive man, proposing the use of fingerprints for identification and raised characters for the blind.

The Scots had sufficient difficulty in accommodating the nineteeth-century developments in their own country with Calvinistic theology and a gentle Jesus, meek and mild: it is not surprising that in Africa and India they had difficulty in finding the way forward. They could see the effects of European ways in eroding old tribal structures, with the demoralization that occurs when peoples have lost their own culture and have not really adopted a new one from outside. The Scots, especially perhaps in Africa, were caught in the clash between a static missionary paternalism and exploitation by business and by modernizing governments. They became deeply involved in the life of colonial societies, having Christianized important parts of the population, and having provided the first elements of European education through their mission schools.

10

The Scottish Nation and the British State

1 The Sense of Nationhood

By 1832 native Scottish culture had suffered a series of dilutions, damaging to a sense of national identity. This had begun with the union of the crowns in 1603 and was accelerated by the union of the parliaments of 1707 and the pacification of the Highlands after 1745. Anglicization was thus a great threat to a unified national consciousness. Geography was another and older one: the Highlands and Lowlands had developed distinct cultures, and a strong mutual distrust. The Lowlander had felt the impulses of the age of Enlightenment and industry, expressed in the English language, while the Highlander, though subject to Anglicization and depopulation, clung to the old ways and his ancient Gaelic tongue.

So far as Lowlanders concerned themselves with Highland culture at all many supported the view of the Scottish Society for the Propagation of Christian Knowledge (SSPCK), that the Gaelic tongue was outmoded and was best replaced by English, the language of industry, commerce, the law and the Lowland churches. Even the Society for the Support of Gaelic Schools (f.1811) though less suspicious of the Gaelic, saw it as a stepping-stone to English. Because Gaelic was largely an oral language, with few books published in it, the Gaels were largely illiterate in their own tongue. Hence literacy in Gaelic was seen as a necessary stepping-stone to the more useful language of English.

So it was that Scott's influence on Scottish consciousness, though powerful in other ways after 1832, could not bind Scotland together against the forces of industrialization. The tartan became an affair of the Highland regiments and of wealthy deer-stalkers. By 1832 the Highland aristocrats had largely lost their Gaelic, speaking a different tongue from their soldiers and tenants. The great Whig triumph of 1832 had cut right across Scotch – English lines: it was a victory of the Scottish urban business class, and not of nationhood. Chartism likewise had had no real nationalist component. The Disruption could perhaps be partly blamed on English obtuseness over Scottish matters, but most Scots saw it as their own affair. The ruling and activist elements in Scottish life, the politicians and the business men, had no cause to appeal to a separate nationhood, for they were gainers from the Union and from the Empire.

From 1832 to the later 1870s Scottish nationalism tended to be a vicarious matter: middle and working-class radicals identified with the aspirations of the oppressed nations and minorities of Europe. This had begun back in the 1820s with sympathy for Greek Independence (after all, Byron was a Scot). It extended to Hungary, Poland and Italy, to Kossuth and Garibaldi.[1] But parallels with an oppressed Scotland were not drawn by these Lowland urban sympathizers.

And yet there were sleeping echoes of Scottish resentment and aspirations for identity: Bannockburn, Flodden and Culloden with their doomed heroes, though they had receded in Scottish consciousness, did not die. The movement to erect a great monument to the Wallace overlooking the valley of the Forth at Stirling was begun in 1856, though it languished for a good many years. The Gaelic Society of Inverness was founded in 1871; it was to become the most important vehicle of the Gaelic revival. Highlanders like John Murdoch told the Crofting Commissioners in 1883 that it had been a disaster to tell the Highlander that his culture was valueless and his language a barbarism, thus striking at his basic self-esteem.

There was a Vindication of Scottish Rights movement formed in 1853, and in the 1860s the Gaelic revival. By the late 1870s and early 1880s the Scottish sense of the past was gaining momentum. It converged with another strand in the national consciousness, namely the beginnings of a reaction against the demands of industrialization and its assaults on the personality and the community. An urge began to express itself among a few for something more warm and intimate than Britain and world empire, in which identity and continuity with a native past could merge. This coincided with a feeling that Scotland had allowed herself to be taken for granted politically by the Liberals, those advocates of free market forces who repudiated paternalism. Moreover a realization was

[1]See chapter 4, section 7 above.

dawning of the extent to which Scotland had been assimilated to English ways and to the Empire. In various parts of Europe there was developing a feeling that advanced industrialization was promoting cultural destruction and perversion, causing some Scots to begin to look back in the hope of recovering old values. The presentation of Scott's novels in the schools and the general reading of them helped Highlander and Lowlander to accept one another, thus closing a fissure in the Scottish sense of self, but the scholarly study of Scottish history was largely a matter of indifference in schools and universities. The fate of the Gaelic language drama-tized this aspect. The process of 'wearing out' or destroying it was well advanced: the Education Act of 1872 made no provision for teaching in Gaelic; by the 1880s most of the teachers and the taught were no longer interested in literacy in the ancient language.

So it was that by the 1880s there was a considerable degree of revival of cultural sensitivity and an urge for Scottish identity. A colourful exponent of this was the author R.B. Cunninghame Graham, of aristocratic origins, who had been a ranching and gold mining adventurer in South America. He was an idealist for Scottish identity and autonomy who combined this with realism, doing so in the sentiment that Scottish nationalism was the right of Scots to see their taxes wasted in Edinburgh instead of London. Confronting such men were the countervailing forces of Angli-cization and the Empire. There could thus be both a question-ing of the Union, stimulated for some by the Irish Question, and an acceptance of economic integration with England together with imperial participation. Most nationalists were of a fairly mild variety, opposed to disrupting the British community to the extent of total separatism, and approving of the monarchy shared with England.

Inevitably Scottish nationalism assumed an anti-English aspect, in more or less direct proportion to its intensity, for though the essence of identity must lie within the nation itself, an important aspect of nationalism is negative in the sense of being an assertion of difference from a dominant people. Indeed the Scots' view of them-selves had always contained a mixture of self-congratulation and denigration of the English.

The mild nationalism of the 1880s and later was not general in class terms. Except in the Highlands it was an affair of the middle classes, though even in the Highlands much of the dynamic came from journalists and lawyers. Even among them and the Highland nationalists, few wanted to go all the way to an autonomous Scottish nation. As Lord Derby correctly put it in the late 1880s, 'no Scotsman, except a handful of Celtic enthusiasts in the Highlands, wants a separate parliament for Scotland.' The Scottish commitment to the Liberal Party continued to be a dampening influence on nationalism.

The Scottish working-class leaders like Alexander McDonald and Keir Hardie placed nationalism low in their practical priorities. Though Hardie could express himself as in favour of Home Rule for Scotland, and though there was such a strand in the Scottish labour movement, its dominant aim was the formation of British trade unions and (with Hardie) a British political party. For them such unified action with their English workmates against their employers was more important than seeking a distinctive Scottish dimension. Industrial Scotland was no place for romantic, messianic or populist nationalism. On the other hand Scottish nationalism from its outset, as in Ireland, contained an element that wanted not only independence but socialism also. This latter aspiration could indeed find support among elements of the industrial labour force. Though this double aspiration was a minority view in such a dominantly middle-class movement, it was a portent of tensions to come. By contrast, the attempt in the Highlands to sustain the Gaelic language and to improve the lot of a poverty-stricken peasantry meant that cultural revival and the claim that the land should be restored to the people converged; land radicalism and Celticism were combined. Thus could Gaelic revivalists and Lowland radicals come together, especially over crofters' rights.

As the reciprocal of Scottish nationalism, what was the English view? It can be argued that apart from the activities of the SSPCK, such cultural imperialism as there was stemmed from Scots modernizers, as with Craik Sellar and Henry Craig in education. The English certainly stood for the continued unity of the United Kingdom, but apart from this primary objective they combined indifference and ignorance of Scottish matters with a willingness to implement a Scottish viewpoint if a sufficiently unified one could be found. Indifference and detachment, however, can be more maddening than oppression.

Scottish national aspirations might be characterized by two extremes, namely what was thought by many in its day to be the lunatic fringe with Professor Blackie a notable exemplar, and the political respectablity of men like Lord Rosebery. John Stuart Blackie (1809-95), born in Glasgow and professor of Greek at Aberbeen then Edinburgh, helped to found the chair of Celtic at Edinburgh, embraced the grievances of the crofters and enthusiastically involved himself in all questions of Scottish nationality and customs, becoming first chairman of the Scottish Home Rule Association. Aggressively attired in plaid and bonnet and carrying a staff, he held, among other eccentric beliefs, the conviction that the Gaelic was descended from Greek, an idea made tenable only by the tenuousness of his grip on both languages, together with a zeal to discover what he hoped to find. Rosebery, too, had his Scottish romantic side, but he was also an imperialist, seeing the British as having a mission on a world scale. He thought in terms of smaller loyalties being contained within the larger so that for him Scottishness should have its own distinctiveness but within a greater whole. Rosebery also had a practical side: he sought to meet Scottish aspirations along the path of administrative devolution.

Party because of this great diversity, depriving Scottish nationalism of obsessive clarity and limiting its class coverage, it did not develop a strong and general activism: much less did it attract the fierce support among expatriates in the United States that characterized the Irish movement. Few of the hard-working students in the universities of Scotland were infused with nationalist zeal.

2 The Devolution of Powers

Because the grievances against London control came mainly from the middle classes they were tempered with moderation and with a strong component of the managerial. This was accompanied by particular profession-based grievances, as with the lawyers who felt Scottish law to be slighted by the final appeal to the House of Lords, and doctors and educators who had their special Scots perspectives.

In 1827 the old system of government and patronage broke up; from the early 1830s the Home Secretary in London became responsible for Scottish matters, drawing upon the advice of the Scottish Lord Advocate. A series of Scottish Boards came into being including the Board of Supervision for the Poor Law (1845), the Prisons Board (1838), the Board for Lunacy and Mental Deficiency (1857), the Scotch Education Department (1872) and the Crofters Commission (1886). But these were *ad hoc* and not directly responsible to Parliament.

The National Association for the Vindication of Scottish Rights had been formed by a group who were affronted by what they saw as the apathy and indifference of Westminster to Scottish problems; it was dissolved in 1856. In 1869 a majority of the Scots MPs asked for the appointment of a Secretary for Scotland, but were refused. In 1883 a Bill for a Scottish Local Government Board failed in the Lords, provoking a mass meeting of protest in Edinburgh.

In terms of legislation too, there was difficulty. Making new law on matters concerning which Scotland already had a body of law was difficult for Westminster. Sometimes it was doubtful how far a statute applied to Scotland: for example it was not clear from the Bank Act of 1826 whether the Bank of England had the power to open branches in Scotland: it wisely refrained from doing so. Scotland had her own Reform Acts in 1832 and 1868. The Health Act of 1848 specifically excluded Scotland, delaying public health legislation there until 1867. A Sanitary Act of 1865 proved impossible to apply in terms of Scots law.

The mid-1880s brought considerable concessions to Scottish feeling. A Scottish Local Government Board was gained in 1894.[2] The electoral reforms of 1884–5 raised the number of Scottish parliamentary seats to make them proportional to her population. In 1885, Largely under pressure from Rosebery, the office of Scottish Secretary was instituted, superseding the Lord Advocate except in legal matters. In 1886 the 'Goschen Formula' was adopted whereby Scotland was to receive a share in United Kingdom public expenditure proportional to taxation: this yielded a ratio of 11 to 80. In response to pressure from the Scots a report on the Financial Relations of England, Scotland and Ireland, begun in the 80s, was published in 1890–1, setting out Scotland's contributions to the national Exchequer and her receipts from it. The Scottish Grand Committee (the Standing Committee on Scottish Bills) was begun in 1894.

It was a curious circumstance that the Conservatives did more to recognize Scottish claims than the Liberal Party so favoured by the Scots. Gladstone had greatly frustrated the young Rosebery who was strongly in favour of the claims of his countrymen. It was Lord Salisbury's Tory governments that initiated the Scottish Secretaryship and had set up the Goschen Formula and the fiscal inquiry

[2]See chapter 6, section 3 above.

of the 1880s both of which were concerned with Scotland's financial contribution to the United Kingdom. Meanwhile events in Ireland helped to inspire the setting up of the Scottish Home Rule Association in 1886. For there were still grievances enough. The Scottish Secretary was not a Secretary of State, and lacked real power, especially to initiate. Though he answered in parliament for the various Scottish Boards, he had little real control over them. They continued to be based in Dover House in London, a set of fragments of government.

Part II

The Edwardian and Georgian Coda

11

The Mature Economy and its Urban Setting

1 The Industrial and Commercial Responses

By 1900 the Scottish economy had reached maturity: that is to say it was committed to a way of life deriving from industry, and from cities together with mining-town outliers, all of which was largely centred in the midland belt. This pattern depended heavily on exports to England, to the empire and to the world at large. In such markets Scotland encountered increasing competition as other nations accelerated in the industrializing race, especially Germany and the United States, pitting their protectionism against Britain's free trade, and their renewed national dynamics against Britain's tendency to relax. The construction by German shipbuilders in 1897 of the *Kaiser Wilhelm Der Grosse* taking the North Atlantic Blue Riband, marked Germany's ability to compete with the premier yards of the Clyde. Though international tension could help Clydeside by providing a demand for ships of war, in the longer run trade and industrial rivalries were more important. Associated with this long-term threat there was short-term instability: Glasgow and its region suffered severely in 1903–5 and 1907–10 when engineering and shipbuilding slumped simultaneously with house building.

But Scottish industry was not passive under these challenges: indeed notable things were achieved. Down to 1914 the Scottish engineering and shipbuilding industries responded vigorously and successfully to competition from abroad. The Clyde continued to launch not far short of one-fifth of the world's output of ships. The Glasgow Exhibition of 1901 was the largest ever held in Britain, with almost 12 million attendances, featuring a Machinery Hall and an Industrial Hall. Its successor of 1911 seemed to confirm this confidence; the following year saw the Centennial Exhibition of Steam Navigation, with the scale and versatility of Clydeside shipbuilding dramatized by the liner *Lusitania* and the warship *Colossus* displacing 20,000 tons. The North British Locomotive Company, formed in 1903 from three Glasgow firms, was Britain's largest centre for producing locomotives and rollingstock: between 1904 and 1913 it built no less than 450 engines per year to precise specifications, with great care. Beardmores not only made the largest forgings then possible, but had diversified into shipbuilding, power units of all kinds, and automobiles leading to aircraft. The West of Scotland was making some 80 per cent of world's sugar processing machinery.

Scots civil engineers held a foremost place in the building of bridges, docks and other capital works, proud of being in the tradition of Smeaton and Telford. Their achievement and reputation were at their peak, having in 1890 completed the great civil engineering triumph of the nineteenth century, the Forth Bridge, with its eight million rivets, 54,000 tons of steel and 250,000 tons of masonry, though it had cost 57 lives and 518 injured.

Colvilles, from a modest beginning in 1860 had by 1914 an ingot-producing capacity of well over 350,000 tons of steel, one of the greatest plants in Britain. Scotland supplied 50 per cent of the UK ironfounding output by 1907. A new Scottish potential in coal had been opened up in the east, in Fife and the Lothians, working at deep levels, giving new life to certain of the small Fife ports like Methil and Wemyss, exporting much of their output to eastern Europe. The merger of Coats and Clark in 1896 had created a Scottish firm that dominated the world's market in sewing thread. In the manufacture of jute and linoleum Scotland held a similar leading position. Edinburgh had the largest breweries north of the Trent and the largest distilleries in the United Kingdom.

The Scots economy was not, of course, all industry. There was the striking achievement of Lowland agriculture, maintaining and indeed increasing its levels of productivity, as high as any in Britain or indeed the world. In finance also the Scots' record was impressive, centring on the banks and the insurance and investment companies of Edinburgh. Scots funds were placed in Australia and Canada, in American real estate and the ranches of Texas or stock market securities. Scottish overseas investment rose from about £300 millions in 1900 to £500 millions in 1914. Much of the capital thus placed overseas was a good deal more speculative than that kept at home. By 1884 some three quarters of British foreign and colonial investment companies were either located in Scotland or promoted by Scotsmen. At home by the early 1890s called up capital in Scottish limited companies totalled some £50 millions, plus some £100 millions in British railway companies; the total of Scottish bank liabilities had risen from £52 millions in 1850 to £168 millions in 1914.

Against these real achievements must be placed important negative aspects. Even the progressive industries and firms could not generate enough employment to keep Scots at home: in the decade before 1914 Scotland lost by emigration not far short of 50 per cent of her natural increase. The labour force that stayed behind received little sympathy from their employers for their demands. The tradition of master and man had confirmed itself with the growth of scale: the workers by 1900 had accepted this, and produced their own response in the form of a confrontational stance: the engineering lockout of 1897 had been an indication that the easier relationships of earlier generations had largely gone. The President of the Institution of Engineers and Shipbuilders in Scotland in 1893 had suggested to its members that they should give thought to the principles of 'equitable industrial remuneration', but there was no response.

Though there were promising beginnings in automobile production, with the Arrol-Johnson, the Argyll and other cars, these failed to come to real fruition. Scottish engineering, in spite of its great achievements (perhaps because of them) could not gain a secure foothold in the revolutionary new development of the internal combustion engine and the vehicles it was to power. Mass production engineering, requiring advanced costing systems and adequate but careful financing, together with a new kind of market sensitivity, did not thrive in Scotland, but centred in the English Midlands where it was serviced by a more suitable mix of auxiliary industries.

The second of the new developments of the later nineteenth century to which Scotland found it difficult to respond was the growth of new consumer industries, beginning to become important as the age of mass consumption began to dawn. Though a shopkeeper-genius like Thomas Lipton (1850–1931) could create his own commercial empire beginning with tiny premises in Finnieston, Glasgow, and though Edinburgh industry had traditionally been close to the upper and middle-class consumer, neither centre could take a lead in the production of the new range of mass-produced goods.

The general pattern of employment did not greatly change between 1901 and 1911. The labour force in defined occupations rose from 1,879.2 thousand to 2,011.2. The decline in textiles, leather and clothing continued (from 327.8 thousand workers to 289.2). Staying more or less static in employment terms were agriculture, forestry and fishing (237.3 to 240.8) and the service trades including building (845.7 to 866.4). The growth of the decade lay in the metal trades (205.8 to 252), miscellaneous manufacture (130.4 to 181.3) and mining and quarrying (132.2 to 181.5): each of these three categories gained some 50,000 workers.

2 The Business Community

By 1900 a complex web of interlocking ownerships and directorates had been formed in Scotland with banking, finance and industry. This confirmed itself down to 1914. Industrial integrations, especially of the vertical kind, linking shipowning, shipbuilding, engineering and steel and coal had been formed. They had arisen largely because in each of these industries the need for heavy capital investment and the instability of markets prompted firms to seek to minimize their risks by reaching backward to the source of their materials and forward to their markets. By the same integrative process Scotland became endowed with great commercial and industrial families, taking their place alongside the landed nobility, and to some extent linked together by marriage.

Business psychology had changed since the 1830s or 1860s: in large measure the exhilaration of founding a firm, especially when associated with inventiveness and direct participation, and running it in direct terms, had given place over much of industry to the new outlook engendered by greater scale and by the impersonalization of the limited liability company. Mandarinism too had grown in the upper echelons. Shipowning for example had become an affair for gentlemen: the leading financiers and industrialists dominated this sector as ships became larger, more complex, and heavily dependent on credit facilities.

Dundee had by 1900 produced a special kind of business man. Its leading figures were ardent free traders, employers of the cheapest labour they could find at home or in Calcutta, housing it as cheaply as possible. In politics, like their workers, they were radicals: their city had returned only one Conservative in its long history. They were highly market conscious, intimate with the maps of India, China and the Americas, steady men, with muted responses in both prosperity and depression. They had a sense of civic duty in the running of their city, but their business perspective kept wages low and housing poor.

It would seem that in the Scotland of the turn of the century the standards of commercial morality were higher than in England, with less fraud and gross mismanagement: this might be related to the more intimate nature of the Scottish financial and business world. Certainly Scottish limited companies, as Professor Payne has shown in his pioneering work, were longer-lived than their English counterparts. Fewer companies aborted, suggesting that members of the business community, large and small, were well informed about investment opportunities and sophisticated in their judgements. But the Scots shipbuilders were prominent in the 'ring' formed about 1910 to put pressure on the Admiralty to build new ships and to allocate them among the yards which might otherwise have engaged in damaging competition.

The business system had shown its instability as early as 1825: this did not diminish with time. But Scottish business men by 1900 had become inured to recurrent cycles, indeed to the point of believing that recovery would always come, keeping the company afloat if need be by calling up unpaid capital. Yet erratic demand accompanied by changing technology were very serious challenges. In tight times the availability of finance could become paramount in determining survival, with liquidity crises killing firms otherwise sound. But works seldom closed down, though they often changed hands, their assets having been revalued downward and thus cleared of debt.

Scottish business was being increasingly weakened by the draw of Britain's financial and business centre in London. A fair number of Scottish companies by 1900 were taken over by London-based companies, thus removing business decision making from Glasgow, Edinburgh or Dundee. Major figures like Sir Charles Tennant or William Mckinnon, in spite of their Scottish feelings, had to join the informational and financial net of the City. But the charge that Scottish business contained too much hereditary management by 1900 or 1914, and that this was damaging, is not very convincing. Colvilles, for example, having sold shares to its senior managers, was from 1916 ruled by John Craig, son of one of the company's furnacemen.

The Scottish banks had received a heavy shock with the failure of the City of Glasgow Bank in 1878. Thereafter they moved toward limited liability and more conservative banking practice: indeed an air of complacency had invaded a once vigorous system since the mid 1880s. No new Scottish banks were founded after 1845; amalgamations had brought their number down by 1880 to 10; between 1900 and 1914 this was reduced to 8. The General Managers Committee had become in effect a cartel from the 1870s, setting agreed rates for borrowing and lending, settling communally other matters of shared interest, and confining competition to service chiefly through the multiplication of branches, but with advertising strictly eschewed. In spite of the wish of Scottish bankers to continue to confine their lending to short-term advances, the demands of heavy industry drew them into renewals that were in effect long-term loans. By 1900 all the Scottish banks had invaded London, servicing Scottish interests there, and adding to their deposits. The professions servicing industry continued to grow, with more lawyers, accountants, insurers, surveyors, stock brokers and engineers expanding the middle classes.

In religious terms the kind of evangelicalism that Chalmers had generated, still powerful in the 1830s, had faded among the major businessmen by 1900. Though a good many like John Craig were elders of their kirk, there was little effort to re-Christianize the lapsed workers as William Collins and John Burns of an early business generation had attempted. But there was a good deal of philanthropic action, as by William Pearce and John Elder and his widow, providing facilities like social centres and libraries.

3 The Captains of Industry and their Workers

By 1900 Scotland had produce a breed of major industrialists whose actions and prestige dominated the economic scene. They included such names as Colville, Baird, Yarrow, Tennant, Lorimer, Elder, Pearce, Neilson and Beardmore. These were the magnates of ship-building, heavy engineering, iron and steel and coal. They were autocrats, their decisions were made, conveyed, and not discussed. They had a strong desire to keep everything in their own hands. A man like Beardmore, perhaps the greatest of them, took his own authority over the concern to be absolute and rightful: he and his peers were not given to self-doubt and self-questioning. Such men acted largely intuitively, with little effective costing or market research. Their heavy fixed investment had however often created a need for capital that made it necessary to go public in the form of limited liability companies: this brought additional jurisdiction from the accountant, the shareholders and the directors. But so far as the last of these was concerned, with the autocrat of the boardroom at the head of the table, though the business might be slipping away or heading into crisis, it would be a courageous junior who would raise his voice. In the wider world the industrial mandarins commanded great respect: those who were seeking phil-anthropic contributions for good causes had no choice but to appeal to the ego of such major donors. A knighthood not infrequently set the seal upon self-esteem.

There was no sense among the magnates of a need to persuade the workers, or to propitiate them, much less to involve labour in the affairs of the firm beyond the ordered task. Contact with the workers as it had operated in many cases in the 1860s had by 1900 given place to the remoteness of increasing scale: labour had become in large measure merely a hired input, with an underlying fear of instant dismissal. The workers were kept without informa-tion about the firm, except such as they could gather from their immediate tasks. Their instructions came to them from the fore-men – the non-commissioned officers of the industrial army. Such foremen might from time to time be consulted about means, but not about ends. The trade unions were resisted, and where possible excluded. Some industrialists were vindictively anti-trade union as James Neilson had been; Beardmore succeeded in keeping the unions out down to 1914.

The magnates of the Scottish basic industries at the end of the century may perhaps be taken as a distillation of the Victorian ethic. It centred upon the dominant male of middle age or over, brooking no interference, speaking only with his equals so far as there was any conferring at all, keeping under authority not only his labour force but also his wives and daughters. Even his sons could be kept under tutelage until old age or death broke the grip. Perhaps some of these magnates saw themselves as living legends, naming their forges *Vulcan, Atlas* or *Phoenix* .

Within the general pattern of Scottish industrial autocracy there was, however, considerable variety. There was the conservative style of management as represented by Sir William Lorimer of the Steel Company of Scotland, whose near autocracy expressed itself in 'sound' management and modest performance. By contrast there were the adventurers of heavy industry, with Beardmore as their great exemplar, a man prepared to try almost anything within his reach. There was a third category of whom Sir Charles Tennant was the leading case, the out-reachers who, finding their base in the west of Scotland becoming confining, operated on a national scale. Thus Tennant was a prime mover in 1890 in the formation of a national enterprise, the United Alkali Company, the world's largest chemicals company combining 45 firms, assimilating his St Rollox chemical works to it. Tennant was a leading figure in the subsequent battle of the giants between United Alkali and Brunner Mond. Finally there were the industrialist-manipulators like Sir James King who could build up a Scottish investment empire sufficiently impressive for him to help Mr Gladstone with his investments: thus King became chairman of the Caledonian Railway, the Clydesdale Bank and the Tharsis Company (the latter at the age of 76). He was also a director of J. & P. Coats, the Lothian Coal Company, the Coltness Iron Company, Young's Paraffin Company and the Irrawaddy Flotilla Company.

There is, of course, the question: why did these industrial magnates behave as they did? Scottish culture played some part. There was a strong didactic and authoritarian element in both the kirk and the schools, together with a long tradition in the country-side and the Highlands of the acceptance of social hierarchy, though perhaps not to the English degree. The dominie traditionally instilled respect not only for himself but for those to whom he himself had to defer. Works schools, as for example at the Shotts Iron works, would have an even stronger effect in this direction. Moreover, though most Scottish workers were made literate by their schooling, they did not gain enough education to be able to take on their masters on anything like equal terms, in argument or negotiation, especially when the masters held a virtual monopoly of information concerning the firm. Often, also, an opaque dialect impaired the workers' confidence and made the assertion of their views and case difficult. A man like Alexander McDonald could break through these barriers by force of character, aided by his self-financed attendance at the University of Glasgow, but few could achieve this. Thus was the hold of the magnates confirmed by the culture.

There was the felt need among the employers to preclude, so far as possible, power sharing with the workers, to resist all pressures from below. By 1900 this posture had become deeply ingrained. Large-scale investment, with its accompaniment, the need to service a heavy debt and to persuade the bankers to grant periodic renewals, involved the industrialists in a dilemma. They needed to expand and to modernize in order to compete, but fixed debt charges could expose them to labour militancy. Morever their undertakings were highly vulnerable to the trade cycle, putting a premium on keeping wages flexible in a downward direction in order to meet bad times. The skilled men, with their own craft protectionism and their desire to maintain their differentials against the unskilled, often accepted the pattern of business command, especially, as frequently happened, they were kept on as a cadre in bad times when unskilled labour was shed.

Riley, J. & T. Thomson and Beardmore provide three examples of the price to be paid for industrial progressiveness. Riley, left on a slack leash by an indulgent board, had landed the Steel Company of Scotland in deep trouble by the mid 1890s. He was too innovative, seeking to work the plant at the known technological limits, involving the company in excess capacity and high fixed capital. Thomsons, among the leading shipbuilders in the 90s, had sunk very large investments in their yards to build steel ships powered by triple expansion engines. These large and more complex craft required that costing and tendering be much more scientific. To this the management proved inadequate: in 1899 John Brown and Company, the Sheffield steel makers, the principal creditor took over. Beardmore provided perhaps the most dramatic case of progressiveness and its implications. By 1902 he had extended his ventures so far that they could not continue as a private company in family control: he had to go public. This meant that Vickers became major shareholders. The notion was that this alliance would not only promote integrated policies, but would keep Beardmore in check. But he was skilful enough in obfuscation and other devices to retain effective control, greatly worrying the Vickers board. Not least, Beardmore, amid his many concerns, lost touch with the steel markets. Riley and Beardmore were the opposite of authoritarian stodge (one way to the bankruptcy court) but represented the entrepreneur as artist, seeking to assert his will over the productive process (another route to collapse of the firm.)

How effective then, were the Scottish magnates of large-scale industry? There is no doubt that on the credit side they as a group produced a striking achievement. The industries of the West of Scotland were by 1914 a world wonder, finding a place in geography textbooks in all parts of the world where these existed. But the pattern was precarious, and in two principal senses. It meant a heavy export dependence that could not continue indefinitely. Secondly the command structure and the labour relations on which it rested, both the result of a peculiar evolutionary process ruled by technology, culture and economics, could not persist. The captains of industry simply assumed that in creating employment and incomes they were doing good, and that anyone who sought to impede them in this was acting contrary to the public interest. Such a posture was inconsistent with the extension of the political franchise and the growth of the unions. So it was that by 1914 industrial failures and inadequacies of leadership were accompanied by success, together with the beginning of the end of labour passivity.

4 The Cities

By 1914 the actions of Scottish business men had created a range of cities that would have astonished the men of 1832. Moreover the cities had taken on a life of their own. They had become vast organisms which, though their primary element was still their product mixes, had generated a range of phenomena in complex inter-relationship. These determined the shifting pattern of location of industry and of homes, the life fulfilment of the working classes and the relationship between the classes. Alongside these primary phenomena, civic policy, even when very active, was a secondary force.

The general shapes of the cities continued largely as they had been set by 1875, though on an increasing scale in the case of Glasgow and to a lesser degree Edinburgh; Glasgow in 1911 had 784,496 people and Edinburgh 423,464. The regional imbalance based on the industrial west of Scotland was greater than ever.

In spite of municipal improvement programmes in Glasgow and Edinburgh the slums were still intractable and dense. Much of the population of Glasgow and Dundee shocked the visitor: the streets were full of people stunted in their growth and impaired in health, made so by poor diet and living conditions. Bodies deformed by rickets were commonplace. Though the provident artisans could escape to better conditions, those without skills and craft unions could not remove themselves from the containment of the east end of the cities. Most of them by now did not want to. The possibility of a return to the land had been effectively blocked for a generation; by 1914 it did not enter the minds of urban workers, for they knew only the city. They had, indeed, come to see it as home, the place that had formed them and whose ways they understood. But the major cities were too big to satisfy the need for identification: there was a strong feeling for the various 'villages' within the cities, the sub-localities of the 'crosses' – in Glasgow the Gorbals, Anderston, Partick and others. The wealthy had moved yet further from the sources of their fortunes, creating a new Edwardian generation of country houses, but typically without the broad acres that had characterized the landed aristocracy, and without the links with the land and those who worked it.

The cities had begun to manifest serious limitations. The larger ones had created intense urban congestion where movement was concentrated: parts of Glasgow, where railway termini and harbour traffic converged, as in Jamaica Street, were as choked as London Bridge. But the ratepayers of the cities would not accept the enormous cost of an operation on the road system at the nerve centre. The horse had become a major pollutor, dropping a massive discharge onto the streets, making them smelly in dry weather and dangerous in wet.

Yet there had been a considerable phase of confidence in the effectiveness of civic government in dealing with the problems of the cities. Glasgow in particular had by 1900 achieved an international reputation with continentals and Americans visiting the city to learn how to manage various municipal enterprises, especially in water and gas supply, sewage disposal, libraries and museums and the tramways system. By 1900 Glasgow had become a world-ranking city, standing just below London, Paris, Berlin and New York. From this eminence she had confronted the principal urban problems, pioneering in many. The golden years of municipal confidence had come between 1891 and 1900, with the city buoyed up by the business upswing and a large extension of the city's boundary in 1891 taking in the populous and prosperous shipbuilding burghs of Partick and Govan.

But from 1900 came a lessening of municipal nerve. A number of elements contributed to this. The population of the city grew hardly at all from 1901 to 1911. There was the worrying question whether the growth of the city and its taxable capacity would be such, given the business climate, as to pay for the increasing costs the city had incurred. The growth of local government was showing signs of bureaucracy and a degree of corruption. Perhaps most frightening of all for the City Treasurer, there was the mounting pressure to attack the social conditions and the bad housing of the lower-income working class. In this respect the Glasgow record was far worse than in most British and American cities, a terrible blemish on her reputation for good government. There was always the danger of a ratepayers' revolt, or of damage to the tax base by burdening business too heavily and causing it to move away. On the other hand the extension of the franchise and the growth of populism made strong demands for new and costly social expenditure. So it was that the halting rate of growth of the city's economy created problems not only for its entrepreneurs but also for its civic politicians and officials. The same syndrome applied to all the Scottish cities in varying degrees.

In a sense the basis of municipal government had not changed greatly since 1833. It was still in 1914 in middle-class hands, with few working-class councillors. But circumstances had indeed altered in important respects. The leading men of business were withdrawing from the council chamber, leaving it to the middle and lower reaches of the business class including the 'shopocracy'. These sat even for the working-class wards in spite of the widening of the franchise. But in order to get elected they had to respond to the pressures from their constituents, and so pushed for advantages for their wards. Though municipal collectivism by 1914 was still run by the middle classes, there was an important though indirect working-class input.

12

The Scottish Version of Industrial Society

1 Population Growth and Movement

Taking population as a primary indicator of Scotland's experience, the years between 1901 and 1911 reflect quite dramatically the state of the nation. The growth of numbers was almost halved to 6.5 per cent, against 11.1 per cent in the 1890s. This was largely due to a net emigration of 253,894 persons, or 46.8 per cent of natural increase. By 1911 the total population was 4,760,904 and was virtually unchanged in 1914 (the figure of five millions was not reached until 1939). The dampening of increase in the first decade of the new century by out-migration was an indication that employment opportunities had diminished, certainly relative to those outwith Scotland.

This continuous adjustment in search of work continued to operate powerfully within Scotland. The predominance of the western lowlands with Glasgow as its focus continued: by 1901 it contained some two million people or 45.6 per cent of Scotland's population (Glasgow itself had 761,000 people) The eastern lowlands centred on Edinburgh increased slightly to some 1.5 millions, holding its share at 31.6 per cent. The north-east with Aberdeen as its leader gained slightly absolutely and lost slightly relatively, with 9.8 per cent. The remaining three regions, the borders, the highland counties and the far north continued their decline in both senses, containing together 13.1 per cent of the Scottish people (the figure in 1831 had been 27.4 per cent). Within the lowlands the degree of urbanization had steadily increased: in the west it grew from 51.9 per cent in 1831 to 72.2 per cent in 1911, in the east from 37.3 per cent to 59.3 per cent. Taken together the two regions contained 88.2 per cent of Sotland's urban population by 1911. By 1914 Glasgow had achieved the magical figure of one million, aided by the massive gains from boundary extensions of 1912.

This was the demographic face of Scotland as a mature industrial society. Its features were urbanization and a concentration on two rival foci. These had distinct regional economies and cultures, but shared a nostalgia for a Scottish past, much of which lay in the abandoned countryside and the Highlands.

2 Working-Class Health and Prospects

Much of the urban population was unhealthy and underweight. Congestion was a condition of life in all cities: Glasgow was the most striking case with some 700,000 people in 1914 living in its three central square miles, the heaviest concentration of people in Europe. Against the inevitable human deterioration the Medical Officers of Health, the doctor and the philanthropists struggled, confronting the impossible odds inherent in low incomes and consequent deterioration, often compounded by drink. There had been some improvement infant mortality rates in Scotland: from a peak of 130 deaths per year per 1,000 live births in the early 1890s the level had fallen to 109 in 1914, but this was still very high. The sanitary staff in the city had been increased from 90 in 1886 to 401 in 1914, involved in the inspection of homes, abattoirs and milk supplies. By 1902 government had become seriously worried by the nation's health as shown by the high number of volunteers for the Boer War who were unfit. The Royal Commission on Physical Training of 1902 was followed in 1903 by the Interdepartmental Committee on Physical Deterioration. Games and physical education were introduced in schools, together with school medical inspections and meals: in short the educational system was seen as a principal means of improving health. Noel Paton, Glasgow's Professor of physiology, appointed in 1906, was a pioneer in the scientific study of the relationship between health and diet. Elements of the working classes were also becoming interested in health provision: from the 1880s the surgical and nursing revolutions in which Scotland played so large a part gave rise to a demand for a large share in such facilities. Through the School Boards and as poor law guardians working-class influence grew. But the provision of public funds for hospitals and other facilities was slight: these continued on the philanthropic principle. The attack on the health problem through the schools was a charge on the local rates.

Health was one ceiling placed upon the prospects of the young. Another was the working of the labour market. Boys of respectable artisan families had a reasonable chance of following their fathers by means of an apprenticeship. Those of unskilled parents had very little prospect of self-improvement. There was a vast body of child and adult casual labour in all the cities: by 1914 they teemed with cabmen, cart drivers, shoe-blacks, newspaper sellers, porters, watchmen, pedlars, messengers, dockers, general labourers in building and in industry as well as in such jobs as boxmaking and sewing sacks. The Victorian middle-class view had been to regard those in such employment as moral delinquents who had failed in the challenge of self-improvement. But by 1914 there was some degree of realization that such people were caught up in a system from which they could not escape. It had been perceived by R.H. Tawney and others that the school system was a major component in this closed circle. Because children could earn, they escaped school attendance when they could. This meant that their subsequent choice of jobs was very limited, with no training facilities for something better. In the short run casual labour paid better than an apprenticeship. Each generation a new cohort of the young moved into blind-alley employment with no security, their employers hiring or firing them according to the need of the moment. They came to accept their fate and that of their children. The Education Act of 1901 helped somewhat in keeping children at school to the age of 14, thus relieving pressure on the labour market. But the casual labour syndrome was a curse to the lower working class.

The Glasgow Distress Committee in 1904 arranged to buy land in order to start a farm colony for the unemployed: Keir Hardie attacked John Burns who as President of the Local Government Board, stopped the purchase. The level of unemployment was so bad in 1908 that the Corporation of Glasgow started work schemes.

3 Urban Life for the High and the Low

By 1900 the great majority of Scots lived in the setting of the street: houses looked across to other houses or to factories or workshops. The eye of the urban Scot suffered a kind of tunnel-vision of life. It ran typically between four or five storey tenements, with few lateral extensions except where streets crossed. The street, however, was also a thoroughfare, a play place and a showplace as small shops and public houses had opened along it. Such shops were the

attempts of their petty owners to become economically independent: at the same time they were the main means of making known
to the working classes what was available to be consumed and at
what price. Along with the pawn shops they were the principal
source of workingclass credit. The pub was the place for social
foregathering and also for oblivion. The street a place where the
slender family budget was spent, the source of excitement and dis-
traction, the matrix of life. Thousands of people never went out of
Glasgow in the whole of their lives: those who did got not much
further than Rothesay, or, more daringly, Blackpool. Only the
army and navy opened up the larger world.

Since the 1830s the streets had been cleaned up a good deal. They
were no longer the recipient of the contents of chamber pots
emptied from the windows, for there was indoor sanitation, though
much of it was still in the form of earth closets. There were now
carriageways with side gutters and sidewalks so that the pedestrian
was separated from the traffic and walked along by the shop-fronts.
The motor vehicle scarcely penetrated working-class streets.

The tenements had no gardens so that the only withdrawal from
the street was in the wynds, back courts, closes and stairheads
where children played and couples courted, and in the house. The
tenement stairs and stairhead were a kind of extension of the street
but with an intimately shared social responsibility for noise and for
cleanliness, especially the stair-head lavatories. With so many
families living in one or two rooms there was little privacy in the
home. The kitchen was the centre of family life, especially the range
for heating and cooking, coming in from the 1880s, and the sink or
'jawbox' where so much was done including food preparation and
ablutions. There were no baths: the local bathhouse or steamie
served to wash both clothes and their wearers.

The closeness of this kind of living in home and street could
produce a united family life and a supportive neighbourliness, or it
could degenerate into a bitter and claustrophobic setting, together
with local hostilities between religious and ethnic groups. The outcome, in the home at least, was largely determined by the character
of the mother. One of the most important budgetary problems was
the provision of the rent, for the Scottish tenement dweller was
typically a tenant. There was little really disorderly street life,
partly because of the rain. But by 1914 the streets of the denser
working-class areas were seen by much of the middle classes as

hostile and menacing. The Glasgow 'keelie' with his cloth cap personified the middle-class view of the lower working class. But it is doubtful how far the bosses of Scottish industry in their grand homes really feared the working classes.

The upper-class districts of the cities were a different world: Edinburgh's New Town and Glasgow's grand terraces on Great Western Road and elsewhere were the scenes of a life-style that was starkly contrasting. Here there were spacious rooms and plenty of them, looked after by living-in servants. Amid such comfort and insulation it was easy to ignore the social costs of industrialization. The jute master of Dundee and his family, for example, could close his mind to Dock Street on a Saturday night: it was a place of violence and degradation, with almost every second door opening onto a public house with frequent brawls and with pavements littered with drunken women and men and stained with the blood of bottle fights. Indeed the great employers may well have felt a need to close their minds to such hopelessness.

And yet the old tradition of territory shared between classes was not entirely dead, especially in Glasgow. Sauchiehall Street had become the epitome of the city – its Piccadilly. George Square had replaced Glasgow Green as the place of general foregathering, though the Green was still used for labour rallies. When Mafeking was relieved in May 1900, releasing the pent-up mass hysteria of the long siege, it was to George Square that the multitude surged. In Edinburgh there was less mixing of classes, with Princes Street still bourgeois territory with only the prostitutes representing the working class.

4 Labour Politics and Values

By 1914 there was a characteristic division in the Scottish Labour movement between skilled and unskilled workers, for though industrial unionism embracing the latter had begun, and though there was an aspiration for the brotherhood of all workers, the movement contained a powerful élitist craft element. There was, too, a division of political loyalties: though the Labour Party had formally existed since 1906, the old Lib – Lab alliance that had helped to keep the Liberal Party dominant in Scotland was still strong. But the visits of Henry George, the single-taxer, in the 1880s and his book *Progress and Poverty* of 1879, with its indictment of landowners both rural and urban, had helped to push the movement in the socialist direction. The strikes of 1911–13 further shifted the balance in favour of independent Labour action. Because of the Home Rule policy of the Liberal Party it was able to retain the loyalty of the Irish in Scotland and their Roman Catholic hierarchy a good deal longer.

Behind all this lay a powerful moralism: the social attitudes and values of the Scottish labour élite continued to carry religious overtones into Union and Labour Party affairs. This tended to widen the gap between them and the unskilled. It took the form not of condemning Christianity, but of rejecting its formal organization, especially the Church of Scotland, seen by many as the enemy of the working classes. Scottish labour politicians still had the Bible as a profound formative influence. The power of church tradition and the frame of mind it had generated were reflected in the Socialist Sunday School Movement from the later 1890s, dominated by the Independent Labour Party. The adoption by the Church of Scotland, the Free Church and the United Presbyterian Church of a social gospel and of social programmes from the 1880s and 1890s came too late to dispel this deep distrust. On the side of the church there was the fear that socialism would also mean atheism, as was believed to be the case on the continent.

The second great moralist element among the Scottish labour élite continued to be temperance: indeed this was one of its characteristic features. Just as it had been part of Chartism and the cooperative movement, so too it permeated much of trade unionism, bringing something of an alliance between the artisan and the lower middle class. Because of the drink problem, temperance had become a profound part of the consciousness of Scottish labour leaders: Keir Hardie was deeply repelled by the drinking of the London socialists and for this reason refused to join the Social Democratic Federation. For many skilled men taking the pledge was a means to respectability and family improvement and a mark of these. The campaigns of the temperance societies against the liquor traffic provided useful experience in the politics of pressure groups. So it was that for the unions temperance was no fad to be urged on others, as it was among a good many middle-class Liberals, but part of a general philosophy of society, a projection of a deep-seated puritan urge for renewal and moral uplift, as well as being part of the indictment of a capitalism which shackled the wage slaves by destroying their will to resist. The brewers and distillers were, in this sense, the most guilty element of capitalism.

Along with moralism the Scottish Labour movement contained a considerable element of romanticism of the William Morris sort: this brotherly utopianism on the basis of the dignity of craftmanship could assume something of the character of a religion.

But moralism and romanticism, though of great importance, were ultimately a block to revolutionary thinking. By 1914, though still realities in Scottish labour politics, such notions had begun to weaken. Yet, with the Labour Party still in embryo, and with the craft unions so strong, far-reaching radicalism was still under severe restraint. The structure of the Scottish labour movement was a further impediment to radical thinking and action: the Trades Councils with their local and regional bias stood in the way of strong policies within the various industries. Scotland by 1914 had produced in general a relatively low level of unionization. And yet unionism and labour politics were an increasingly important reality. The miners, as in England, were at the core of the labour movement, with a long history of conflict with their employers. From around 1900 severe depressions in the coal industry had broken the old Liberal, class collaborationist attitude among them: the mining unions began to be radicalized, turning to the Labour Party. In 1910 William Adamson (1863–1963) became West Fife's first miner MP sitting as a Labour member.

Scottish labour and union politics had acquired a special flavour before 1914, as described by Harry McShane in his reminiscences of Glasgow. The skilled workers who dominated Clydeside unionism were respectable Protestants, running their unions on principles as democratic as their Calvinist Churches, attending meetings in their blue Sunday suits, bowler hats and often rolled umbrellas. The 'scientific socialism' of Marx had a fascination for them with its historical inevitability not far removed from the predestination their forefathers had learned from John Knox. But this did not make many of them convinced revolutionaries: having abandoned inevitability in its religious garb they were cautious about embracing it in its secular form. At the other end of the scale there was the extraordinary world of the political and religious zealots, with their varying compounds of the two starting points. There were the ferociously self-convinced autodidacts, the free thinkers who demonstrated their catholicism by flaying Protestant and Catholic alike, the ranters of the Orange Order jumping on rosary beads and the worker parents who baptized their children into socialism with rose petals, four white for purity and one red for revolution. Tom Johnston (1881–1965) published in 1909 *Our Noble Families* with an approving introduction by Ramsay MacDonald, charging the Scottish nobility with enjoying landed fortunes gained by generations of 'pillage, butchery and theft'. The oratory of the street corner and the public parks was at its colourful peak, together with attempts to reconcile religion with the urge for a new order of society.

In the Glasgow case there was a complex interplay between the new welfare Liberalism as centred on the reforms that followed 1906 and the emergent socialism that found its strongest expression in the ILP. The unemployment crisis of 1908 had the effect of shifting a significant element of the workers, including skilled men, away from amelioration of the market system and toward a socialist alternative. In March 1910 there was an attempt to introduce industrial unionism among the 10,000 workers at Singers but the firm defeated the strike by a direct appeal to the labour force, accepted by 6,500 of them. The ILP had kept clear of the Trades Councils, had repudiated religion and patriotism, rejected 'fads' like temperance and the singletax, and urged the end of capitalism. But this was not to come by insurrectionist, revolutionary means, but by erosion and gradualism.

5 The Countryside

While life in the cities was thus intensifying itself, life in the countryside changed at a slower pace, continuing to rely on much that was traditional, but beginning to feel the impact of industrial society. The horse continued to 1914 to be the principal source of power and was a component of the life of the countryman at all levels. After the harvest came the ploughing matches – competitions of skill and elegance that could make a ploughman a local celebrity, guiding his mighty Clydesdales with their gleaming brasses and polished leather. The substantial lowland farms still employed large permanent labour forces, making each of them a kind of community. But most farm labourers were tenant cottagers, a circumstance that gave their employers additional power over them.

The bothy, grubby and bare, still thrived, with its bachelor dormitory life. Though it could produce a kind of folk culture through its songs and stories, the life of the bothy could also be degrading in its lewd songs and gross talk, its drinking, its fights and the general deadness of aspiration it could induce. The bothy contrasted strongly with the carefully kept and comfortable living room of a Border shepherd, or of a Lowland or Highland game-keeper, men who were often well read, with well formed characters. At harvest time there was still a migrant labour force of men and women with many Irish and Highland people, moving from farm to farm. Much of the work in the fields and elsewhere was done by hand.

But there were elements of change. Steam farming had made a beginning in the Lothians and others such areas where the scale of the farms made it appropriate. This was done by means of self-powered steam engines, by 1914 a familiar sight on country roads, drawing the thresher and often a baler with the rear brought up by the van in which the three-man crew lived. The steam engine could not traverse the fields, but from its stationary position at one side, aided by an anchoring device on the other, it could draw large ploughs by cable across the field. The Lothian farmers were famous for their skill and progressiveness, operating on the most scientific principles of the day, often using 30 to 40 tons of farmyard manure per acre.

The landowner or his factor watched over the efficiency of farmer tenants as closely as ever. Good husbandry together with the harvest yield had traditionally governed rent-paying capacity. Since the 1880s there had been the need to compete with the cheap cereals of North America: a challenge that was met by diversification of crops and continuous pressure on best practice, together with resistance to farm labourers' wage claims.

The wealth of the landowner was still manifest in the rural landscape. There were over one hundred mansions in the Lothians with their parks, woodlands, cornfields and meadows. The traditional landed class was joined in Edwardian times with an increasing influx of men of business seeking to live the landed life. Their new country houses were artificial creations, sometimes attempting to combine irreconcileable notions, as for example an impression of wealth combined with pre-industrial romanticism, with interiors of marble, mahogany and shining brass. All of this was dusted and cleaned by an army of servants, making the brass bedsteads glisten and panelling shine. Ardkinglass in Argyllshire, begun in 1905 for Sir Andrew Noble, chairman of the engineering and armaments firm of Armstrong, Whitworth, was an overwhelming architectural assertion, having among other features a complex shower in the main bathroom set in a kind of pergola of chrome. This was the most ambitious work of the most popular Scottish architect for the building of new country houses, Sir Robert Lorimer (1864–1929), regarded by some as the Lutyens of Scotland. Much of his work provided settings for the way of life available to the Scottish high Victorian and Edwardian bourgeoisie. But usually he was able to mute the crasser elements, projecting good manners in architecture, using a sober but attractive Scots baronial style. For example Lorimer was commissioned by Frederick Sharps who had made a fortune in jute followed by finance in the form of investment trusts. Sharp bought Hill of Tarvit in Fife in 1904 and Lorimer made it an example of the kind of reconciliation of wealth and taste to which much of his career was dedicated.

Another form of reaching back into the traditional past expressed itself in an interest in folk song. In 1904 the New Spalding Club charged Gavin Greig, schoolmater, and James Duncan, United Free Church minister, with gathering 'the traditional minstrelsy' of Aberdeenshire: they wrote down no less than 3,500 texts, and 3,300 tunes, to which the bothies made a major contribution. Between them they recorded the song-stories of kings and queens, dukes and duchesses, sailors and soldiers, together with adventures amorous and otherwise closer to home. Bawdry, an important part of the whole, was sternly excluded by schoolmaster and minister.

The British fisheries thrived greatly, with an especially astonishing growth in the Aberdeen area where 2.27 million hundredweight were landed in 1914 as against one million in 1900.

6 The Highlands

Since the break-up of the clans there had emerged two levels of agrarian society in the Highlands, namely landlords and a peasantry working small farms. The substantial tenant of the first half of the nineteenth century, usually an incomer from the Lowlands, had been heavily depleted since the 1860s because of the conversion of former sheep walks to deer forests. The crofter continued to be the focus of Highland grievances. In 1908 the Congested Districts Board was placed in a position to lease land to crofters and others and to undertake public works such as pier and road building and fencing. In 1912 the Board became part of the new Board of Agriculture. A Land Court was set up in 1911. But the basic problem remained, namely how could such a regional economy be made to generate a reasonable standard of living for the crofters and their families?

The life of the Highlander to 1914 continued to be hard, involving much primitive housing and narrow horizons, often presided over by an austere minister. As in the past, alcoholism was a problem there as in the great cities. The long dark Highland winter with the ticking of the clock in the otherwise silent cottage could produce either a largely self-taught scholarship, or all too often a recourse to the bottle. The Highlander's horse sometimes facilitated toping because it could safely bring its master home without his guidance. Doctors paid in whisky could all too easily succumb. The excise man or gauger was a Highland figure of some note. These who went to remote Highland villages as ministers or teachers could suffer a death of the mind, for the manual toil of the local people did not encourage intellectual effort.

The pall of a Highland Sabbath was a further constraint on the spirit. The Free Church had greatly flourished in the Highlands; with the setting up of the Free Presbyterian Church (the 'Wee Frees') in 1892, the religious perspective of much of the Highlands had become more Calvinistically austere than ever.[1] There was much insistence on the solemn realities of evil and on the lesson that redemption from it should be the chief concern of man. So it was that religion laid its strong hand on many, sometimes bringing a certain refinement of mind, as shown by the supplications of elders and others at prayer meetings.

And yet Gaelic society could preserve the warmth, support and character formation of the family, as well as keeping its members close to the natural world from which the urbanite had been by 1900 largely cut off. It was still the case that many a 'lad o' pairts' was discovered in the local school and given his chance. Indeed the notion of getting into a wider world and 'getting on', perhaps to one of the professions, was strong in families that could rise above the constraints of low incomes and bad housing. The Highlander could thus reach out beyond his Gaelic culture only by deserting it. There was however little penetration the other way: the gramophone in 1914 was still too expensive to encroach upon the bagpipes and the fiddle. The clan spirit could also be sustaining: the tradition was still real of closing ranks against outsiders (though often quarrelling fiercely within the family), together with support for even its most inadequate and troublesome members. There was a new optimism that the decay of the Gaelic culture could be arrested. Gaelic conferences

[1] See chapter 7, section 7 above.

were called in 1905 and 1906 to consider the future of the language: as a result the Scottish Secretary awarded an annual grant of £10 to each Gaelic-speaking teacher.

At the other end of the social scale were the great landowners and those who rented their moors and rivers. By 1914 the best 'lets' came from the brewers and distillers, the Basses, Walkers, Haigs, Edwards and Ushers. Page after page of *The Field* listed the number and size of the salmon lifted by them and their guests from Scottish rivers. An under-keeper 'well up in pheasant rearing and a good vermin trapper and able to work a retriever' was paid 17 shilling per week and one suit of clothes per year.

7 The Churches and Society

The new century began with the union in 1900 of the majority of the Free Church and the United Presbyterian Church, to form the United Free Church. This reflected the feeling that, after all, the Scottish Presbyterian churches shared one faith and one common order. The easing of old theological acerbities made this easier: all the main branches of Presbyterianism, like other protestant churches the world over, were confronted with the same challenge, namely how to come to terms with science, secularism and socialism. By 1900 General Assemblies and the divinity faculties and colleges of Scotland, having resisted the new ideas, and having indeed put some of their advocates on trial before church courts, in effect accepted that it was improper any longer to attempt to enforce uniformity of belief. The threat of scientific materialism, with its cold eye brought to bear upon the origins and authenticity of the Bible, was now the great enemy.

The Church of Scotland had successfully resisted its own disestablishment, so that this was pretty well a dead issue by 1900. Though its internal travails and its confrontation with the new thoughts of the new age had been more muted than those of the Free Church, it was moving along with other Scottish churches in the direction of the social gospel: in 1904 its General Assembly set up its Committee on Social Work. This was largely in response to the efforts of the Reverend David Watson who, along with others, wished the Church of Scotland to take the social welfare initiative. In 1901 he had founded the Scottish Christian Social Union. To some Churchmen this kind of amelioration at the bottom of society, helping the old, the orphans, the inebriates, the prostitutes and the hard-pressed working-class woman was not enough. The Rev. Professor Henry Reid of Glasgow University in 1904 charged the clergy of the Church of Scotland with being 'little more than chaplains in the central fortress of power, wealth and privilege'.

All the churches except the Roman Catholic shared the same problem, namely that being so largely middle-class. They could not, in spite of a good deal of heart-searching and self-reproach, make real contact with the churchless million, represented by Glasgow's Gallowgate, the lower part of Edinburgh's Leith Walk or Dundee's Dock Street. A second wave of American evangelism reached Scotland between 1904 and 1907, that of Torry and Alexander. It had a considerable impact, though less than that of Moody and Sankey, and one that faded more quickly.

Roman Catholicism could still stir strong emotions among Scots conditioned for generations to the idea of the Pope as anti-Christ. The life chances of the young Irish Catholics in Scotland were considerably inferior to those of the majority of the population. The Scottish Catholics, having rejected participation in the work of the School Boards set up after 1872, had embarked on their own system of schools: from 1918 the government assumed the cost of maintenance of Catholic school buildings and of the non-religious part of the teaching within them.

8 The Civic Gospel

Meanwhile the civic gospel, closely related to the social gospel among the churches, was strong in Scotland, especially so in Glasgow. There the idea of the city as an ethical Christian community had taken a strong hold in an element of the middle class. For such people the way to renewal and to the redemption of society from the corruption of industrialization lay through the city, its government and its philanthropy. Thus spiritual regeneration and national renewal could come through the practical socialism of the city: indeed the effort to do so could promote internationalism as cities exchanged experiences. To this Edward Caird who, through 30 years of teaching had made Glasgow University the centre of British philosophic idealism, had contributed much. The Christian bourgeois values of social responsibility were especially embodied in two businessmen Lord Provosts, Sir Samuel Chisholm (1836–1923) and Sir Daniel Macaulay Stevenson(1851–1944). Both ardent churchmen, they and others sought to make of the city a model

Christian municipality. Earnest American visitors, in search of guidance based upon a morality appropriate to their own urban and national problems, came to Glasgow to learn.[2] There was an echo here of Thomas Chalmers's emphasis on community of almost a century earlier, but using the city rather than the parish as the unit of succour, redemption, social responsibility and social regeneration. The movement did a good deal of good, but, as with Chalmers, it under-estimated what needed to be done, the scale of national effort required, and the depth of critique of society on which it had to rest.

Moreover something of the vitality of Scottish municipal life was lost after 1902. By 1907–8 municipal socialism had also suffered a setback. Both the managerial municipalizers and the civic socialists felt that they were up against the severe limitations on municipal initiatives set by parliament. This caused a transference of emphasis to parliament and the political process at the national level.

9 Identity and Ethos Again

What is there to say of the elusive soul of Scotland by 1914? The thinking Scot, contemplating the 77 years since Victoria became Queen, might well have asked two great questions, namely 'what has happened to us?' and 'who are we?' The answer to the first was, of course, industrialization, together with the greater assimilation to Great Britain that it brought. The answer to the second depended on whether industrialization and assimilation had destroyed or fragmented the Scottish psyche.

Scots from different parts of the country knew they were different from one another. The same was true in terms of class. The regional differences did not make for fissures in the national consciousness, for the Scots recognized the various sub-societies, both urban and rural, of which they were members, and indeed took pride in these. The old mutual disregard between Lowlander and Highlander had largely gone. In class terms there was indeed a tendency to draw apart, more especially in the industrialized areas. But even here, in spite of tensions that were growing stronger, the feeling of a shared nationhood was real. There was a feeling that Scotland had an identity that distinguished it and its people from other nations, including England. At the time of the accession of Edward VII in 1901 there was a Scottish petition bearing several hundred thousand signatures

[2]See chapter 11, section 4 above.

protesting that this was not Scotland's seventh Edward but its first. This was the kind of issue which, though minor in itself, indicated resentment at the assumption that Scotland's past was simply part of that of England.

For most Scots, at home and abroad, there was a spiritual country where their identity lay. As the French historian, Elie Halevy, put it with illuminating exaggeration: 'All Scotsmen, whatever their religious persuasion, are Scottish and proud to be Scottish. They are filled with admiration for their fellow countrymen and with a contempt for the English.' But the overt and organized expressions of a national spirit were few. Nationalism as a cultural programme had begun to stir, though only slightly. As a political programme, apart from some degree of pressure for further administrative devolution, Scottish nationalism was feeble. Though a good many thought, perhaps at the unconscious level, in terms of a national identity and community formed by history and distinct from that of England, few saw it as serving as a practical and inspirational framework for a separate self-assertive Scottish society that would revive an integral past and serve as a basis for national renewal. Rather there was a sense of distinctiveness that did not require the assertion of separateness. It is for this reason that in studies of the world's nationalisms in the nineteenth and early twentieth centuries the Scottish case barely receives a mention.

The Scottish sense of distinctiveness by 1914 was embodied in nature, in culture and in institutions. There was the possession of a marvellous landscape where beauty, history and romanticism could infuse the view. There was the Gaelic language and culture, now beginning to be seen from the urban intellectual world, with its need for escape from rationalism and utilitarianism, as the embodiment of the pristine virtues of man close to nature; the Highlander was perceived by many Scots as one whose speech was full of colourful metaphor, deep symbolism and amusing hyperbole, and who could sense the presence of forces that a rational culture had tried to expel. There was the powerful feeling among Scots of a shared history, full of travail, in which both internal strife and the external enemy of England played large parts. There was a sense that though with only one-tenth the population of England, Scotland as a world nation was almost England's equal, through the energies and initiatives of the Scottish diaspora. At home there was still a separate body of Scottish law, the principles of Presbyterianism, a distinctive educational system and the prevalence of the notes of Scottish banks when the

English were still relying on coin. Scotland, too, had a real capital in Edinburgh, a city that could hold its own against all comers. There was a Scottish literature, together with proud philosophical, scientific and medical traditions. With these went, at the level of the working population, a splendid range of skills, the world's envy. Finally there was the Scottish sense of virility, taking pride in the fighting men of the Scottish regiments.

Much of this was present at a subliminal level at a rugger international against England. The stand would be full of the sons of the Scottish race, every man and boy both a patriot and an expert, with no women, as at Twickenham, with their uncomprehending questions to reduce concentration and tension. Thus could be released the pent-up feelings from the depths of the Scottish psyche, seeking to assert a Scottish identity, providing eighty minutes of purgative atavism, reviving for an afternoon the spirit of Bannockburn against the auld enemy.

A Note on Further Reading

General

Place of publication is London except where otherwise stated

There are many books dealing with this period having 'Britain' in their title: their Scottish content varies, but is usually minimal. In recent years scholars have related Scottish experience to that of other societies, and have brought to bear insights from the various social sciences, thus affecting historical writing and giving Scottish experience a wider significance.

For overall coverage the volumes of the *Second and Third Statistical Accounts of Scotland* are invaluable. For omnibus discussion, see

R.H. Campbell, *Scotland since 1707* (Oxford, 1965)
W. Ferguson, *Scotland 1689 to the Present* (Edinburgh, 1968)
D. Daiches, ed., *A Companion to Scottish Culture* (1981)
M. Flinn, ed., *Scottish Population History from the Seventeenth Century to the 1930's* (Cambridge, 1977)

Among the journals there is much to be found in
The Scottish Historical Review (*SHR*)
Scottish Journal of Economic and Social History (*SJESH*)
Scottish Studies (School of Scottish Studies, Edinburgh) (*SS*)
Scottish Industrial History (*SIH*)

Chapter 1: Entrepreneurs and Industries: Useful general discussions include the following: David Bremner, *The Industries of Scotland* (new ed. J. Butt and I. Donnachie eds., Newton Abbot, 1969), R.H. Campbell, *The Rise and Fall of Scottish Industry* (Edinburgh, 1980), M.S. Moss and J.R. Hume, *Workshop of the British Empire* (1977), P.L. Payne, ed., *Studies in Scottish Business History* (1967) especially T.J. Byers, 'Entrepreneurship in the Scottish heavy industries, P.L. Payne, *The Early Scottish Limited Companies* (Aberdeen, 1980), A. Slaven, *The Development of the West of Scotland 1750–1860* (1975).

The pictorial and archaeological aspects are represented by I. Donnachie, J.R. Hume and M.S. Moss, *Historic Industrial Scenes, Scotland*

(1977), J. Butt, *The Industrial Archaeology of Scotland* (Newton Abbot, 1967) and J. Hume, *The Industrial Archaeology of Glasgow* (Glasgow 1974).

Various sectors are treated in P.L. Payne, *Colvilles and the Scottish Steel Industry* (Oxford, 1979), J.R. Hume and M.S. Moss, *History of William Beardmore and Co., 1837–1977* (1979); also their *Clyde Shipbuilding from Old Photographs* (1975), M.S. Moss and J.R. Hume, *Engineering and Shipbuilding in the West of Scotland* (1976), M.S. Moss, 'William Todd Lithgow – Founder of a fortune' (*SHR* 1983), A. Slaven, 'Management and shipbuilding, 1890–1938: structure and strategy in the shipbuilding firm on the Clyde', in A. Slaven and D. Aldcroft, eds., *Business, Banking and Urban History* (Edinburgh, 1982), N. Crathorne, *Tennant's Stalk: the story of the Tennants of the Glen* (1973), S.G. Checkland, *The Mines of Tharsis* (1967), C. Mair, *A Star for Seamen: The Stevenson Family of Engineers* (1978), J. Butt, 'The Scottish Oil mania of 1864–66' *SJPE* Vol. 12 (1965), E. Gauldie, ed., *The Dundee Textile Industry, 1790–1885* (Edinburgh, 1969), C. Gulvin, *The Tweedmakers . . . 1690–1914* (Newton Abbott, 1973), I. Donnachie, *A History of the Brewing Industry in Scotland* (Edinburgh, 1979), M. Gray, *The Fishing Industries of Scotland, 1790–1914* (Oxford, 1981).

For transport see: J. Lindsay, *The Canals of Scotland* (Newton Abbott, 1968) J.F. Riddell, *Clyde Navigation. A History of the development and deepening of the River Clyde* (Edinburgh, 1979), C.J.A. Robertson, *The Origins of the Scottish Railway System 1722–1844* (Edinburgh, 1983), O.S. Nock, *Scottish Railways* (1961), W. Vamplew, 'Railways and the transformation of the Scottish economy' *Economic History Review* (*EcHR*, 1971), J.R. Kellett, 'Glasgow's Railways, 1830–80: a study in 'Natural Growth' (*EcHR*, 1964), John Thomas, *The North British Railway* (Newton Abbott, 1969). .

On Banking and finance there are S.G. Checkland, *Scottish Banking. A History 1695–1973* (London and Glasgow, 1975), C.W. Munn, *The Scottish Provincial Banking Cos, 1747–1864* (Edinburgh, 1981), Norio Tamaki, *The Life Cycle of the Union Bank of Scotland, 1830–1954* (Aberdeen, 1983), R.C. Michie, *Money, Mania and Markets* (Edinburgh, 1981).

Chapter 2: The urbanization of Scotland: Comprehensive discussions of Scottish urban experience are to be found in: G. Best, 'The Scottish Victorian city' *Victorian Studies*, (1968), I.H. Adams, *The Making of Urban Scotland* (1978), D.F. Macdonald, *Scotland's Shifting Population, 1770–1850* (Glasgow, 1937), C. McWilliam, *Scottish Townscape* (1975), J.R. Kellett, *The Impact of Railways on Victorian Cities* (1969). G. Gordon and B. Dicks, eds., *Scottish Urban History* (Aberdeen, 1983), R.G. Roger, 'The invisible hand. Market forces, housing and the urban forms in Victorian cities' in D. Fraser and A. Sutcliffe, eds., *The Pursuit of Urban History* (1983).

For particular cities the most important sources are the volumes of the *Second and Third Statistical Accouts of Scotland*. See also A.J. Youngson, *The Making of Classical Edinburgh* (Edinburgh, 1966), C.S. Minto, *Victorian and Edwardian Edinburgh from Old Photographs* (1971), S.G. Checkland, *The*

Upas Tree: Glasgow 1875-1981 (Glasgow University Press, 1982), P.J. Smith, 'Planning as environmental improvement: slum clearance in Victorian Edinburgh', in A. Sutcliffe, ed., *The Rise of Modern Urban Planning 1800-1914* (1980), A. Gibb, *Glasgow, The Making of a City* (1983), M.A. Simpson, 'The West End of Glasgow, 1830-1914', in Simpson, T.H. Lloyd, eds., *Middle Class Housing in Britain* (Newton Abbott, 1977), J.G. Robb, 'Suburb and slum in Gorbals, social and residential change, 1800-1900,' in Gordon and Dicks, ed., W. Forsyth, 'Urban economic morphology in nineteenth century Glasgow', in A. Slaven and D.H. Aldcroft, eds., and in the same volume, T. Hart, 'Urban growth and municipal government: Glasgow in a comparative context, 1864-1914', C.M. Allan, 'The genesis of British urban redevelopment with special reference to Glasgow' *EcHR* (1965).

Chapter 3: The rural and the Highland Scot: For the general aspects of agrarian change see J.E. Hanley, *The Agricultural Revolution in Scotland* (Glasgow, 1963), M.L. Parry and T.R. Slater, *The Making of the Scottish Coutryside* (1980), I. Carter, 'The Changing image of the Scottish peasantry, 1745-1980', in S. Raphael, ed., *People's History and Socialist Theory* (1981), T. Devine, 'Social stability during the Scottish industrial revolution, 1760-1840', in T.M. Devine, ed., *Lairds and Improvement in the Scotland of the Enlightenment* (Glasgow, 1979).

For a more regional perspective there are I. Carter, *Farm Life in Northeast Scotland, 1840-1914* (Edinburgh, 1979), T.M. Devine, 'Social stability and agrarian change in the Eastern Lowlands of Scotland, 1810-1840', *Social History* (1978).

The Highlands have generated a large and vigorous literature, in which feature M. Gray, *The Highland Economy* (Edinburgh, 1957), D.W. Crowley, 'The Crofters' Party 1885-1892' *SHR*, Vol. 35 (1956), E. Richards, *The Highland Clearances*, Vol. I, *Agrarian Transformation and the Evictions, 1746-1886* (1982), J. Hunter, *The Making of the Crofting Community* (Edinburgh, 1977), I.F. Grigor, *Mightier than a Lord* (Stornoway, 1979), P. Gaskell, *Morvern Transformed* (Cambridge, 1968), I.R.M. Mowat, *Easter Ross, 1750-1850: The Double Frontier* (Edinburgh, 1981), R.W. Clark, *Balmoral: Queen Victoria's Highland Home* (1981).

Chapter 4: Class, power and politics: The background is illuminated by J.J. Saunders, *Scottish Democracy, 1815-40* (Edinburgh, 1950), G. Pryde, *Central and Local Government in Scotland* (1960), H. Cockburn, *Memorials of his Time* (Edinburgh, 1856), new ed., F. Gray, ed. (1945), A.A. MacLaren, ed., *Social Class in Scotland: Past and Present* (Edinburgh, 1976), A.A. MacLaren, *Religion and Social Class, the Disruption Years in Aberdeen* (1974). Various aspects of class and power are discussed in L.C. Wright, *Scottish Chartism* (Edinburgh, 1953) and A. Wilson, *The Chartist Movement in Scotland*

(Manchester, 1970), W.H. Fraser, 'Scottish Trades Councils in the Nine-teenth Century', (*Bulletin of the Society for the Study of Labour History*, XIX) also his 'The Glasgow Cotton Spinners, 1837' in J. Butt and J.T. Ward, eds., *Scottish Themes. Essays in Honour of S.G.E. Lythe* (Edinburgh, 1976), N. Murray, *The Scottish Handloom Weavers* (Edinburgh, 1978), F. Reid, *James Keir Hardie: The Making of a Socialist* (Newton Abbott, 1977), J. McCaffrey, 'The Irish vote in Glasgow in the later nineteenth century' *Innes Review* (1970), also his 'Origins of Liberal Unionism in the West of Scotland' *SHR* (1971), J.G. Kellas, 'The Liberal Party in Scotland, 1876–1895' *SHR* (1965), D.W. Unwin, 'The Development of the Conservative Party Organisation in Scotland until 1912' *SHR* (1965), J.T. Ward, 'Some aspects of working-class Conservatism in the nineteenth century', in Butt and Ward, *op. cit.*

Chapter 5: The Scottish urban working classes: The following discuss the quality of social life: I. Levitt and T.C. Smout, *The State of the Scottish Working Class in 1843* (Edinburgh, 1980), T.C. Smout, *The Social Condition of Scotland in the 1840's* (Dow Lecture, University of Dundee, 1980), J. Butt, 'Working class housing in Glasgow 1851–1914' in S.D. Chapman, ed., *The History of Working Class Housing* (1971), F. Worsdall, *The Tenement: a Way of life* (Edinburgh, 1979), R. Smith, 'Multi-dwelling building in Scotland, 1750–1970,' in A. Sutcliffe, ed., *Multi-Storey Living: the British Working Class Experience* (1974), J. Handley, *The Irish in Scotland* (Cork, 1945), W.M. Walker, 'Irish immigrants in Scotland: their priests, politics and parochial life' (*Historical Journal*, 1972), J. Butt, *History of the SCWS* (Manchester, 1981).

The workers' responses to their condition are treated in: I. MacDougall, ed., *Essays on Scottish Labour History: a tribute to W.H. Marwick* (Edinburgh, 1978), J.D. Young, *The Rousing of the Scottish Working Class* (1979), R.Q. Gray, *The Labour Aristocracy in Victorian Edinburgh* (Oxford, 1976), W.M. Walker, *Juteopolis, Dundee and its Textile Workers, 1885–1923* (Edinburgh, 1979), K.D. Buckley, *Trade Unionism in Aberdeen, 1878–1900* (Edinburgh, 1955), N. Murray, *The Scottish Handloom Weavers* (Edinburgh, 1978), J.W. Ward, 'The factory movement in Scotland' *SHR* (1962).

Whereas the coal industry is poorly treated in the literature, the miners fare better: R. Page Arnott, *A History of the Scottish Miners* (1955), A.B. Campbell, *The Lanarkshire Miners – A Social History of their Trade Unions 1775–1874* (Edinburgh, 1979), J.A. Hassan, 'The landed estate, pater-nalism and the coal industry in Midlothian, 1800–1880' *SHR* (1980), G.M. Wilson, *Alexander McDonald, Leader of the Miners* (Aberdeen, 1982), K.O. Morgan, *Keir Hardie* (1975), L. Thompson, *The Enthusiasts. A Biography of John and Katherine Bruce Glasier* (1971).

Chapter 6: The welfare and education of the people: The development of the various aspects of welfare may be somewhat unevenly studied in the following: T. Ferguson, *The Dawn of Scottish Social Welfare* (Edinburgh, 1948), *Scottish Social Welfare, 1864–1914* (Edinburgh, 1958), O. Checkland, *Philanthropy in Victorian Scotland* (Edinburgh, 1980), R.A. Cage, *The Scottish Poor Law* (Edinburgh, 1981), A. Paterson, 'The Poor Law in Scotland after 1845' in D. Fraser, ed., *The New Poor Law in the Nineteenth Century* (1976), E. Gauldie, *Cruel Habitations. A History of Working Class Housing 1780–1918* (1974), J.H.F. Brotherston, *Observations on the Early Public Health Movement in Scotland* (1952), O. Checkland and M. Lamb, eds., *Health Care as Social History, The Glasgow Case* (Aberdeen, 1982), A.K. Chalmers, ed., *The Health of Glasgow, 1818–1925* (Glasgow, 1930), I. Levitt, 'The Scottish Poor Law and Unemployment, 1890–1929' in T.C. Smout, ed., *The Search for wealth and stability: essays in economic and social history: presented to M.W. Flinn* (1979), J. Scotland, *A History of Scottish Education* (1970), R.M. Knox, *250 Years of Scottish Education* (Edinburgh, 1953) and *Studies in the History of Scottish Education, 1872–1939* (1970), J.M. Roxburgh, *The School Board of Glasgow 1873–1919* (1971), M. Cruickshank, *A History of the Training of Teachers in Scotland* (1970), M. Skinnender, 'Catholic Education in Glasgow', in R.M. Knox (1970).

Chapter 7: Religion, morals and social responsibility: The standard works are A.L. Drummond and J. Bulloch, *The Scottish Church 1688–1843: the Age of the Moderates* (Edinburgh, 1973), *The Church in Victorian Scotland, 1843–74* (Edinburgh, 1975), *The Church in Late Victorian Scotland, 1874–1900* (Edinburgh, 1978). See also S. Mechie, *The Church and Scottish Social Development* (Oxford, 1960). A compehensive reappraisal of a major figure is Stewart J. Brown's *Thomas Chalmers & The Godly Commonwealth in Scotland* (Oxford, 1983), also A.A. Cheyne, ed., *The Practical & The Pious: Thomas Chalmers (1780–1847), Bicentenary Essays,* (Edinburgh, 1983). M. Lochhead, 'Episcopal Scotland in the nineteenth century' *SHR* (1968), I.A. Muirhead, 'Catholic Emancipation in Scotland: the debate and the aftermath' *Innes Review* (Vol. XXIX, 2), T.C. Smout, 'Scottish marriage, 1500–1940', in R.S. Outhwaite, ed., *Marriage and Society. Studies in the Social History of Marriage* (1981), D. McRoberts, *Modern Scottish Catholicism, 1878–1978* (Glasgow, 1979), I.A. Muirhead, 'The revival as a dimension of Scottish Church history' *Records of the Scottish Church History Society*, Vol. XX. part 3, 1980. C.D. Rice, *The Scots Abolitionists: 1833–1861* (Louisiana, 1982).

Chapter 8: The intellect, the arts and the sciences: The religious aspect is discussed under Chapter 7, especially in Drummond and Bulloch and Mechie, though the links made with culture are weak. For the Enlightenment see R.H. Campbell and A.S. Skinner, eds., *The Origins and Nature of the Scottish Englightenment* (Edinburgh, 1982). The literary achievement is to be found in D. Craig, *Scottish Literature and the Scottish People* (1961), F. Hart, *The Scottish Novel* (Cambridge, Mass. 1978), I. Campbell, ed., *Nineteenth*

Century Scottish Fiction (Manchester, 1979), G. McMaster, *Scott and Society* (Cambridge, 1982), D. Daiches, *Sir Walter Scott and his World* (1971), J. Calder, ed., *Stevenson and Victorian Scotland* (Edinburgh, 1980), E. Campbell, *Kailyard: A New Assessment* (Ramsay Head, 1981).

A general survey of music is to be found in F. Collinson, *The Traditional and National Music of Scotland* (1966). The Scottish influence of the great 18th and 19th century composers is discussed in R. Fiska, *Scotland in Music* (Cambridge, 1983)

There are two major studies of painting, namely, D. and F. Irwin, *Scottish Painters at Home and Abroad 1700–1900* (1975), and W. Hardie, *Scottish Painting*, 1837–1939 (1976). More particular aspects are illuminated by M. McKerrow, *The Faeds* (Edinburgh, 1982), G. and C. Larner, *The Glasgow Style* (Edinburgh, 1979), T.J. Honeyman, *Three Scottish Colourists* (1950), T. Howarth, *Charles Rennie MacKintosh and the Modern Movement* (1977). Bridging the artist and the photographer is R. Taylor, *George Washington Wilson, 1823–93* (Aberdeen, 1981). For architecture see H. Petzch, *Architecture in Scotland* (1971), A. Gomme and D. Walker, *Architecture of Glasgow* (1968), A.M. Young and A.M. Doak, *Glasgow at a Glance* (1965), A. Fenton and B. Walker, *The Rural Architecture of Scotland* (Edinburgh, 1981).

An attempt to distinguish myth from reality in terms of the life of the Gael is to be found in M. Chapman, *The Gaelic Vision of Scottish Culture* (Newton Abbott, 1978). Folk tales collected between 1859 and 1870 are presented in *The Dewar Manuscripts*, Volume I, (Edinburgh, 1964), folk songs in P. Shuldham-Shaw and E.B. Lyle, eds., *The Greig-Duncan Folk Song Collection* (Aberdeen, 1981) and in J. Ord, *Bothy Songs and Ballads* (Edinburgh, 1969).

Science is treated generally in A.G. Clement and R.H.S. Robertson, *Scotland's Scientific Heritage* (Edinburgh, 1961) and N. Campbell and R.M.S. Smellie, *The Royal Society of Edinburgh (1783–1983). The First Two Hundred Years* (Edinburgh, 1983). Biographies of Scotland's two greatest scientists are A.G. King, *Kelvin the Man* (1925), H.I. Sharlin, *Lord Kelvin: the dynamic Victorian* (Pennsylvania State University Press, 1979), C.W.F. Everitt, *James Clerk Maxwell: physicist and natural philosopher* (New York, 1975).

Debate on the universities has centred on G.E. Davie, *The Democratic Intellect, Scotland and her Universities in the Nineteenth Century* (Edinburgh, 1961), See also P.L. Robertson, 'The finances of the University of Glasgow before 1914' *History of Education Quarterly* (Winter 1976).

Medicine is effectively covered by D.N.H. Hamilton, *The Healers: A History of Medicine in Scotland* (Edinburgh, 1981) and in Checkland and Lamb, *op. cit.* The two giants are depicted in R.B. Fisher, *Joseph Lister 1827–1912* (1977) and A.K. Bowman, *The Life and Teaching of Sir William Macewen* (1942).

Patrick Geddes view of society is discussed in P. Kitchen, *A Most*

Unsettling Person (1975) and in H. Meller, 'Cities and evolution, Patrick Geddes as an international prophet of town planning before 1914' in A. Sutcliffe ed., *The Rise of Modern Urban Planning, 1800–1914* (1980).

Chapter 9: The outward impact: the Empire and beyond: G. Donaldson, *The Scots Overseas* (1966) provides a general perspective. More particular ones are presented in J.M. Gibson, *The Scots in Canada* (Toronto, 1971), W.S. Reid, ed., *The Scottish Tradition in Canada* (Toronto, 1976), D.S. MacMillan, *Scotland and Australia, 1788–1950: Emigration, Commerce and Investment* (1967), W.T. Jackson, *The Enterprising Scot: Investors in the American West after 1873* (Edinburgh, 1968), W.G. Kerr, *Scottish Capital on the American Credit Frontier* (Austin, 1976), J.D. Hargreaves, *Aberdeenshire to Africa. Northeast Scots and British Overseas Expansion* (Aberdeen, 1982).

Chapter 10: The Scottish nation and the British state: The aspiration for a distinct identity is discussed in C. Harvie, *Scotland and Nationalism, Scottish Society and Politics, 1770–1977* (1977), J. Brand, *The National Movement in Scotland* (1977), R. Mitchison, 'Nineteenth century Scottish nationalism' in R. Mitchison, ed., *The Roots of Nationalism: Studies in Northern Europe* (Edinburgh, 1980), A.C. Turner, *Scottish Home Rule* (Oxford, 1952). Wider perspectives are suggested in T.C. Smout, 'Centre and periphery in history – Scotland', *Journal of Common Market Studies* (1980).

On the administrative side see H.J. Hanham, 'The creation of the Scottish Office, 1881–7', *Juridical Review* (1965), D. Milne, *The Scottish Office* (1957).

Chapter 11: The mature economy and its urban setting: Previous sources listed above often continue their coverage over Edwardian and Georgian England. Additionally, see C.W. Hill, *Edwardian Scotland* (Edinburgh, 1977), C.H. Lee, *Regional Economic Growth in the United Kingdom since the 1880's* (1971), B. Aspinwall, 'The Scottish Religious Identity in the Atlantic World, 1880–1914' *Studies in Church History* (1982), J.G. Kellas, *Modern Scotland, The Nation since 1870* (1968), A.C. Macdonald, *History of the Motor Industry in Scotland* (Institution of Mechanical Engineers, 1961).

Chapter 12: The Scottish version of industrial society: See earlier sources, but also: E.H. Phelps Brown, *The Growth of British Industrial relations: a study from the standpoint of 1906–14* (1959), J.H. Treble, 'The market for unskilled male labour in Glasgow, 1891–1914' in I. MacDougall (1978), T. Johnston, *Memories* (1952), H. McShane and J. Smith, *No Mean Fighter* (1978), W. Kendal, *The Revolutionary Movements in Britain, 1900–21* (1969), J. Butt, 'Working class housing in Scottish cities, 1900–1950' in Gordon and Dicks 1983; also the same author, 'Working Class housing in Glasgow, 1900–1939' in MacDougall (1978), S. Damer, 'State, class and housing: Glasgow 1885–1919' in J. Melling, ed., *Housing, Social Policy and the State* (1980), B. Aspinwall, 'Glasgow trams and American politics 1894–1914' *SHR* (1977), G. Gordon, 'The status areas of Edinburgh in 1914' in Gordon and Dicks, eds., (1983), J. Brown, 'Scottish and English land legislation 1905–11' *SHR* (1968), F.F. Darling, *West Highland Survey* (Oxford, 1955), W. Orr, *Deer forests, Landlords and Crofters: the Western Highlands in Victorian and Edwardian Times* (Edinburgh, 1982).

Appendix: Chronological Table

Abbreviations *E* Election, PM Prime Minister, RC Royal Commission, CS Church of Scotland, MOH Medical Officer of Health, f. founded

1832 Reform Act (Scotland); *E* Grey PM; Cholera epidemic; Death of Sir Walter Scott.

1833 Factory Act; Burgh Reform Acts restructuring Scottish burgh government; First government grant for education; slavery ended in British Empire.

1834 Evangelicals gain majority in General Assembly of CS; pass the Veto Act; Central Board of Scottish Dissenters.

1835 *E* Jan. & Feb., Peel PM.

1836 Highland potato crop fails; cotton spinners' strike (1836–7); first Scottish Teachers Training College, Glasgow.

1837 Death of William IV; Accession of Victoria; *E* Jul. & Aug., Melbourne PM; Depression; British Chartism launched in Glasgow; typhoid and typhus (to 1839).

1838 Cotton spinners' trial.

1839 General Prisons Board for Scotland; Highland migrations quicken; Eglinton Tournament; launch of first clipper ship, Aberdeen.

1840 Opium war in China (1840–2); Scottish handloom weavers peak; Chair of Engineering in Glasgow University f.

1841 *E* July Peel PM; YMCA f.; Hugh Miller, *The Old Red Sandstone*; David Napier purchased Parkhead Forge.

1842 Typhoid and typhus; Chadwick's *Report on the Sanitary Condition of the Labouring Population of Great Britain*; industrial unrest in cotton, textile and other industries; RC on Coal Mines; Coal Mines Act; Victoria's first visit to Scotland.

1843 Disruption of the CS, formation of the Free Church of Scotland.

1844 Bank Charter Act; *Report of the Royal Commission of the Poor Law (Scotland)*; North British Railway Co.; Robert Chambers (but published anonymously) *Vestiges of the Natural History of Creation*.

1845 Bank Act (Scotland); Poor Law (Scotland) Amendment Act; *New Statistical Account of Scotland* complete.

1846 Potato famine in Highlands and in Ireland; Repeal of Corn Laws.

1847   *E* Jul. & Aug. Russell PM; United Presbyterian Church formed
         by merger of the Burghers, Anti-Burghers and the Relief; Further
         potato blight in Highlands; Depression; Educational Institute of
         Scotland f.; typhoid and typhus.
1848   Chartism fades; cholera.
1851   Exploitation of Lothian shale oil deposits begins.
1852   *E* July & Aug. Derby PM (February to December); Aberdeen
         PM (December –); Highland Emigration Society f. in London.
1853   Public Libraries (Scotland and Ireland) Act; Association for Vin-
         dication of Scottish Rights (to 1856); Public House Act (Forbes
         Mackenzie Act); Edinburgh Trades Council. cholera; Elder and
         Randolph's marine compound expansion engine; jute mills
         begun in Calcutta.
1854   Crimean war; Scottish Registration Act, effective from 1 January
         1855.
1855   *E* March & April Palmerston PM; United Coal and Iron Miners'
         Association of Scotland.
1856   Crimean War ends; Nuisance Removal Act (Scotland); Joint-
         stock Companies Act.
1857   *E* March & April Palmerston PM; Lunacy (Scotland) Act; Indian
         Mutiny; Failure of Western Bank.
1858   Derby PM; RC on Scottish Universities; Universities
         (Scotland) Act; Glasgow Trades Council; National Miners Asso-
         ciation.
1859   *E* April & May Palmerston PM; Loch Katrine water to Glasgow.
1860   Coal Mines Regulation Act; Lister in Glasgow (to 1869), anti-
         septic surgery developed there.
1861   American Civil War (to 1864).
1862   General Police and Improvement (Scotland) Act; Glasgow Police
         Act; Dr. Henry Littlejohn 1st MOH, Edinburgh; Howden's
         'Scotch' marine boiler.
1863   Factory Act; Dr. William T. Gairdner 1st MOH, part-time,
         for Glasgow.
1864   Compulsory Vaccination Act (Scotland); hymn singing
         authorized in CS.
1865   *E* July Russell PM; Report on the Sanitary Condition of
         Edinburgh.
1866   Glasgow Improvement Act; first Japanese studying in Glasgow,
         Yozo Yamao at Napier's Yard.
1867   Public Health (Scotland) Act; isolation hospitals permitted;
         Public Libraries (Scotland) Act; Edinburgh Improvement Act;
         Singer Sewing Machine Co. at Clydebank.
1868   Reform Act (Scotland); *E* Nov. & Dec. Disraeli PM, briefly,
         later Gladstone PM; Scottish Co-operative Wholesale Society;
         Edinburgh Association for Improving the Condition of the Poor;
         Argyll Commission on Education.

1870   Denny's launch Cutty Sark at Dumbarton; Glasgow University moved to Gilmorehill.

1872   Education (Scotland) Act; *Endowed Schools and Hospitals (Scotland) Commission*; Steel Co. of Scotland f.

1873   First Moody and Sankey Revivalist Campaign; death of Livingstone.

1874   *E* Jan. & Feb., Disraeli PM; Factory Act; Glasgow Association for Improving the Condition of the Poor; Patronage Act of 1712 repealed; Kirk's triple expansion engine.

1875   Housing Act; Edinburgh Improvement Act.

1876   Rivers Pollution Prevention Act; Mary Slessor in Calabar.

1877   Factory Act; Prisons (Scotland) Act; 'Trial' of Robertson Smith by Church of Scotland begins (ends 1881).

1878   City of Glasgow Bank failure; Roman Catholic hierarchy restored in Scotland; Education (Scotland) Act; Public Parks Act.

1879   Gladstone's Midlothian campaign; first steel hulled ocean going vessel launched at Dumbarton; Lanarkshire coal strikes; Tay Bridge collapse.

1880   *E* April & May Gladstone PM; Macewen developed aseptic surgery in 1880s.

1881   Married Women's Property Act (Scotland); Householders of Scotland Act (some women can vote locally); University College Dundee f.

1882   Crofters' War.

1883   Factory and Workshops Act; Napier Commission on the Highlands; Highland Land League; Boys' Brigade; Chair of Celtic in Edinburgh University.

1884   Reform Act; Scottish National Society for Prevention of Cruelty to Children f.

1885   *E* Nov. & Dec. Salisbury PM; Scottish Secretaryship established; National Liberal Federation of Scotland; Royal Commission on Housing.

1886   *E* Jul. & Aug., Gladstone, PM; later, Salisbury; Home Rule Bill, Liberal-Unionist Party; Crofters' Holdings (Scotland) Act, Crofters' Commission; Scottish Home Rule Association.

1887   Victoria's Golden Jubilee; Scottish Office in Whitehall; Public Libraries Consolidation (Scotland) Act.

1888   J.B. Russell publishes *Life in One Room*; Goschen formula re government grants to Scotland; Scottish Labour Party f; Denny's shiptesting tank; first Glasgow International Exhibition.

1889   Local Government (Scotland) Act; Universities of Scotland Act; West Highland Railway opened; Glasgow City Chambers opened; Universities Act.

1890   Housing of the Working Classes Act; Infections Diseases (Notification) Act; Forth Railway Bridge completed; Glasgow Police (Amendment) Act.

1891	Highland Association f.; Glasgow Presbytery Housing Inquiry.
1892	*E*; Gladstone PM; Burgh Police (Scotland) Act; Royal Commission on Crofting; Scottish Land Restoration League; First National Mod held in Oban; Free Presbyterians (Wee Frees) split from Free Church; Keir Hardie MP for South West Ham.
1893	First public electricity supply (in Dundee); Rosyth Naval Base; Independent Labour Party f.
1894	Rosebery PM; Local Government (Scotland) Act; Public Libraries Act; Scottish Grand Committee; Scotland's first automobile; first Glasgow Sewage Purification Works; ILP absorbs Scottish Labour Party.
1895	Salisbury PM; Factory and Workshop Amendment Act; London-Aberdeen railway races begin.
1896	Glasgow underground opened; merger of Coats and Clark.
1897	Victoria's Diamond Jubilee; Public Health (Scotland) Act; Scottish Trade Union Congress; Congested Districts Board set up; engineering lockout.
1898	Burgh Police and Public Health (Scotland) Act.
1899	Boer War began.
1900	Free Church and the United Presbyterian Church merge in the United Free Church; Scottish Workers' Parliamentary Election Committee; Relief of Mafeking.
1901	Death of Victoria; accession of Edward VII; Factories and Workshops Act; Education Act (Scotland); Second Glasgow International Exhibition.
1902	Boer War ends (May); Balfour PM (July).
1903	Educational Code; Interdepartmental Committee on Physical Deterioration; North British Locomotive Co. f.
1904	Glasgow Distress Committee proposes a farm colony for the unemployed; CS sets up its Committee on Social Work.
1905	Royal Commission for the Relief of the Poor.
1906	*E* Jan., Campbell Bannerman PM; Scottish Labour Party f.
1908	Asquith PM (April); heavy unemployment; Childrens Act; Education (Scotland) Act; Old Age Pensions.
1909	*Report of RC on the Poor laws and Relief of Distress*; medical inspection of school children begins; Housing and Town Planning Act; Liberal budget.
1910	*E* Jan. & Dec., Death of Edward VII; accession of George V; world's largest armour plate rolling mill at Parkhead, Glasgow.
1911	Series of strikes to 1913; National Insurance Act; Coal Mines Act; Agriculture (Scotland) Act; Reform of House of Lords; third Glasgow International Exhibition.
1912	Scottish Liberal Unionists and Conservatives merge as Unionists; RC on Scottish Housing; Board of Agriculture.
1913	Mental Deficiency and Lunacy (Scotland) Act.
1914	Irish Home Rule crisis; Housing of the Working Classes Act; Declaration of War on Germany (August 4).

Index